# 4th Workshop on Computational Linguistics for the Political and Social Sciences (CPSS 2024)



Vienna, Austria
13 September 2024

ISBN: 979-8-3313-0481-2

**Printed from e-media with permission by:**

Curran Associates, Inc.
57 Morehouse Lane
Red Hook, NY 12571

CURRAN ASSOCIATES INC. proceedings.com

**Some format issues inherent in the e-media version may also appear in this print version.**



Association for Computational Linguistics
209 N. Eighth Street
Stroudsburg, Pennsylvania 18360

Phone: 1-570-476-8006
Fax: 1-570-476-0860

acl@aclweb.org

**Additional copies of this publication are available from:**

Curran Associates, Inc.
57 Morehouse Lane
Red Hook, NY 12571 USA
Phone: 845-758-0400
Fax: 845-758-2633
Email: curran@proceedings.com
Web: www.proceedings.com

CPSS 2024

# The 4th Workshop on Computational Linguistics for the Political and Social Sciences (CPSS)

## Proceedings of the Workshop

September 13, 2024

Order copies of this and other ACL proceedings from:

Association for Computational Linguistics (ACL)
209 N. Eighth Street
Stroudsburg, PA 18360
USA
Tel: +1-570-476-8006
Fax: +1-570-476-0860
acl@aclweb.org

The CPSS organisers gratefully acknowledge the support from the German Society for Computional Linguistics and Language Technology.

**Sponsor**

GSCL German Society for **Computational Linguistics** and **Language Technology**

# Preface

Welcome to the 4th Workshop on Computational Linguistics for the Political and Social Sciences (CPSS)!

CPSS provides a venue to bring together researchers and ideas from computational linguistics/NLP and the text-as-data community from political and social science, to foster collaboration and catalyse further interdisciplinary research efforts between these communities.

This year's workshop takes place in-person and consists of invited talks, contributed papers, and non-archival abstracts. We received 44 submissions, spanning a wide range of topics related to issues in the computational political and social sciences. We accepted 8 long and 3 short paper submissions to be presented at the workshop, either as oral presentations or as posters. In addition, we accepted 16 non-archival abstracts that describe work in progress, hoping that this will encourage discussions and provide valuable feedback to the authors.

We thank our invited speaker, **Lisa Argyle**. Lisa is an assistant professor of political science at Brigham Young University and is affiliated with the Center for the Study of Elections and Democracy in Provo, Utah. Her talk is titled "TITLE" and focusses on "INSERT CONTENT".

The workshop also features a **Panel on LLMs in Political and Social Science Research** and we would like to thank our panelists for agreeing to share their insights on this topic:

- Anna-Carolina Haensch (LMU Munich)
- Jana Lasser (University of Graz)
- Anne Lauscher (University of Hamburg)
- Alexander Wuttke (Geschwister-Scholl-Institut for Political Science, Munich)

Finally, we would like to thank the KONVENS organisers and the GSCL for their support.

The CPSS Organisers,

Christopher Klamm, Gabriella Lapesa, Simone Paolo Ponzetto, Ines Rehbein, and Indira Sen

# Organising Committee

### Program Committee

Christian Arnold, Cardiff University
Dennis Assenmacher, GESIS - Leibniz Institute for the Social Sciences
Lukas Birkenmaier, GESIS - Leibniz Institute for the Social Sciences
Tanise Ceron, University of Stuttgart
Chung-Hong Chan, GESIS - Leibniz Institute for the Social Sciences
Clint Claessen, University of Basel
Julian Dehne, GESIS - Leibniz Institute for the Social Sciences
Daryna Dementieva, Technical University of Munich
Aditi Dutta, University of Exeter
Lukas Erhard, University of Stuttgart
Agnieszka Falenska, University of Stuttgart
Johannes Gruber, Vrije Universiteit Amsterdam
Valerie Hase, LMU Munich
Annette Hautli-Janisz, University of Passau
Zlata Kikteva, University of Passau
Christopher Klamm, University of Mannheim
Verena Kunz, GESIS - Leibniz Institute for the Social Sciences
Andreas Küpfer, TU Darmstadt
Gabriella Lapesa, GESIS - Leibniz Institute for the Social Sciences and Heinrich-Heine University Düsseldorf
Hauke Licht, University of Cologne
Max Pellert, University of Konstanz
Ines Rehbein, University of Mannheim
Tatjana Scheffler, Ruhr-Universität Bochum
Indira Sen, University of Konstanz
Melanie Siegel, Hochschule Darmstadt
Dominik Stammbach, ETH Zürich
Philine Widmer, ETH Zurich
Sukayna Younger-Khan, University of Konstanz

### Workshop Chairs

Christopher Klamm, University of Mannheim
Gabriella Lapesa, GESIS - Leibniz Institute for the Social Sciences and Heinrich Heine University Düsseldorf
Simone Paolo Ponzetto, University of Mannheim
Ines Rehbein, University of Mannheim
Indira Sen, University of Konstanz

# Table of Contents

## Conference Program

**Friday, September 13, 2024**

**9:00–9:10** ***Opening Remarks***

**9:10–10:30** **Session 1: Oral presentations**

9:10–9:30 *Detecting Calls to Action in Multimodal Content: Analysis of the 2021 German Federal Election Campaign on Instagram*
Michael Achmann-Denkler, Jakob Fehle, Mario Haim and Christian Wolff

9:30–9:50 *Multilingual Bot Accusations: How Different Linguistic Contexts Shape Perceptions of Social Bots*
Leon Fröhling, Xiaofei Li and Dennis Assenmacher

9:50–10:10 *Operationalising the Hermeneutic Grouping Process in Corpus-assisted Discourse Studies*
Philipp Heinrich and Stephanie Evert

10:10–10:30 *A Few Hypocrites: Few-Shot Learning and Subtype Definitions for Detecting Hypocrisy Accusations in Online Climate Change Debates*
Paulina Garcia Corral, Avishai Green, Hendrik Meyer, Anke Stoll, Xiaoyue Yan and Myrthe Reuver

10:30–10:50 *Language Complexity in Populist Rhetoric*
Sergio E. Zanotto, Diego Frassinelli and Miriam Butt

**10:50–11:20** ***Coffee break***

**Friday, September 13, 2024 (continued)**

**11:20–12:30 Session 2: Posters (non-archival)**

**12:30–14:00** ***Lunch***

**14:00–15:00 Session 3: Posters (long/short + non-archival)**

*ChatGPT as Your n-th Annotator: Experiments in Leveraging Large Language Models for Social Science Text Annotation in Slovak Language*
Endre Hamerlik, Marek Šuppa, Miroslav Blšták, Jozef Kubík, Martin Takáč, Marián Šimko and Andrej Findor

*Detecting emotional polarity in Finnish parliamentary proceedings*
Suvi Lehtosalo and John Nerbonne

*Topic-specific social science theory in stance detection: a proposal and interdisciplinary pilot study on sustainability initiatives*
Myrthe Reuver, Alessandra Polimeno, Antske Fokkens and Ana Isabel Lopes

*The Echoes of the 'I': Tracing Identity with Demographically Enhanced Word Embeddings*
Ivan Smirnov

*TPPMI - a Temporal Positive Pointwise Mutual Information Embedding of Words*
Paul Schmitt, Zsófia Rakovics, Márton Rakovics and Gábor Recski

*Augmented Political Leaning Detection: Leveraging Parliamentary Speeches for Classifying News Articles*
Charlott Jakob, Pia Wenzel, Salar Mohtaj and Vera Schmitt

**Friday, September 13, 2024 (continued)**

**15:00–16:00 Keynote Lisa Argyle**

**16:00–16:30** ***Coffee***

**16:30–17:45 Session 4: Panel**

**17:45–18:00 Closing**

# Detecting Calls to Action in Multimodal Content: Analysis of the 2021 German Federal Election Campaign on Instagram

**Michael Achmann-Denkler**
Media Informatics Group
University of Regensburg
Regensburg, Germany
michael.achmann@ur.de

**Jakob Fehle**
Media Informatics Group
University of Regensburg
Regensburg, Germany
jakob.fehle@ur.de

**Mario Haim**
Department of Media and Communication
Ludwig-Maximilians-Universität
Munich, Germany
haim@ifkw.lmu.de

**Christian Wolff**
Media Informatics Group
University of Regensburg
Regensburg, Germany
christian.wolff@ur.de

## Abstract

This study investigates the automated classification of Calls to Action (CTAs) within the 2021 German Instagram election campaign to advance the understanding of mobilization in social media contexts. We analyzed over 2,208 Instagram stories and 712 posts using fine-tuned BERT models and OpenAI's GPT-4 models. The fine-tuned BERT model incorporating synthetic training data achieved a macro F1 score of 0.93, demonstrating a robust classification performance. Our analysis revealed that 49.58% of Instagram posts and 10.64% of stories contained CTAs, highlighting significant differences in mobilization strategies between these content types. Additionally, we found that FDP and the Greens had the highest prevalence of CTAs in posts, whereas CDU and CSU led in story CTAs.

## 1 Introduction

In this study, we experiment with the automated classification of Calls to Action (CTAs) from the 2021 German Instagram campaign to advance the understanding of mobilization in social media election campaigns. Our primary goal is to determine the efficacy of several computational approaches for binary classification of the presence or absence of CTAs in Instagram posts and stories from the 2021 Federal election in Germany. To this end, we fine-tuned a BERT model (Devlin et al., 2019), experimented with synthetic training data to enhance the model, and contrasted these approaches with zero- and few-shot prompting using OpenAI's GPT-4 model family. Through our study, we aim to address the three gaps in computational text analysis for the social sciences identified by Baden et al. (2022): 1) We experiment with a non-English language, 2) We evaluate all classifications against human annotations for external validation (Birkenmaier et al., 2023), and 3) We investigate the potential of LLMs for overcoming the specialization before integration gap.

The 2021 election marked a shift in Germany's political landscape, with the long-serving Chancellor Angela Merkel stepping down. The key parties in the race included the CDU/CSU, SPD, Greens, FDP, AfD, and The Left. In 2021, Instagram was used by almost the same share of the German population as Facebook and was particularly popular among younger users under the age of 30 (Koch, 2022). About half of the candidates had profiles on Instagram, with notable differences between parties (Kelm et al., 2023). We are interested in the front-runner and party accounts and how they utilized CTAs on Instagram to gain insight into their mobilization and audience engagement strategies. Understanding these strategies reveals how political actors use Instagram to engage voters. Thus, our secondary goal is to use the CTA classifications to contrast mobilization strategies between Instagram stories and posts, filling a gap as ephemeral stories have often been overlooked. Therefore, we want to answer the following research questions:

**RQ1a** *Which of the currently available GPT-4 model variants, when tested with few-shot and zero-shot prompts, achieves the highest performance in automated detection of CTAs in German-language Instagram content?*

**RQ1b** *Does incorporating synthetic training data enhance the performance of a fine-tuned BERT model in detecting CTAs in German-language Instagram content?*

**RQ1c** *When comparing the best-performing GPT*



*Proceedings of the 58th Annual Meeting of the Association for Computational Linguistics*, pages 1–13

*and BERT models, what are the performance differences in detecting CTAs between different types of Instagram content (stories vs. posts) and text types (OCR vs. caption vs. transcript)?*

**RQ2** *How does the usage of CTAs vary between different types of Instagram content (stories vs. posts) and between different political parties?*

### 1.1 Political Communication on Instagram

Instagram's role in political communication has been extensively studied, addressing various political actors and nations. Studies commonly reveal that political figures use Instagram to project positive imagery rather than for policy discussion or voter engagement (Bast, 2021). Studies of the 2021 German Federal election have focused on visual personalization and political issues in posts (Schlosser et al., 2023; Haßler et al., 2023; Geise et al., 2024), and Instagram stories were compared to regular posts using topic modeling (Achmann and Wolff, 2023).

Voter engagement and mobilization on social media have been the focus of recent studies: Magin et al. (2017) illustrated that about half of the posts in the 2013 German and Austrian election campaigns on Facebook included CTAs, primarily focusing on mobilization. Larsson et al. (2024) proposed a framework for comparing political actors' campaign strategies across social media platforms. They investigated the Norwegian parliamentary election campaign on three social media platforms: Facebook, Instagram, and Twitter. Wurst et al. (2023) examined the mobilization strategies used by German political parties during the 2021 election campaign on Facebook and Instagram. Their findings revealed that 43% of Instagram posts from parties and candidates included mobilization calls. The study found notable differences in mobilization strategies among parties, with the Greens using calls to vote more frequently than others.

The current research offers a comprehensive view of how CTAs are used in social media campaigns. This paper aims to extend the analysis to include both Instagram posts and Stories, offering a more holistic view of political campaigning on this platform.

### 1.2 Ephemeral Instagram Stories

Few studies have investigated ephemeral Instagram stories in the context of political campaigns and communication: Towner and Muñoz (2022) analyzed stories from 2020 U.S. presidential candidates. They collected 304 images one week before and after the election campaign. They found the campaigns missed opportunities to share user-generated content and inconsistently followed communication norms for Instagram Stories. Towner and Muñoz (2024) studied how gubernatorial candidates utilized Instagram Stories during the 2018 elections. They found that candidates primarily used stories to mobilize voters and showcase indoor events, preferring static images to videos. This area remains relatively unexplored compared to the analysis of Instagram posts.

### 1.3 Text-Mining in Political Communication

Textual analysis of Instagram content includes a frequency study to analyze Islamist extremist content (Clever et al., 2023), and an analysis of political advertisements on Instagram and Facebook, utilizing computational text classification methods (Vargo and Hopp, 2020).

The computational detection of CTAs in social media content has, for example, been investigated by Rogers et al. (2019). They classified CTAs on VKontakte, focusing on their role in mobilization and potential for censorship. Their model demonstrates a classification performance of F1=0.77. They used a relatively small ground-truth dataset (n=871) and employed RuBERT, a Russian version of BERT. Similarly, Siskou et al. (2022) developed a rule-based Natural Language Processing (NLP) pipeline to identify CTAs in Spanish social media posts. Their approach yields F1 scores between 0.81 and 0.85. Gupta et al. (2020) report in their working paper on training a fine-tuned BERT model for classifying political tweets and Facebook posts from the 2016 US General Election. They achieved an F1 score of 0.92 for CTAs on Twitter and 0.95 for Facebook.

In conclusion, these studies highlight the potential of using advanced NLP approaches and BERT variants to detect political CTAs in different languages and social media platforms.

### 1.4 Large Language Models for Social Science Tasks

LLMs have shown proficiency in various text classification tasks, including social sciences tasks, with some studies indicating performance superior to human annotators (Liu et al., 2023; Törnberg, 2023; Gilardi et al., 2023). While they are promising for tasks with clear and well-defined criteria, such as identifying misinformation or distinguishing political stances, applying LLMs requires caution, particularly in tasks needing deep semantic understanding (Ziems et al., 2023).

Beyond prompting, LLMs may also be used to augment training data: Bertaglia et al. (2024) explored using GPT-3.5 Turbo to generate synthetic Instagram captions for detecting sponsored content. Combining synthetic with real data improved their classification F1 score from 0.71 to 0.78, demonstrating that synthetic data can enhance classifier training.

In summary, Instagram is a critical platform for political communication. Prior research validates the potential of advanced NLP models, including BERT variants and LLMs, for detecting CTAs. Our study aims to compare GPT-4 and a fine-tuned BERT model to classify CTAs in German Instagram texts, using synthetic training data for enhanced performance.

## 2 The Corpus

We collected two types of Instagram content: permanent posts that may include multiple images or videos with a caption and stories that typically consist of a single image or video. Captions in posts represent the primary textual content on Instagram, varying in length and often featuring hashtags. While captions are the primary text elements, many images and videos incorporate embedded text or spoken words.

For our computational analysis, we deconstructed each Instagram post and story into smaller units to analyze text in various forms: captions, embedded text (through Optical Character Recognition, OCR), and speech (transcriptions) for video audio. This approach resulted in up to two text documents per image and up to three documents per video. As a post can contain multiple images, this leads to a maximum of $3 \cdot n_{\text{images}}$ documents per post, plus an additional document for the caption. In contrast, Instagram stories typically comprise a single image or video, resulting in one OCR document and an optional transcription document per story. See table 1 for an overview of corpus statistics for each text type, and table 2 for examples.

### 2.1 Data Collection & Preprocessing

We collected stories and posts published by eight parties, namely *AfD* (@afd_bund), *CDU* (@cdu), *CSU* (@christlichsozialeunion), *Die Grünen* (@die_gruenen), *Die Linke* (@dielinke), *FDP* (@fdp), *FW* (@fw_bayern), and *SPD* (@spdde), and 14 front-runners[1] (see table 7 in the appendix). Data collection started two weeks before election day, from Sept. 12th until Sept. 25, 2021, excluding election day. During this time, parties and politicians shared 712 posts and 2208 stories. Posts were collected retrospectively using CrowdTangle, amounting to 1153 images and 151 videos. Stories were collected daily at 0:00 using the `selenium` Python package to simulate a human user browsing the stories.[2] A majority of the posted stories are videos (n=1246).

Table 1: Corpus statistics grouped by post- and text-type.

| Post Type | Text Type | Documents | | Tokens | | |
|---|---|---|---|---|---|---|
| | | # | % | # | mean | % |
| Post | Caption | 720 | 15.57 | 48449 | 67.29 | 34.02 |
| Post | OCR | 1093 | 23.64 | 15529 | 14.21 | 10.90 |
| Post | Transcription | 138 | 2.99 | 22099 | 160.14 | 15.52 |
| Story | OCR | 2157 | 46.66 | 41850 | 19.40 | 29.38 |
| Story | Transcription | 515 | 11.14 | 14499 | 28.15 | 10.18 |
| | **Overall** | 4623 | 100 | 142426 | 289.19 | 100 |

Many images contain embedded text, which we extracted using OCR (`easyocr`). We transcribed videos using the *whisper-large-v2-cv11-german* model,[3] a version of OpenAI's Whisper model (Lucas et al., 2022) fine-tuned for German. We also applied OCR to the first frame of videos.

## 3 Methods

We have operationalized CTAs as a binary variable, indicating their presence or absence in documents, simplifying our model's classification process. Each social media post or story is analyzed by decomposing it into several text documents, enabling the computational analysis of multimodal data. To answer questions on a post/story level, we assign 'True' for an entire post or story if Call to Action is marked as 'True' in any of the associated documents. This section defines CTAs, describes our annotation study, and the prompt engineering

[1]We only collected stories from verified accounts. In case of missing accounts or verification marks, we followed the hierarchy Chancellor-Candidate > Front-Runner > Head of Party > Deputy Head of Party. CDU and CSU are running a joint campaign; therefore, just one candidate each is included.

[2]We can not guarantee completeness for Sep 14 due to technical problems.

[3]https://huggingface.co/bofenghuang/whisper-large-v2-cv11-german

Table 2: A sample of text documents and their human annotations for the presence (✔) or absence (✘) of Call to Action (CTA).

| Post Type | Text Type | Example | CTA | Username |
|---|---|---|---|---|
| Post | Caption | Jede*r vierte Erwerbstätige arbeitet für weniger als 12 Euro pro Stunde. Das reicht selbst bei Vollzeitarbeit kaum zum Leben. Deshalb sorgen wir für höhere Löhne und gesunde Arbeitsbedingungen. Denn Arbeit muss gerecht bezahlt werden. Du willst, dass alle Menschen von ihrer Arbeit leben können. Dann wähl Grün am Sonntag. | ✔ | @die_gruenen |
| Post | OCR | ROT-ROT-GRUN WURDE FUR MILLIONEN MENSCHEN IN BAYERN EINE VERSCHLECHTERUNG DER LEBENSSITUATION BEDEUTEN. MARKUS SÖDIR CSU | ✘ | @markus.soeder |
| Story | Transcription | Nicht verpassen, heute einschalten, einundzwanzig Uhr fünfzehn, Home Sweet Germany mit mir. | ✔ | @cdu |

and model training steps.

### 3.1 Calls to Action

A "Call to Action" (CTA) refers to statements or prompts that explicitly encourage the audience to take immediate action (Ilany Tzur et al., 2016). Larsson et al. (2024) connect CTAs in political campaigns to three of Magin et al.'s (2017) campaign functions: Informing, Mobilizing, and Interacting. The first function aims at disseminating messages and positions on important issues. Mobilizing encourages supporters to take active steps such as voting, participating in events, or sharing campaign messages. Interacting facilitates dialogue between politicians and citizens, enhancing engagement and potentially persuading voters more effectively through reciprocal communication (Magin et al., 2017). Wurst et al. (2023) relate to these functions and define three types of CTA: "Calls to Inform" encourage the audience to seek further online or offline information. This could include directing users to the party's website or inviting them to read party-related materials. "Calls to Interact" aim to increase engagement through dialogue, such as inviting users to comment on a post or participate in discussions. Finally, "Calls to Support" are direct appeals for actions that benefit the party, such as voting, donating, or sharing posts to increase the campaign's visibility.

We consider CTAs as a dichotomous variable marking the presence or absence of *any* CTA in a document. While this reduction from three types into a singular CTA reduces the analytical value of our work, we see it as a simplification to create a robust classification model. Such a model can then be used to develop more nuanced classification models in future studies.

### 3.2 The Annotation Process

Preparing our corpus, we drew a stratified sample across text (caption, OCR, transcript) and content type (story, post) combinations. The documents were annotated across two batches: We started with a 20 % sample in the first batch (n=925) and increased the sample size to 1,388 documents (app. 30 %) through a second batch.[4] Each document was independently annotated by at least three randomly assigned annotators. A total of nine annotators contributed to the annotation. Alongside one of the authors who participated in the annotation process, we recruited eight non-expert annotators from our staff and students. The latter were rewarded with participant hours for their work. The majority (8) of annotators were native German speakers. Participants received a detailed annotation guide, including examples and the GPT classification prompt (see appendix, figure 2). They had to pass a short quiz to ensure they read the manual before being invited to the annotation project. Annotations were collected remotely using the Label Studio software. Participants coded one document at a time, marking the presence of CTAs with "True" or "False". "Unsure" responses were coded as NA.

Items with disagreement were passed into a second round of annotations to increase the number of votes. Overall, nine coders created 5290 annotations. Using a majority decision, we deduced the ground truth CTA labels. Ties were resolved through the author's annotation. The interrater agreement measured by Krippendorff's $\alpha$ reached a moderate level of $\alpha$=0.67 (Krippendorff, 2004). Notably, the agreement between the major-

[4] Overall, our text corpus comprises 4,614 documents; sample sizes were rounded when balancing the text- and content-type distribution.

Table 3: An overview of the annotated corpus. About one-fifth of text documents contain (✔) Calls to Action.

| Post Type | Text Type | ✔ | | ✘ |
|---|---|---|---|---|
| Post | Caption | 106 | (49.30%) | 109 |
| Post | OCR | 52 | (15.85%) | 276 |
| Post | Transcription | 11 | (26.19%) | 31 |
| Story | OCR | 91 | (14.04%) | 557 |
| Story | Transcription | 8 | (5.16%) | 147 |
| | **Overall** | 268 | (19.31%) | 1,120 |

ity decisions and the annotating author reached a strong level (McHugh, 2012), with Cohen's $\kappa$=0.88 (n=892, excluding ties) (Cohen, 1960). This alignment with the author's labels confirms the validity of our final dataset, demonstrating that the majority decision effectively captures *Calls to Action*, despite the expected variability among non-expert student annotators.

### 3.3 Classification Approaches

We compare several classification approaches using transformer architectures and large language models to detect the presence of *Call for Actions* within posts and stories shared during the election campaign. Specifically, we compare two main classification methods: fine-tuning the gbert-large German BERT model and utilizing OpenAI's GPT-4 large language model. We tested different variations for each method: we trained two BERT models—one with the original dataset and another with an extended dataset augmented by GPT-4o. For the GPT approach, we tested GPT-4, GPT-4 Turbo, and GPT-4o models in both zero-shot and few-shot settings.

### 3.4 Fine-tuned BERT models

We fine-tuned the pre-trained 'deepset/gbert-large' model for our German language classification task using the `tansformers` library (Wolf et al., 2022). GBERT is a state-of-the-art BERT model trained on German text (Chan et al., 2020). We trained two classification models: **gbert-cta** trained on the original dataset, and **gbert-w/-synth-cta** trained on the original dataset + synthetic data generated using GPT-4o to mitigate the class imbalance of the original dataset.

Both models went through the same preprocessing and training steps. Input documents were tokenized, with truncation and padding to a maximum length of 512 tokens. The training took place on Google Colab, using Nvidia A100 graphics cards. We used wandb[5] to find the best hyperparameters, focusing on achieving the highest F1 score. To address the class imbalance in the gbert-cta model, we calculated class weights and added them to the loss function. After optimizing the hyperparameters, we validated each model with a five-fold cross-validation. This means we split the dataset into five parts stratified by the call to action variable, trained the model in four parts, and tested it on the remaining part. We added one-fifth of the synthetic data to the training data per fold for the model incorporating the synthetic dataset. We repeated this process five times, each with a different part as the test set, ensuring a robust evaluation.

### 3.5 Synthetic Dataset

To improve the quality of our BERT classification model, we generated synthetic data to counter the class imbalance of our ground truth dataset. We generated three synthetic texts for each of the documents classified to contain a CTA using the prompt in the appendix, see figure 1. During the training of the gbert-w/-synth-cta model[6], we appended the synthetic data to the training set, paying attention to not leaking any synthetic data into the evaluation dataset and, vice-versa, to not leak any evaluation or test data through synthetic data based on these datasets, into the training data. We used the following parameters for our API requests: `gpt-4o-2024-05-13`, `temperature=0` and `top_p=1`. The `max_tokens` were set individually: We calculated the number of tokens for each original text using the `tiktoken` package provided by OpenAI and used the original token count as `max_tokens`.

### 3.6 Zero- and Few-Shot using GPT

Following Törnberg's (2024) recommendations, we initiated the prompt engineering process by having one author annotate a small random sample of 150 documents. Next, we hand-crafted a preliminary classification prompt: "Given any user input, classify whether the input contains any calls to action". We tested the initial draft on ChatGPT to classify one document at a time. Responding to misclassifications, we provided nuanced examples and instructed ChatGPT to modify and im-

[5] wandb.ai

[6] Available at https://huggingface.co/chaichy/gbert-CTA-w-synth

prove the original prompt accordingly.[7] Thus, we started to improve the prompt by conversation with GPT-4.0 on the ChatGPT platform. Once the classifications on ChatGPT appeared satisfactory, we used the prompt with the API and inferred classifications for all 150 sampled captions. This iterative prompt development process has been previously demonstrated to be effective (Pryzant et al., 2023). Through the iterations, we added examples, as few-shot prompts have also been proven effective (Brown et al., 2020).

During this prompt optimization process, we compared the classification results to the author's annotations and calculated Cohen's $\kappa$ as a benchmark for the prompt's quality. Ultimately, we settled on a prompt incorporating Törnberg's advice to construct prompts around context, the question, and constraints. The context was provided in the objective part of the prompt, the question in the instructions part, and the constraints in the formatting part. Additionally, we enumerated the instructions and potential types of CTAs. Within the instructions, we employed the chain-of-thought approach (Wei et al., 2022), as the model was prompted to split input messages into sentences, classify each sentence, and then return the final classification. See figure 2 in the appendix for the final result. We deleted the examples from the few-shot prompt to convert it into the zero-shot prompt.

Our commands were sent as system prompts to the API, while each document was sent as user messages. We used the following settings for our API requests: `temperature=0`, `max_tokens=5`, and `top_p=1`. We used the following model versions: `gpt-4-0613`, `gpt-4-turbo-2024-04-09`, and `gpt-4o-2024-05-13`.

### 3.7 Evaluation Approach

We evaluated our classification approaches using established machine learning evaluation metrics: precision, recall, macro F1-score, and binary F1-score. The metrics were calculated using `scikit-learn` (Pedregosa et al., 2011). Additionally, we calculated Cohen's $\kappa$ to measure the interrater agreement between our ground truth data and the model classifications for comparison with social science research.

We used an independent test dataset to evaluate our BERT model. The corpus was stratified by

Table 4: Evaluation of CTA detection across different GPT-4 model variations and prompt types (few-shot vs. zero-shot). The highest values are marked in bold.

| | | | $F_1$ | | | |
|---|---|---|---|---|---|---|
| Model | Prompt | $\kappa$ | Macro | Binary | Precision | Recall |
| GPT-4o | Few | **0.81** | **0.91** | **0.84** | 0.82 | 0.87 |
| GPT-4 Turbo | Few | 0.77 | 0.89 | 0.81 | 0.72 | **0.92** |
| GPT-4 | Few | 0.80 | 0.90 | 0.84 | **0.95** | 0.75 |
| GPT-4o | Zero | 0.79 | 0.90 | 0.82 | 0.86 | 0.78 |
| GPT-4 Turbo | Zero | **0.81** | **0.90** | **0.84** | 0.85 | **0.83** |
| GPT4 | Zero | 0.70 | 0.85 | 0.76 | **0.94** | 0.64 |

"Call to Action" and split into two sets: 80% for training and 20% for testing. The 80% training set was used for hyperparameter tuning and cross-validation, while the 20% test set was reserved for the final evaluation. To evaluate the GPT classifications, we excluded rows containing phrases from the few-shot examples (n=16) and used the entire annotated dataset.

## 4 Results

In the first part of this section, we will answer our primary questions **RQ1a–c** regarding the computational classifications through the external evaluation based on human annotations. At the end of the section, we will answer our secondary interest **RQ2**, uncovering the differences between stories, posts, and parties.

### 4.1 Evaluation of GPT Models

The performance across all tested GPT models is consistently high: The macro F1 scores[8] range from F1=0.85 to F1=0.91 (compare table 4). GPT-4o, with the few-shot prompt, achieves the highest classification performance, answering **RQ1a**. Upon closer inspection, the model performs best when classifying captions, followed by OCR in posts and post transcriptions. For stories, the performance drops to F1=0.85 for OCR and even lower for transcription text.

### 4.2 Evaluation of BERT Models

Both BERT models display a comparatively high classification quality ranging from F1=0.92 for the model trained on the original data to F1=0.93 for the model incorporating the synthetic training data (see table 5). Thus, to answer **RQ1b**: incorporating synthetic training data generated by GPT-4o

[7] for example: https://chatgpt.com/share/fdd306b0-ff2d-4971-bad2-92eb6e8f07a7

[8] Subsequently, we always refer to macro F1 scores unless stated otherwise.

Table 5: Classification metrics on the independent test dataset for the fine-tuned gbert models.

| Model Name | $F_1$ Macro | $F_1$ Binary | Precision | Recall |
|---|---|---|---|---|
| **gbert-cta** | 0.92 | 0.87 | 0.86 | 0.89 |
| **gbert-w/-synth-cta** | **0.93** | **0.89** | **0.98** | **0.81** |

improved classification performance. Since the performance has only improved by the second decimal place, the synthetic text generation prompt should be revisited to introduce greater linguistic variety, and the overall results should be interpreted with caution. The small quality improvement might be influenced by other factors, suggesting that the answer to RQ1b is not universally valid. A five-fold cross-validation evaluated the model hyperparameters. The mean F1=0.90 score for the gbert-w/-synth-cta model demonstrates its ability to generalize well across different subsets of the data, and the standard deviation of 0.02 suggests a stable performance with minimal variability.

### 4.3 Performance Across Text-Type and Post-Type Combinations

To answer **RQ1c**, we investigated the classification performance for each text-type and post-type combination (compare table 6). Notably, the poor results for the classification of story transcriptions and the excellent results for post transcriptions stand out. These outliers may be partly attributed to the low number of cases: of the 12 post transcriptions in the test set, one contains a call to action. Both models classified the document correctly; the F1 score is perfect without false positives. However, across story transcriptions, the BERT model missed three out of four CTAs across 26 documents. Coincidentally, two out of the three false negatives are Calls to Interact. They have been neglected in posts of the 2021 campaign (Wurst et al., 2023), indicating that the training data contains few documents of this type.

The lower classification performance of GPT-4o across OCR texts compared to the BERT model is striking. Across both post types, OCR documents constitute about 70% of all text documents and show the lowest mean token count per document. The OCR process introduces noise by recognizing irrelevant text, i.e., street and shop signs in the background and incorrectly recognized words. The OCR text bits are concatenated and do not necessarily follow the right word order. For captions, the OpenAI model is on par with the BERT model and exceeds the fine-tuned model in transcriptions.

### 4.4 Calls to Action in Posts and Stories

We used the gbert-w/-synth-cta classifications to answer **RQ2**: Instagram posts display a higher relative mention of Calls to Action. Almost half of all captions (44.7%) contain CTAs, followed by 16.8% of transcriptions and 15.9% of OCR documents. In stories, we found the most CTAs in the embedded text (10.5%) and a very low number in transcriptions (2.3%). On the post/story level, almost half of all posts contain a Call to Action (49.58%), compared to only 10.64% of all stories. The difference between CTAs in posts and stories is significant ($\chi^2(1) = 501.84$, $p < .001$), with a medium effect size (Cramer's V = 0.42).

Next, we tested the use of CTAs across parties for all post types: The analysis indicates a significant difference in their usage between different parties ($\chi^2(15) = 604.13$, $p < .001$), with a medium effect size (Cramer's V = 0.46). We accounted for the interaction between party and post type to ensure this difference was not due to varying distributions of post types between parties. This suggests that the parties varied in their use of calls to action in their Instagram election campaigns, even considering the different use of stories and posts across parties. For posts, the FDP displayed the highest use of CTAs (70.45%), followed by the Greens (60.23%). On the low end, the SPD made the least use of CTAs (31.97%), followed by AfD (40.54%). In stories, the parties acted differently: The CDU (18.76%) and CSU (14.78%) show the highest use of calls. Similarly, the Freie Wähler party (14.97%) and the Left (14.56%) display relatively high numbers of CTAs in their stories. The CTA leaders for posts, the Greens (5.12%) and the FDP (5.66%), are at the bottom of the list for stories.

## 5 Discussion

Our experiments confirm the efficacy of large language models for the binary classification of Calls to Action in social media election campaigns. Overall, the GPT-4 models performed well in zero- and few-shot settings. Regarding Cohen's Kappa, there is a strong agreement between language model classifications and ground truth labels.

Fine-tuning the gbert-large BERT model, however, exceeds the performance of the LLMs. The relatively low number of 1,388 human-annotated

Table 6: Evaluation results per document and post type combination for the best classification models for the test dataset. The highest values between models are marked in bold.

| | | gbert-w/-synth | | | GPT-4o | | | |
|---|---|---|---|---|---|---|---|---|
| Post Type | Text Type | $\kappa$ | $F_1$ Macro | $F_1$ Binary | $\kappa$ | $F_1$ Macro | $F_1$ Binary | n |
| Post | OCR | **0.81** | **0.91** | **0.83** | 0.73 | 0.87 | 0.75 | 59 |
| Post | Caption | **0.86** | **0.93** | **0.92** | **0.86** | **0.93** | **0.92** | 44 |
| Post | Transcription | **1** | **1** | **1** | **1** | **1** | **1** | 12 |
| Story | OCR | **0.91** | **0.95** | **0.92** | 0.78 | 0.89 | 0.81 | 137 |
| Story | Transcription | 0.36 | 0.67 | 0.4 | **0.76** | **0.88** | **0.80** | 26 |

documents, with 270 positive cases, yielded a well-performing classification model. Adding synthetic training data generated by the GPT-4o model improved the model further. Both models surpass the performance of CTA classification approaches reported for Russian (Rogers et al., 2019) and Spanish (Siskou et al., 2022) social media texts. Compared to a fine-tuned version of BERT for classifying CTAs in English Twitter and Facebook messages (Gupta et al., 2020), our models perform similarly well while using only a third of the training data.

A closer look at the classification quality on a text- and post-type level reveals problems with classifying story transcripts. CTAs in these documents account for only 5.16% of the overall training data. This highlights the potential for further improvements in data augmentation using synthetic documents: A qualitative inspection of synthetic training data generated based on transcripts revealed less similarity to original transcripts than to, for example, post captions. Improving the synthetic data prompt to generate more realistic transcripts might improve the classification performance for this type of text while increasing the linguistic variance across synthetic training data might further increase the overall classification performance.

Striving for the best possible annotation quality, we chose the gbert-w/-synth-cta for our classification task. However, training a robust classification model takes several steps, from annotation through hyperparameter tuning to the final evaluation. Conversely, the GPT-4 models are readily available, and prompt engineering was comparatively uncomplicated in our context. With decreasing prices, evolving models, and the availability of open-source alternatives, like Llama 3, this study further confirms the utility of large language models for computational social science tasks and political science analyses.

After applying the model, we uncovered significant differences between political actors' use of CTAs in stories and posts. We found a slightly higher prevalence of CTAs across posts compared to previous studies (Wurst et al., 2023), which may be attributed to our sample: We collected data close to election day, CTAs have been shown to increase closer to election day (Stromer-Galley et al., 2021; Wurst et al., 2023). Our study contributes to the study of election campaigns mainly by uncovering a significant difference between posts and stories and between parties. The Greens, for example, have been highlighted before as the party with the highest prevalence of CTAs across their posts. At the same time, we found the party's stories contain the lowest number of CTAs relative to the number of stories posted. Overall, the use of CTAs in stories was low, which contrasts with Towner and Muñoz's (2024) observations of the 2018 U.S. gubernatorial election, raising questions about what other elements or content constituted political stories in the 2021 election.

### 5.1 Limitations

Our study has several limitations. We observed the campaign for a relatively short period – two weeks – due to the necessary effort to capture ephemeral stories. Additionally, we limited our study to verified accounts only. We also limited the analysis to the first frame of each video to decrease complexity, possibly dismissing embedded text in any other frame.

### 5.2 Future Work

The literature on calls to action in election campaigns distinguishes between different types of CTAs that fulfill various campaign functions. To gain a more holistic understanding of election campaigns and increase the analytical power of our approach, we see future work to build on top of our classification model: Using the positive classifications, future studies can collect human annotations to train a multi-label classification model. Following Törnberg's argumentation, future work should evaluate the classification performance of open-source LLMs.

### 5.3 Ethical Considerations

We collected publicly available data posted by parties and verified party officials only. We followed the recommendations towards a conscientious approach to data collection by Venturini and Rogers, who considered scraping a "necessary evil" (Venturini and Rogers, 2019). In our article, we do not address personal or sensitive data.

## References


Michael Achmann and Christian Wolff. 2023. Policy issues vs. Documentation: Using BERTopic to gain insight in the political communication in Instagram stories and posts during the 2021 German Federal election campaign. *Digital Humanities in the Nordic and Baltic Countries Publications*, 5(1):11–28.

Christian Baden, Christian Pipal, Martijn Schoonvelde, and Mariken A C G van der Velden. 2022. Three Gaps in Computational Text Analysis Methods for Social Sciences: A Research Agenda. *Communication methods and measures*, 16(1):1–18.

Jennifer Bast. 2021. Politicians, Parties, and Government Representatives on Instagram: A Review of Research Approaches, Usage Patterns, and Effects. *Review of Communication Research*, 9.

Thales Bertaglia, Lily Heisig, Rishabh Kaushal, and Adriana Iamnitchi. 2024. InstaSynth: Opportunities and Challenges in Generating Synthetic Instagram Data with ChatGPT for Sponsored Content Detection.

Lukas Birkenmaier, Clemens M Lechner, and Claudia Wagner. 2023. The Search for Solid Ground in Text as Data: A Systematic Review of Validation Practices and Practical Recommendations for Validation. *Communication methods and measures*, pages 1–29.

Tom B Brown, Benjamin Mann, Nick Ryder, Melanie Subbiah, Jared Kaplan, Prafulla Dhariwal, Arvind Neelakantan, Pranav Shyam, Girish Sastry, Amanda Askell, Sandhini Agarwal, Ariel Herbert-Voss, Gretchen Krueger, Tom Henighan, Rewon Child, Aditya Ramesh, Daniel M Ziegler, Jeffrey Wu, Clemens Winter, Christopher Hesse, Mark Chen, Eric Sigler, Mateusz Litwin, Scott Gray, Benjamin Chess, Jack Clark, Christopher Berner, Sam McCandlish, Alec Radford, Ilya Sutskever, and Dario Amodei. 2020. Language Models are Few-Shot Learners.

Branden Chan, Stefan Schweter, and Timo Möller. 2020. German's next language model. In *Proceedings of the 28th International Conference on Computational Linguistics*, pages 6788–6796, Barcelona, Spain (Online). International Committee on Computational Linguistics.

Lena Clever, Tim Schatto-Eckrodt, Nico Christoph Clever, and Lena Frischlich. 2023. Behind Blue Skies: A Multimodal Automated Content Analysis of Islamic Extremist Propaganda on Instagram. *Social Media + Society*, 9(1).

Jacob Cohen. 1960. A Coefficient of Agreement for Nominal Scales. *Educational and psychological measurement*, 20(1):37–46.

Jacob Devlin, Ming-Wei Chang, Kenton Lee, and Kristina Toutanova. 2019. BERT: Pre-training of deep bidirectional transformers for language understanding. In *Proceedings of the 2019 Conference of the North American Chapter of the Association for Computational Linguistics: Human Language Technologies, Volume 1 (Long and Short Papers)*, pages 4171–4186, Minneapolis, Minnesota. Association for Computational Linguistics.

Stephanie Geise, Katharina Maubach, and Alena Boettcher Eli. 2024. Picture me in person: Personalization and emotionalization as political campaign strategies on social media in the German federal election period 2021. *New Media & Society*.

Fabrizio Gilardi, Meysam Alizadeh, and Maël Kubli. 2023. ChatGPT outperforms crowd workers for text-annotation tasks. *Proceedings of the National Academy of Sciences of the United States of America*, 120(30).

Shloak Gupta, S. Bolden, Jay Kachhadia, A. Korsunska, and J. Stromer-Galley. 2020. Polibert: Classifying political social media messages with bert. Working paper presented at the Social, Cultural and Behavioral Modeling (SBP-BRIMS 2020) Conference.

Jörg Haßler, Anna-Katharina Wurst, and Katharina Pohl. 2023. Politicians over issues? Visual personalization in three Instagram election campaigns. *Information, Communication and Society*, pages 1–21.

Naama Ilany Tzur, Lior Zalmanson, and Gal Oestreicher-Singer. 2016. The dark side of user participation - the effect of calls to action on trust and information revelation. *SSRN Electronic Journal*.

Ole Kelm, Michael Angenendt, Thomas Poguntke, and Ulrich Rosar. 2023. Which candidates benefit from social media? An analysis of the 2021 German federal election. *Electoral studies*, 86:102701.

Wolfgang Koch. 2022. Reichweiten von social-media-plattformen und messengern. *Media Perspektiven*, 10:471–478. Ergebnisse der ARD/ZDF-Onlinestudie 2022.

Klaus Krippendorff. 2004. *Content Analysis: An Introduction to Its Methodology.* Sage.

Anders Olof Larsson, Hedvig Tønnesen, Melanie Magin, and Eli Skogerbø. 2024. Calls to (what kind of?) action: A framework for comparing political actors' campaign strategies across social media platforms. *New Media & Society*.

Yiheng Liu, Tianle Han, Siyuan Ma, Jiayue Zhang, Yuanyuan Yang, Jiaming Tian, Hao He, Antong Li, Mengshen He, Zhengliang Liu, Zihao Wu, Lin Zhao, Dajiang Zhu, Xiang Li, Ning Qiang, Dingang Shen, Tianming Liu, and Bao Ge. 2023. Summary of ChatGPT-Related Research and Perspective Towards the Future of Large Language Models.

Luis Lucas, David Tomás, and Jose Garcia-Rodriguez. 2022. Exploiting the Relationship Between Visual and Textual Features in Social Networks for Image Classification with Zero-Shot Deep Learning. In *16th International Conference on Soft Computing Models in Industrial and Environmental Applications (SOCO 2021)*, pages 369–378. Springer International Publishing.

Melanie Magin, Nicole Podschuweit, Jörg Haßler, and Uta Russmann. 2017. Campaigning in the fourth age of political communication. A multi-method study on the use of Facebook by German and Austrian parties in the 2013 national election campaigns. *Information, Communication and Society*, 20(11):1698–1719.

Mary L. McHugh. 2012. Interrater reliability: the kappa statistic. *Biochemia Medica (Zagreb)*, 22(3):276–282.

F. Pedregosa, G. Varoquaux, A. Gramfort, V. Michel, B. Thirion, O. Grisel, M. Blondel, P. Prettenhofer, R. Weiss, V. Dubourg, J. Vanderplas, A. Passos, D. Cournapeau, M. Brucher, M. Perrot, and E. Duchesnay. 2011. Scikit-learn: Machine learning in Python. *Journal of Machine Learning Research*, 12:2825–2830.

Reid Pryzant, Dan Iter, Jerry Li, Yin Tat Lee, Chenguang Zhu, and Michael Zeng. 2023. Automatic Prompt Optimization with "Gradient Descent" and Beam Search.

Anna Rogers, Olga Kovaleva, and Anna Rumshisky. 2019. Calls to Action on Social Media: Detection, Social Impact, and Censorship Potential. In *Proceedings of the Second Workshop on Natural Language Processing for Internet Freedom: Censorship, Disinformation, and Propaganda*, pages 36–44, Hong Kong, China. Association for Computational Linguistics.

Katharina Schlosser, Jörg Haßler, and Anna-Katharina Wurst. 2023. Visuelle Personalisierung des Negative Campaigning: Eine Konzeptualisierung anlässlich des Wahlkampfes auf Instagram. In Christina Holtz-Bacha, editor, *Die (Massen-) Medien im Wahlkampf: Die Bundestagswahl 2021*, pages 155–177. Springer Fachmedien Wiesbaden, Wiesbaden.

Wassiliki Siskou, Clara Giralt Mirón, Sarah Molina-Raith, and Miriam Butt. 2022. Automatized Detection and Annotation for Calls to Action in Latin-American Social Media Postings. In *Proceedings of the 6th Joint SIGHUM Workshop on Computational Linguistics for Cultural Heritage, Social Sciences, Humanities and Literature*, pages 65–69, Gyeongju, Republic of Korea. International Conference on Computational Linguistics.

Jennifer Stromer-Galley, Patrícia Rossini, Jeff Hemsley, Sarah E Bolden, and Brian McKernan. 2021. Political Messaging Over Time: A Comparison of US Presidential Candidate Facebook Posts and Tweets in 2016 and 2020. *Social Media + Society*, 7(4):20563051211063465.

Petter Törnberg. 2023. ChatGPT-4 Outperforms Experts and Crowd Workers in Annotating Political Twitter Messages with Zero-Shot Learning.

Petter Törnberg. 2024. Best Practices for Text Annotation with Large Language Models.

Terri L Towner and Caroline L Muñoz. 2024. Tell Me an Instagram Story: Ephemeral Communication and the 2018 Gubernatorial Elections. *Social science computer review*.

Terri L Towner and Caroline Lego Muñoz. 2022. A Long Story Short: An Analysis of Instagram Stories during the 2020 Campaigns. *Journal of Political Marketing*, pages 1–14.

Chris J Vargo and Toby Hopp. 2020. Fear, Anger, and Political Advertisement Engagement: A Computational Case Study of Russian-Linked Facebook and Instagram Content. *Journalism & mass communication quarterly*, 97(3):743–761.

Tommaso Venturini and Richard Rogers. 2019. "API-Based Research" or How can Digital Sociology and Journalism Studies Learn from the Facebook and Cambridge Analytica Data Breach. *Digital Journalism*, 7(4):532–540.

Jason Wei, Xuezhi Wang, Dale Schuurmans, Maarten Bosma, Brian Ichter, Fei Xia, Ed Chi, Quoc Le, and Denny Zhou. 2022. Chain-of-Thought Prompting Elicits Reasoning in Large Language Models.

Thomas Wolf, Lysandre Debut, Victor Sanh, Julien Chaumond, Clement Delangue, Anthony Moi, Perric Cistac, Clara Ma, Yacine Jernite, Julien Plu, Canwen Xu, Teven Le Scao, Sylvain Gugger, Mariama Drame, Quentin Lhoest, and Alexander M. Rush. 2022. Transformers: State-of-the-Art Natural Language Processing.

Anna-Katharina Wurst, Katharina Pohl, and Jörg Haßler. 2023. Mobilization in the Context of Campaign Functions and Citizen Participation. *Media and Communication*, 11(3).

Caleb Ziems, William Held, Omar Shaikh, Jiaao Chen, Zhehao Zhang, and Diyi Yang. 2023. Can Large Language Models Transform Computational Social Science?

# A Appendix

→ See next page.

Table 7: Selected politicians' accounts and their positions and party affiliation at the time of data collection.

| Name | Party | Position | Username |
|---|---|---|---|
| Alice Weidel | AfD | Front-Runner | @alice.weidel |
| Jörg Meuthen | AfD | Head of Party | @joerg.meuthen |
| Armin Laschet | CDU | Chancellor Candidate | @armin_laschet |
| Markus Söder | CSU | Head of Party | @markus.soeder |
| Annalena Baerbock | GRÜNE | Chancellor Candidate | @abaerbock |
| Robert Habeck | GRÜNE | Front-Runner | @robert.habeck |
| Ates Gürpinar | Die Linke | Deputy Head of Party | @atesgurpinar |
| Susanne Henning-Wellsow | Die Linke | Head of Party | @susanne_hennig_wellsow |
| Christian Lindner | FDP | Front-Runner | @christianlindner |
| Nicola Beer | FDP | Deputy Head of Party | @nicola_beer |
| Engin Eroglu | FW | Deputy Head of Party | @engin_eroglu |
| Gregor Voht | FW | Deputy Head of Party | @grey_gor |
| Olaf Scholz | SPD | Chancellor Candidate | @olafscholz |
| Saskia Esken | SPD | Head of Party | @saskiaesken |

```
Review the text below. It is a {text_type} {post_type} from the 2021 German Federal Election campaign, shared by one of the political parties. Human annotators identified calls to action in this text, which may be explicit or implicit. These calls to action could, for example, include urging viewers to vote for a particular party, attend an event, or visit a website for more information.

Your task is to generate an additional text that mimics the style, type, and features of the provided example. The text will be used as synthetic examples to train a BERT model, so it must be representative and diverse.

## Task Details:
- The text should clearly fit the defined content type: {post_type}.
- The style should align with the descriptor: {text_type}.
- The example has been posted by the Instagram user {row['username']}, representative of the party {row['party']}
- The length of the generated text should match the length of the example below (approx. {len(example)} characters).
- Text text should incorporate exactly one call to action in each text

## Instructions:
1. Analyze the provided example to maintain consistency in tone and style, and party affiliation.
2. Include one distinct call to action in each generated text.
3. Tailor each text to the context of the 2021 German Federal Election campaign.
4. Produce all texts in German to maintain authenticity and relevance to the election context.
5. Ensure that each text aligns with the political affiliation with {row['party']} to maintain variety and minimize bias in the training dataset.

## Formatting:
- Output should consist solely of the generated {post_type} {text_type} texts.
- Do not include any additional text, commentary, or formatting elements in your response.

## Example:
{example}
```

Figure 1: The text generation prompt used with GPT-4o to generate synthetic training data.

You're an expert in detecting calls-to-action (CTAs) from texts.

##Objective:
Determine the presence or absence of explicit and implicit CTAs within German-language content sourced from Instagram texts such as posts, stories, video transcriptions, and captions related to political campaigns from any user input.

##Instructions:
1. Examine each input message.
2. Segment the content into individual sentences.
3. For each sentence, identify:
    a. Explicit CTA: Direct requests for an audience to act which are directed at the reader, e.g., "beide Stimmen CDU!", "Am 26. September #FREIEWÄHLER in den #Bundestag wählen."
    b. Explicit CTA: A clear direction on where or how to find additional information, e.g., "Mehr dazu findet ihr im Wahlprogramm auf fdp.de/vielzutun", "Besuche unsere Website für weitere Details."
    c. Implicit CTA: Suggestions or encouragements that subtly propose an action directed at the reader without a direct command, e.g., "findet ihr unter dem Link in unserer Story."
4. CTAs should be actions that the reader or voter can perform directly, like voting for a party, clicking a link, checking more information, etc. General statements, assertions, or suggestions not directed at the reader should not be classified as CTAs.
5. If any CTA is detected return 'True'. Otherwise, return 'False'.

##Formatting:
Just return your classification result, either True or False.

Figure 2: The few-shot CTA detection prompt. It was converted into the zero-shot prompt by deleting the examples.

# Multilingual Bot Accusations: How Different Linguistic Contexts Shape Perceptions of Social Bots

**Leon Fröhling**
GESIS - Leibniz Institute for the Social Sciences
leon.froehling@gesis.org

**Xiaofei Li**
RWTH Aachen
xiaofei.li1@rwth-aachen.de

**Dennis Assenmacher**
GESIS - Leibniz Institute for the Social Sciences
dennis.assenmacher@gesis.org

**Abstract**

Recent research indicates that the online use of the term "bot" has evolved over time. In the past, people used the term to accuse others of displaying automated behavior. However, it has gradually transformed into a linguistic tool to dehumanize the conversation partner, particularly on polarizing topics. Although this trend has been observed in English-speaking contexts, it is still unclear whether it holds true in other socio-linguistic environments. In this work we extend existing work on bot accusations and explore the phenomenon in a multilingual setting. We identify three distinct accusation patterns that characterize the different languages.

## 1 Introduction

Social bots are described in academia as automated accounts in online media that have the ability to manipulate public opinion on large scale. While a plethora of current work on bots focusses on their detection, researchers are increasingly interested in how people perceive social bots and how they talk about them in the online sphere. In this work we extend a recent study by Assenmacher et al. (2024) who look at accusation situations, i.e. those instances where a user on Twitter (𝕏) accuses another user of being a bot. While earlier work only focused on the English speaking landscape of the platform we want to investigate the phenomenon in a multi-lingual setting, examining the following research question:

> *What are the differences in how users accuse each other of being a bot across different languages, and can we identify a taxonomy of these accusation types?*

## 2 Related Work

Up until recently, the largest part of research on social bots has been concerned with developing methods for their detection, trying to expose and characterize their efforts to systematically influence the discourse on social media (Yaojun Yan and Yang, 2023). While most of these approaches focus on the platform Twitter and only look on the English parts of it by default (Orabi et al., 2020), few methods are available that are by design multilingual (Martin-Gutierrez et al., 2021; Lundberg et al., 2019), helping to grapple with a phenomenon that has been found to impact the online public discourse and events in countries around the world (Woolley, 2016), cascading across cultural and linguistic borders (Xu et al., 2024). While researchers developing these methods have to start out from the difficulty of operationalizing a phenomenon that has been found to be changing in meaning even within the academic discourse (Grimme et al., 2017), recent work by Assenmacher et al. (2024) has found an even more drastic shift in the understanding of the concept bot by social media users, away from the academic definition of *a program that automatically produces content and interacts with humans on social media* (Ferrara et al., 2016) towards one that locates bots in the context of polarizing debates and insulting or even dehumanizing comments, effectively denying a (human) social media user their ability to meaningfully participate in the public discourse. Their empirical finding, restricted to the English linguistic context, has been backed up by evidence from a survey conducted by Kats and Sharif (2022), who report that more than a third of participants define bots as "fake accounts", "posing as actual humans", thereby trying to "sway public opinion". The findings by Schmuck and Von Sikorski (2020) further indicate that users might be impacted by the threat they perceive from bot campaigns on social media by exposure to news coverage on them, opening up a channel for different perceptions across regional contexts. Given such conceptual difficulties, it might not come as a surprise that researchers



*Proceedings of the 58th Annual Meeting of the Association for Computational Linguistics*, pages 14–32
July 5–10, 2020. 

report for different platforms and linguistic and cultural contexts, including Russian (Kolomeets et al., 2024), Chinese (Tian and Fussell, 2024) and English (Kenny et al., 2024), how platform users struggle to distinguish human from bot accounts. On top of this general confusion, recent research on human perceptions of bots has found that users tend to perceive accounts with opposing viewpoints as non-human (Wischnewski et al., 2021), easily dismissing their opinions (Schweitzer et al., 2024).

## 3 Data

To extend the study conducted by Assenmacher et al. (2024) to a multi-lingual context, we combine different datasets collected and annotated for complimentary purposes.

### 3.1 Multilingual Data Collection

The first step was to replicate the data collection for different languages of interest. In the English-only study by Assenmacher et al. (2024), they first collected all tweets containing the keyword bot, before then developing their own bot accusation classifier to select those tweets that could actually be considered bot accusations. We used the findings of Pfeffer et al. (2023) to select some of the most popular languages on Twitter for inclusion in our analysis, as well as Korean as a language for which we knew of existing research and general media coverage on popular bot campaigns (Keller et al., 2020) and German as the language of our own linguistic background. For each included language, we conducted extensive checks on the relevant keyword for our purpose of first collecting all tweets containing the language-specific version of the term bot, used in the same sense as the term bot in the social media context in the English language. We did so by comparing different translation tools applied to the term bot used in different constellations and contexts, as well as by searching Twitter with candidate keywords, to see whether potentially relevant tweets would show up. For all languages, we additionally consulted with colleagues who are native speakers of the respective language and asked for confirmation that the keyword we selected for the language would actually be the most likely keyword to refer to a bot on Twitter. We collected the data directly from the Twitter v2 API full-archive endpoint via the academic access. The data collection covered the twelve-year period from January 2011 to January 2023. We constructed the API queries following the pattern

[keyword]*is:reply lang:*[language],

where [keyword] and [language] are replaced with the respective keyword and language code for any of the considered languages. By design of the keyword-matching of the API, this query returns only reply-tweets in the specified language that contain the keyword either as a freestanding word or preceded and/or followed by a punctuation mark. Table 1 gives an overview of the included languages, the keywords used in the API queries, as well as the number of tweets collected.

| Language | Keyword | Tweets |
|---|---|---:|
| Arabic | بوت [bot] | 333,221 |
| French | bot | 579,004 |
| German | bot | 289,260 |
| Japanese | ボット [bot] | 607,188 |
| Korean | 봇 [bot] | 2,976,879 |
| Portuguese | bot | 1,920,350 |
| Russian | бот [bot] | 267,614 |
| Spanish | bot | 2,395,066 |
| Turkish | bot | 385,631 |

Table 1: Languages considered for the data collection, the language-specific equivalents of the English term bot used in the API query construction and the number of collected tweets.

### 3.2 Training Datasets

For some of the bot accusation detection methods presented below, we make use of the training dataset used by Assenmacher et al. (2024). They manually annotated a subset of 2,000 English-language tweets potentially containing bot accusations, reporting an inter-annotator agreement of $\kappa = 0.83$. While they fine-tune and evaluate exclusively for the English-language context, we hope to transfer some of their classifier's strong performance in detecting English bot accusations to the languages we are studying.

To supplement the use of the English-language dataset in developing the language-specific classifiers, we also sample training datasets directly from the tweets collected for each of the considered languages. These datasets are random samples of 3,200 tweets per language and form the basis for two different versions of training datasets. First, the tweets in their original languages are annotated using OpenAI's GPT-3.5,[1] leveraging the

[1]https://platform.openai.com/docs/models/

large language model's (LLM) zero-shot capabilities (prompt details in Appendix A). Second, the tweets are translated into English using Google Translate.[2] We acknowledge the potential for (systematic) errors when relying on LLMs and machine learning models for these tasks in the section on Limitations below, but concede that our work on such a broad range of languages on such a large scale would otherwise be infeasible.

### 3.3 Validation Datasets

To ensure that the bot accusation classifiers we introduce below still produce sufficiently valid results, we ask human crowdworkers - picked for their proficiency in the corresponding language and their familiarity with Twitter - to annotate subsets of 200 randomly sampled tweets per language, thereby generating high quality, groundtruth datasets. We collect three annotations per tweet, and label tweets as an *accusation* if at least two annotators considered it as such, and label them as *no accusation* otherwise. Appendix A provides details on the crowd annotations.

## 4 Methods

The core challenge in multilingual research is the handling of texts that the researcher is not familiar with. In our particular endeavor of studying the linguistic phenomenon of bot accusations across different languages, the ability to reliably discern tweets in which other users are actually accused of being bots from mere discussions of the concept or unrelated posts on potential synonyms is essential to the subsequent analysis methods, which, nonetheless, also need to be adjustable to a multilingual setting.

### 4.1 Multilingual Accusation Detection

In the following, we develop different methods for the detection of bot accusations from tweets mentioning the keyword bot in different languages. All of these approaches do not require the researcher to be able to read or understand the language, building on either pretrained models that are inherently multilingual or specialized on a specific language, or on classifiers trained on the different versions of the training datasets introduced above. Apart from the difficulties of dealing with different languages, these methods are further constrained by compute and financial budgets. While the evaluation of the GPT-3.5 annotations on the training datasets described above is very promising, it would be prohibitively expensive to annotate the full datasets using the model, available only through a paid API.

#### 4.1.1 NLI Classifier

The first method (subsequently referred to as $\mathbf{Model_{NLI}}$) to detect bot accusations from tweets containing the (language-specific) keyword frames the classification task as a natural language inference (NLI) problem to leverage the zero-shot capabilities of pre-trained, language-specific NLI models. The biggest advantage of this approach is that it does neither require expensive annotated data nor access to expensive state-of-the-art models. While NLI models were originally developed to classify whether a hypothesis is either a contradiction, an entailment or neutral to a given premise, they can also be used for any classification tasks, by presenting the instance to be annotated as the premise and by phrasing the available labels as the hypotheses to be classified. Based on the entailment scores assigned to the different labels presented to the model in form of the hypotheses, a final label can then be constructed for any instance presented as the premise.

We directly use the texts of the tweets as premises, and construct hypotheses both for the *accusation* and the *no accusation* label. The templates used for hypothesis-creation were not selected for linguistic sophistication, but rather to be universally applicable, following the English example "This text is about [label]", where [label] for English would either be *accusing user of being bot* or *not accusing user of being bot*. Appendix B provides details on the pre-trained NLI models and the templates used to construct the hypotheses.

#### 4.1.2 Multilingual BERT

The second method ($\mathbf{Model_{Multi}}$) consists in fine-tuning a pre-trained, multilingual language model on the expert-annotated English language data used by Assenmacher et al. (2024). We use the *bert-base-multilingual-cased* model, [3] a BERT (Devlin et al., 2019) variant that has gained remarkable multilingual capabilities thanks to its pre-training on a corpus covering a total of 104 different languages. Most importantly, previous research has shown that fine-tuning the model to a task on data from one language also leads to improved performance on the task in other languages

[2]https://translate.google.com/

[3]https://huggingface.co/bert-base-multilingual-cased

(Pires et al., 2019). In contrast to the first method, the fine-tuning approach requires the existence of annotated training data. However, our hope in using this method is that by fine-tuning the model on the high quality English training data (some of) the strong performance reported by Assenmacher et al. (2024) for detecting bot accusations in English would transfer to the other languages included here. Appendix B details our fine-tuning setup.

#### 4.1.3 Ensemble

The third method (**Model$_{\textbf{Ensemble}}$**) is designed to combine linguistic cues as best manifested in the data originally collected in the respective language with the expert annotations available only for the English language data. First, we fine-tune language-specific, pre-trained classification models on the training datasets in the original language, annotated using the GPT-3.5 model as described above. Second, we fine-tune an English-only, pre-trained BERTweet classifier (Nguyen et al., 2020) on the expert-annotated dataset provided by Assenmacher et al. (2024). To then annotate a tweet, we apply the language-specific classifier to the original version and the English-only classifier to the translated version. Only if both classifiers indicate that the tweet contains a bot accusation do we label it as such, otherwise it is considered to not be an accusation. We hope that the combination of these two crucial aspects improves the precision of the method, with the original-language classifier catching instances where important information is lost in translation and the English-only classifier catching instances where the annotation informed by zero-shot-GPT-3.5 deviates too much from the more precise expert annotations.

### 4.2 Multilingual Accusation Analysis

Once the tweets collected in the different languages have been classified using the accusation detection approaches presented above, the final step is to identify universal as well as language-specific patterns in the development of the phenomenon of social media users accusing each other as bots. Our choice of methods is inspired by Assenmacher et al. (2024), but we had to find ways to apply them across nine different languages and to make the results they produce comparable.

#### 4.2.1 Word Embeddings Over Time

We use the proximity of the term bot to other terms in a language-specific word embedding space as an indication of the usage of the term and to detect shifts in its meaning. Word embeddings capture semantic relationships based on the co-occurrences of different terms by projecting words as vectors in a shared embedding space. To identify terms most closely associated with the term bot at different points in time, we calculate the cosine similarity between the vector for bot and those of all other vectors in the different embedding spaces that we trained using Word2Vec (Mikolov et al., 2013) for each language-year combination. The embeddings cover all years from 2011 to 2023 individually, aggregating only years with insufficient data into single embeddings. Since word embeddings are non-deterministic, we report those ten nearest neighbors of the term bot that show up consistently in five different runs of the embedding model, initialized with different random seeds.

#### 4.2.2 Toxicity Measurement

To check whether tweets containing bot accusations are generally more toxic than their non-accusation counterparts, and to track the general development of the level of toxicity of accusation tweets over time, we measure the toxicity of accusations using the pre-trained Detoxify model (Hanu and Unitary team, 2020). While these models were optimized to measure toxicity across a number of languages, they do not cover Arabic, German, Japanese, and Korean. For these languages, we measure the toxicity of tweets translated into English using the English model variant.

#### 4.2.3 Context Clustering

Shifting focus from the accusations themselves to the contexts in which they occur, we apply unsupervised clustering techniques to the original tweets preceding the bot accusations. We use multilingual sentence transformers (Reimers and Gurevych, 2020) to transform the original tweets into document embeddings, representing the tweets' semantic contents. By using cosine similarity to measure the distance between the embeddings of the different tweets, we are able to identify clusters of tweets that are supposedly concerned with similar topics and contexts, again per language-year combination as described above.

To help us interpret the resulting clusters, we first extract the most significant tokens of each cluster via cTFIDF scores. Based on these tokens that best summarize each cluster in contrast to the remaining clusters in the same embedding space, we

| | Model$_{Multi}$ | | | Model$_{NLI}$ | | | Model$_{Ensemble}$ | | | |
|---|---|---|---|---|---|---|---|---|---|---|
| | P | R | F1 | P | R | F1 | P | R | F1 | S% |
| Arabic | 0.250 | 0.011 | 0.022 | 0.600 | **0.862** | **0.708** | **0.716** | 0.667 | 0.690 | 3.31 |
| French | 0.794 | 0.476 | 0.595 | 0.684 | **0.762** | **0.721** | **0.805** | 0.629 | 0.706 | 7.45 |
| German | 0.877 | 0.475 | 0.616 | 0.789 | **0.750** | **0.769** | **0.919** | 0.658 | 0.767 | 6.35 |
| Japanese | 0.500 | 0.048 | 0.087 | 0.400 | 0.024 | 0.045 | **0.650** | **0.619** | **0.634** | 2.17 |
| Korean | **0.538** | 0.125 | 0.203 | 0.344 | **0.750** | 0.472 | 0.494 | 0.714 | **0.584** | 1.53 |
| Portuguese | 0.633 | 0.310 | 0.416 | 0.570 | **0.610** | 0.589 | **0.720** | 0.590 | **0.648** | 3.59 |
| Russian | **0.925** | 0.270 | 0.418 | 0.792 | **0.891** | **0.838** | 0.901 | 0.533 | 0.670 | 14.4 |
| Spanish | 0.833 | 0.429 | 0.566 | 0.740 | **0.771** | **0.755** | **0.919** | 0.564 | 0.699 | 9.76 |
| Turkish | 0.273 | 0.049 | 0.083 | 0.323 | **1.000** | 0.488 | **0.575** | 0.754 | **0.652** | 1.13 |
| Overall | **0.769** | 0.281 | 0.412 | 0.594 | **0.720** | 0.651 | 0.747 | 0.620 | **0.678** | |

Table 2: Performance of accusation detection models across nine different languages, as well as the percentage share (S%) of accusations detected by **Model$_{Ensemble}$** for each language. The highest value for each metric and language is emphasized in bold. **Model$_{NLI}$** tends to achieve higher recall, while **Model$_{Ensemble}$** prioritizes precision over recall and has the highest F1-score overall.

prompt (details in Appendix B) GPT-3.5 to assign each cluster one of the provided labels for different topical contexts. The available labels were *automated behavior, polarizing debates, insults*, and *other*. The idea of this rather superficial approach is to still get a sense of the contexts in which bot accusations occur across different languages. The proportions of clusters are then tracked across time to observe shifts in the contexts that trigger bot accusations.

## 5 Results

In the following, we first evaluate the performance of the different accusation detection methods, before presenting the analysis results on the accusations detected via our method of choice.

### 5.1 Evaluation of Accusation Detection Methods

To select the most appropriate method for annotating the full datasets of tweets collect for the nine languages and reported upon in Table 1, we compare the performance of the different methods presented above on the validation datasets annotated by crowdworkers. In Table 2, we report the precision (P), recall (R) and F1-score (F1) of the different methods, with the F1-score being the harmonic mean of precision and recall and thus representing a trade-off between these two performance indicators.

For this specific task of classifying candidate tweets, that is, tweets containing the keyword bot in any of the considered languages, into those that contain bot accusations and those that do not, a high precision means that a high share of the

| | Japanese | German | Russian |
|---|---|---|---|
| 2011 - 2016 | tweet, person, account, statement, laugh, block, follow, response, bot, thought | automatic, easy, tweet, word, programmed, account writes, reacts, think, probably | ban, pay, russia, dick, stupid, writes, really idiot, judging, people |
| 2022 - 2023 | account, block, person, tweet, fraud, thank you, probably, polite, think, bot | ukraine, easy, putin, twitter, russia, account, propaganda, profile, actually, russian | people, russia, stupid, really, idiot, putin, idiot, russian, judging, writes |

Table 3: English translations of words closest to the term bot in the Japanese, German and Russian embedding spaces. Terms associated with automation highlighted in blue and those that are insulting or from a political context in red. We see that for Japanse, the term bot almost exclusively appears together with neutral, account-automation-related other terms, both for the first and the last years of data. In contrast, in Russian the term bot appears almost exclusively in company of insults or politics and patriotism related terms. For German, we see how the meaning of the term shifted over time - in the early years, it was associated with terms related to (account) automatization, while in the later years, it appears close to five different terms related to the highly politicized Russian war on Ukraine. Lists of nearest neighbors across all languages and years may be found in Appendix C Tables 9 to 17.

tweets labelled as accusations actually are accusations, while a high recall means that many of the actually existent accusations have been labelled as such. Similar to the argumentation by Assenmacher et al. (2024), we strive to balance precision and recall, but would consider precision to be the slightly more important measure, as we build our subsequent analyses on the assumption that we are working with tweets in which other users are accused of being bots. Since our initial data collection described above was designed to be as inclusive towards candidate tweets as possible, favoring recall over precision by requiring only the presence of the keyword bot, we now deliberately select an accusation detection method that does well on the precision metric across all considered languages. These criteria are fulfilled only by the $\mathbf{Model}_{\mathbf{Ensemble}}$ method, exhibiting F1-scores larger than 0.58 for each language and an overall F1-score of 0.678, as well as the highest precision for seven of the nine languages covered. In the last column of Table 2, we report the share of tweets that are classified as accusations when applying $\mathbf{Model}_{\mathbf{Ensemble}}$ to all tweets containing the keyword bot collected for each language.

## 5.2 Results of Accusation Analysis

We analyze the development of bot accusations on those tweets that have been classified as bot accusations by $\mathbf{Model}_{\mathbf{Ensemble}}$. We carefully tried to balance considerations regarding the precision and recall in the detection method as well as to validate the classifier using human annotations as groundtruth data, but still have to acknowledge that our final datasets used for analysis likely include tweets that do not actually contain a bot accusation (false positives), and that we likely missed tweets that actually are bot accusations (false negatives). However, we are confident that the datasets presented here still allow for a good enough approximation to the phenomenon of bot accusations, especially given the difficulties of conceptualizing and implementing any data collection and processing pipeline across nine different languages.

Based on the results of the different methods used for analysis, we assign the nine languages into three different groups, such that languages within the same group broadly exhibit the same development in the use of bot accusations over the years. We structure our presentation of the results along these groups.

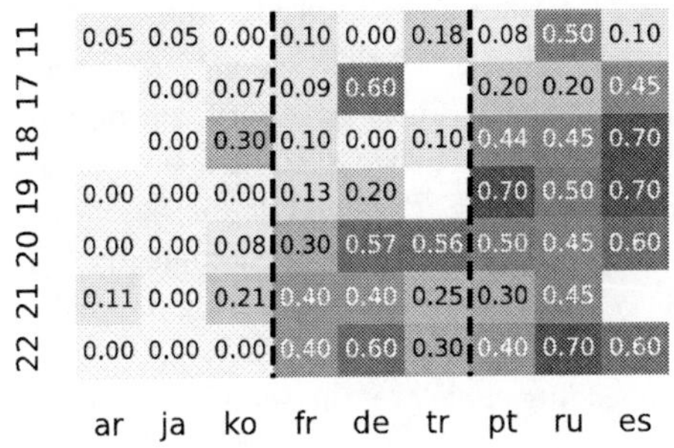


Figure 1: Share of original tweet clusters related to insults and political or politicized issues. Bot accusations in languages from Group 3 (pt, ru, es) consistently occur in contexts that are dominated by insults or discussions around political or politicized topics, which accusations in languages from Group 2 (fr, de, tr) only start doing in later years. Accusations in languages from Group 1 (ar, ja, ko) only rarely appear in these contexts.

### 5.2.1 Group 1 - Stable Automation

For accusations in Arabic, Japanese and Korean, we find that the term bot is consistently used in its original sense and in the context of terms related to automation and tweet technicalities (see Table 3). This continued use of the term in a non-derogatory, more neutral manner is also reflected in the toxicity level of the term in these languages, which - with the slight exception of Arabic during the years 2019 to 2022 - remains stable at a relatively low level, especially when directly compared with languages from the other groups (see Figure 3). Finally, when looking at the proportions of clusters characterized by insults and polarization (Figure 1) versus the proportions of clusters concerned with aspects of automation (Figure 2), we see that the first type of discourse only plays a minor or even negligible role in the original tweets leading up to the accusations, while automated behaviour is over the years consistently featured in the contexts of bot accusations.

We find that especially for Japanese and Korean the accusations were centered around gaming related content, for example:

> @USER 偶然ですよ。ボットだったから。私が勝たないと、負ける所だった (笑) [@USER It was a coincidence. Because it was a bot. I had to win or I would have lost lol.]

### 5.2.2 Group 2 - Shift in Meaning

For the languages in the second group - French, German and Turkish - we observe a pattern similar to what Assenmacher et al. (2024) report for bot accusations in English. While for these languages terms of automation are predominantly found in the vicinity of the term bot during the early years, this shifts in the years 2017 and 2018, with word embeddings in later years showing insults and dehumanizing language as well as political references much more closely associated with the concept bot (see Table 3). For the three languages from the second group, we also find a constant rise in toxicity in the accusing tweets starting around the year 2018 (see Figure 3), which is neither found in the toxicity of the languages in the first group, nor paralleled by a similarly pronounced rise in the non-accusing tweets (see Appendix C Figure 5). However, this reported shift from the term referring to technical aspects of automated behavior on the platform to an insult used in polarized and politicized contexts is best observed through the contents of the original tweets that precede the bot accusation. While Twitter users posting in French, German and Turkish discussed the concept bot predominantly in the context of automation up until the year 2019 (see Figure 2), this shifted drastically, with the years 2020 to 2023 showing a much higher prevalence of clusters related to insulting discussions and polarized debates (see Figure 1).

An important theme of politicization in this group was the alleged role of Russians in bot operations, for example:

> Brauchst nicht weiter mit dem Kerl zu diskutieren der ist ein Russen Bot.... [No need to argue with the guy, he's a Russian bot]

### 5.2.3 Group 3 - Stable Problematization

Similarly to languages included in Group 1, those in Group 3 - Portuguese, Russian and Spanish - do not show any significant shifts in the usage of the term bot. However, we find that the term has been constantly used with insulting and political connotations, right from the start of our data in 2011. Looking at the word embeddings for Russian in Table 3, we see that already in 2011 a number of insults are found close to the term bot, as well as references to foreign politicians or to Russia, potentially as an indicator of patriotic sentiments. This composition of terms associated with bot remains highly stable over the full period covered by our data. Looking at the toxicity measured in the accusations from these languages (see Figure 3), we observe relatively high levels from the beginning on, with slight increases over the full period, but no pronounced shifts as found for the languages in Group 2. Complimenting this impression, we see from the accusation contexts in Figure 1 that accusations in Portuguese, Russian and Spanish are already in the early years oftentimes found in the context of debates around political topics or in conversations that feature insulting and even dehumanizing language, much more so than languages from the other groups.

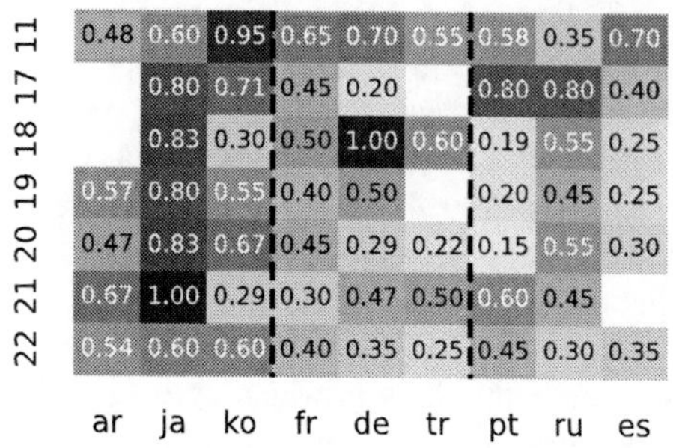


Figure 2: Share of original tweet clusters related to automated behavior. Bot accusations in languages from Group 1 (ar, ja, ko) appear over the years oftentimes in reaction to tweets that are discussing aspects of actual automation.

The following Russian tweet from 2012 is an early example of bot being associated both with insult as well as political motives:

> Нереально тупой бот @USER пытается пихнуть мне гламур Путинских вечеринок для гопоты. [The unrealistically stupid bot @USER is trying to shove the glamor of Putin's gopot parties at me.]

## 6 Discussion

In this study, we expand on existing research about social bot accusations by examining linguistic settings beyond English. We developed an ensemble of language-specific and translation-based models to detect bot accusations in nine different languages. Using this approach, we identified bot accusations on Twitter (𝕏) for each language from 2011 to 2023. Our findings reveal that the previously noted shift in bot accusations in English

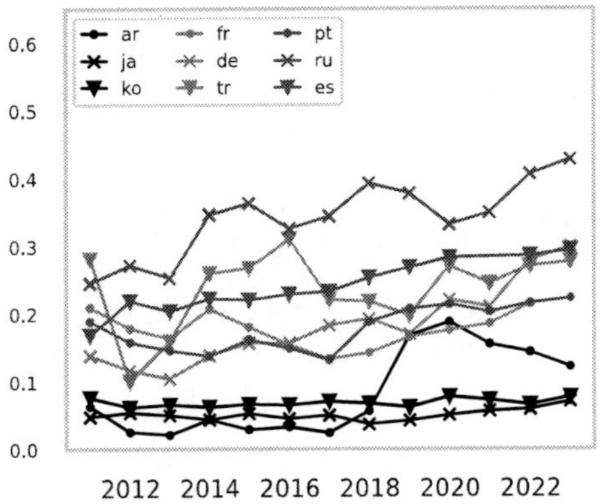


Figure 3: Development of toxicity scores for bot accusation tweets in different languages. Languages from Group 1 (ar, ja, ko) exhibit a relatively stable low level of toxicity in their bot accusations, while languages from Group 3 (pt, ru, es) exhibited (relatively) high levels of toxicity across the years. The bot accusations for the languages in Group 2 (fr, de, tr) started with low toxicity levels that and only started to permanently increase after 2018.

does not occur in every language. Specifically, discussions in East Asian languages, such as Korean and Japanese, show different patterns of bot accusations, with a stronger focus on automation-related topics, particularly in the context of gaming. In contrast, accusations related to polarizing political debates were seldom observed in these languages. On the other hand, we identified languages such as Russian, in which bot accusations were consistently associated with insults. Our findings have several implications. From a moderation perspective, it is important to understand that these accusations should not be treated equally. While it is true that we need to acknowledge that "bot" is often systematically used as an insult, delegitimizing users' opinions and thus undermining constructive dialogue, the context and connotation of such accusations can vary significantly across different languages and cultures and, therefore, require different moderation strategies. We therefore highlight the risk of detection systems trained on English data only to fall short in generalizing to other context, emphasizing the need for diverse linguistic training to ensure accuracy and fairness.

## 7 Ethical Considerations

For our empirical study of the bot accusation phenomenon across a range of different languages, we are relying purely on publicly-accessible, user-generated Twitter posts. Using this type of data carries the usual privacy risks known from social media studies, which we, however, try to counteract by anonymizing all data immediately after its collection. We are not interested in studying individual-level bot accusations, but rather focus on societal-level patterns. We do not try to identify any of the individuals included in our datasets, and explicitly point out that the bot accusations we observe on the platforms are oftentimes directed towards actual human beings instead of automated accounts, as indicated both by our findings and those of Assenmacher et al. (2024). We therefore discourage anyone from trying to infer the status and degree of automation of an account from a bot accusation found in our datasets or elsewhere. In recruiting annotators and collecting their annotations, we followed the ethical considerations and best practices put forth by the platform provider Prolific,[4] including the guarantee that every annotator would receive an hourly pay equivalent (far) exceeding the required minimum pay as well as the informed consent and the possibility to withdraw from participation. To follow established practice in sharing research data collected from social media and still ensure full reproducibility and transparency of our results, we invite other researchers to contact us to mutually explore potentials for collaboration and the sharing of our collected research data.

## 8 Limitations

Most of this paper's limitations originate from its main conceptual and methodological challenge, the inherent multilinguality of the ambitious endeavor to study the same social media phenomenon across nine different languages. While we tried to handle this challenge as carefully as possible, we acknowledge a number of limitations that we were not able to overcome. First, and maybe most importantly, we rely on a number of pre-trained resources, particularly models. While the impressive zero-shot performances of advanced LLMs like GPT-3.5 has already been widely reported and used across a number of tasks and languages, the use of such general purpose, 'black-box' models should still be met with high attention and increased scrutiny. We tried to counterbalance our

[4]https://www.prolific.com/resources/ethical-considerations-in-research-best-practices-and-examples

reliance on the LLM's annotations in our different detection methods by ensuring that we validate the resulting classifier, by evaluating its performance on datasets that have been annotated by humans, without the mediating effects of any other methods or models. We decided to use the LLM-based method only after we observed satisfying performance relative to human annotations on the relevant task of identifying bot accusations across different languages. Regarding the use of the LLM for purposes of the (exploratory) data processing and analysis, particularly its role in labelling the different context clusters, we did not validate the model through crowd annotations, but rather relied on our own judgments and experiments. We manually checked many of the automatically annotated clusters, represented through their (translated) significant tokens, and found that the clustering decisions of the LLM were sufficiently reliable, particularly given the open-ended, exploratory nature of the task. A further limitation lies in the difficulty of reliably detecting bot accusations from tweets that are merely mentioning the keyword bot. This is already a challenging task for a single language, and even more so for nine different languages. As argued above, we tried to optimize for recall, i.e., the inclusion of as many accusations as possible, through a very broad initial data collection strategy, before then optimizing for precision, i.e., making sure that the tweets we identify as bot accusations actually are accusing other users of being a bot. We do so through our choice for the $\textbf{Model}_{\textbf{Ensemble}}$ method, the bot accusation method with the best F1-scores overall and - conceptually - the best setup to only label those tweets as accusations that are identified as such by different types of classifiers.

Related to the limitation of being unable to achieve perfect accuracy in the bot accusation detection task, we acknowledge systematic biases that might occur because of linguistic particularities of and around the term bot. For instance, the German keyword we used, "bot", does not just refer to the concept we are interested in with this paper, but also translates to "offered". Similarly, the Arabic keyword "بوت" may also translate to "boot". We hope that, again, our choice of the ensemble model ameliorates such translation issues by combining a classifier that acts upon the original tweets with another classifier that works on a translated version of it. We hope that this study, as imperfect as it might be, still helps to advance our collective understanding of this interesting phenomenon beyond the much studied, English-only part of a social media platform like Twitter.

## References


Dennis Assenmacher, Leon Fröhling, and Claudia Wagner. 2024. You Are a Bot! –Studying the Development of Bot Accusations on Twitter. *Proceedings of the International AAAI Conference on Web and Social Media*, 18:113–125.

Jacob Devlin, Ming-Wei Chang, Kenton Lee, and Kristina Toutanova. 2019. BERT: Pre-training of Deep Bidirectional Transformers for Language Understanding. In *Proceedings of the 2019 Conference of the North*, pages 4171–4186, Minneapolis, Minnesota. Association for Computational Linguistics.

Emilio Ferrara, Onur Varol, Clayton Davis, Filippo Menczer, and Alessandro Flammini. 2016. The rise of social bots. *Communications of the ACM*, 59(7):96–104.

Christian Grimme, Mike Preuss, Lena Adam, and Heike Trautmann. 2017. Social Bots: Human-Like by Means of Human Control? *Big Data*, 5(4):279–293.

Laura Hanu and Unitary team. 2020. Detoxify. Github. https://github.com/unitaryai/detoxify.

Daniel Kats and Mahmood Sharif. 2022. "I Have No Idea What a Social Bot Is" : On Users' Perceptions of Social Bots and Ability to Detect Them. In *Proceedings of the 10th International Conference on Human-Agent Interaction*, pages 32–40, Christchurch New Zealand. ACM.

Franziska B. Keller, David Schoch, Sebastian Stier, and JungHwan Yang. 2020. Political Astroturfing on Twitter: How to Coordinate a Disinformation Campaign. *Political Communication*, 37(2):256–280.

Ryan Kenny, Baruch Fischhoff, Alex Davis, Kathleen M. Carley, and Casey Canfield. 2024. Duped by Bots: Why Some are Better than Others at Detecting Fake Social Media Personas. *Human Factors: The Journal of the Human Factors and Ergonomics Society*, 66(1):88–102.

Diederik P. Kingma and Jimmy Ba. 2017. Adam: A Method for Stochastic Optimization. *arXiv preprint*. ArXiv:1412.6980 [cs].

Maxim Kolomeets, Olga Tushkanova, Vasily Desnitsky, Lidia Vitkova, and Andrey Chechulin. 2024. Experimental Evaluation: Can Humans Recognise Social Media Bots? *Big Data and Cognitive Computing*, 8(3):24.

Jonas Lundberg, Jonas Nordqvist, and Mikko Laitinen. 2019. Towards a language independent Twitter bot detector. In *Proceedings of 4th Conference of The Association Digital Humanities in the Nordic Countries*, Copenhagen.

David Martin-Gutierrez, Gustavo Hernandez-Penaloza, Alberto Belmonte Hernandez, Alicia Lozano-Diez, and Federico Alvarez. 2021. A Deep Learning Approach for Robust Detection of Bots in Twitter Using Transformers. *IEEE Access*, 9:54591–54601.

Tomas Mikolov, Kai Chen, Greg Corrado, and Jeffrey Dean. 2013. Efficient Estimation of Word Representations in Vector Space. *arXiv preprint*. ArXiv:1301.3781 [cs].

Dat Quoc Nguyen, Tanh Vu, and Anh Tuan Nguyen. 2020. BERTweet: A pre-trained language model for English Tweets. In *Proceedings of the 2020 Conference on Empirical Methods in Natural Language Processing: System Demonstrations*, pages 9–14.

Mariam Orabi, Djedjiga Mouheb, Zaher Al Aghbari, and Ibrahim Kamel. 2020. Detection of Bots in Social Media: A Systematic Review. *Information Processing & Management*, 57(4):102250.

Jürgen Pfeffer, Daniel Matter, Kokil Jaidka, Onur Varol, Afra Mashhadi, Jana Lasser, Dennis Assenmacher, Siqi Wu, Diyi Yang, Cornelia Brantner, Daniel M. Romero, Jahna Otterbacher, Carsten Schwemmer, Kenneth Joseph, David Garcia, and Fred Morstatter. 2023. Just Another Day on Twitter: A Complete 24 Hours of Twitter Data. *Proceedings of the International AAAI Conference on Web and Social Media*, 17:1073–1081.

Telmo Pires, Eva Schlinger, and Dan Garrette. 2019. How Multilingual is Multilingual BERT? In *Proceedings of the 57th Annual Meeting of the Association for Computational Linguistics*, pages 4996–5001.

Nils Reimers and Iryna Gurevych. 2020. Making Monolingual Sentence Embeddings Multilingual using Knowledge Distillation. In *Proceedings of the 2020 Conference on Empirical Methods in Natural Language Processing (EMNLP)*, pages 4512–4525, Online. Association for Computational Linguistics.

Desirée Schmuck and Christian Von Sikorski. 2020. Perceived threats from social bots: The media's role in supporting literacy. *Computers in Human Behavior*, 113:106507.

Shane Schweitzer, Kyle S. H. Dobson, and Adam Waytz. 2024. Political Bot Bias in the Perception of Online Discourse. *Social Psychological and Personality Science*, 15(2):234–244.

Xinhe Tian and Susan R. Fussell. 2024. Could Chinese Users Recognize Social Bots? Exploratory Research Based on Twitter Data. In Constantine Stephanidis, Margherita Antona, Stavroula Ntoa, and Gavriel Salvendy, editors, *HCI International 2024 Posters*, volume 2119, pages 146–156. Springer Nature Switzerland, Cham. Series Title: Communications in Computer and Information Science.

Magdalena Wischnewski, Rebecca Bernemann, Thao Ngo, and Nicole Krämer. 2021. Disagree? You Must be a Bot! How Beliefs Shape Twitter Profile Perceptions. In *Proceedings of the 2021 CHI Conference on Human Factors in Computing Systems*, pages 1–11, Yokohama Japan. ACM.

Samuel C. Woolley. 2016. Automating power: Social bot interference in global politics. *First Monday*.

Wentao Xu, Kazutoshi Sasahara, Jianxun Chu, Bin Wang, Wenlu Fan, and Zhiwen Hu. 2024. A multidisciplinary framework for deconstructing bots' pluripotency in dualistic antagonism. *arXiv preprint*. ArXiv:2402.15119 [cs].

Harry Yaojun Yan and Kai-Cheng Yang. 2023. The landscape of social bot research: a critical appraisal. In Simon Lindgren, editor, *Handbook of Critical Studies of Artificial Intelligence*, pages 716–725. Edward Elgar Publishing.

# A Appendix Data

## A.1 Crowd Annotations

Crowdworkers are recruited on the Prolific platform [5] and selected to be native-speakers of the relevant language, fluent in English, as well as regular users of Twitter. We required these criteria to ensure both sufficient linguistic capability to reliably comply with the annotation task and to be sufficiently accustomed to the jargon and customs of Twitter. We recruited twelve annotators per language and asked each annotator to label 50 candidate tweets, ensuring that each tweet would be annotated by three different annotators. We implemented two annotation checks and retrospectively checked the individual annotations for unusual patterns, but could not find any signs of low annotator attention or suspicious annotation behavior. Annotators were informed about the contents of the study before consenting to participate and were paid the equivalent of an hourly wage of 9 GBP, significantly exceeding the minimum wage requirement imposed by Prolific (6 GBP per hour).

In the following, we present our codebook used to instruct the annotators. We created slightly differing, language-specific versions, the example below is the German version. Figure 4 shows the annotation interface and Table 4 shows the number of accusations and non-accusations per language resulting from the crowd annotations.

[5]https://www.prolific.com/academic-researchers

**Annotation Codebook for Bot Accusations Study**

Available Labels

- **Yes** Choose 'Yes' to indicate that the tweet contains a bot accusation, i.e., that some specific user is said to be a bot.
- **No** Choose 'No' to indicate that the tweet does not contain a bot accusation, i.e., that no specific user is said to be a bot.
- **Not Sure** Choose 'Not Sure' to indicate that you cannot determine from the tweet alone whether a specific user is being accused of being a bot.
- **The text is not written in German / I do not understand the text** Choose this label if the tweet is written in a language other than German or if you just cannot make any sense of it.

Examples for tweets that are bot accusations

- A user is directly accused of being a bot
  - "@USER you're a bot!"
  - "I am sure that this is just another bot account..."
  - "This finally proves that Elon Musk is a bot - I knew it!" [*Accusations may also include people of public interest who are clearly not bots*]
  - "@USER Of course you are a bot, otherwise you wouldn't have these laser eyes." [*Accusations may also be meant sarcastically or ironically*]
- A user is addressed as a bot
  - "@USER a name with 8 numbers? bye, bot!"
  - "@USER ok bot"
- It is indicated that the previous user in a conversation (thread) is a bot
  - "@USER ^ bot" [*On XTwitter, the ^ is sometimes used as an upward pointing arrow, pointing towards the previous user in a conversation*]
  - "Default profile pic and joined 12/2023? #botalert"
- It is put into question whether a user is a bot or something else
  - "@USER Either you are incredibly stupid or just another bot?!"
  - "@USER So you admit you are a bot?"
- It is said that some part of an user' s behavior is bot-like
  - "@USER stop it with your bot tweets"
  - "@USER why are you behaving like a bot then?"

Examples for tweets that are no bot accusations

- The word 'bot' is just being talked about, no accusation is being made
  - "there are too many bots on this platform..."
  - "@USER what am i supposed to do on bot lane???" [*The word 'bot' may sometimes be used in a different context, for example gaming*]
- A user is self-identifying as a bot
  - "I am a bot!"
  - "@USER how can you be sure that I am not just another bot?"
- A bot accusation is negated
  - "@USER At first I thought you were a bot, but now I am pretty sure you actually have a brain."
  - "@USER this does not seem to be a bot to me..."

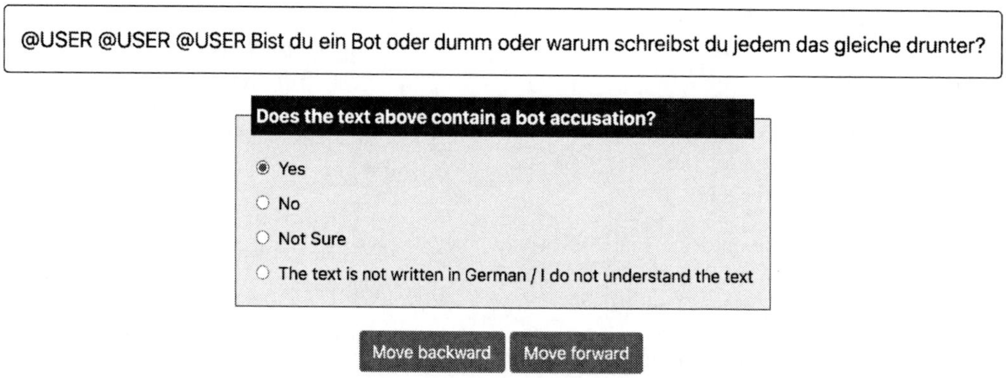


Figure 4: Annotation interface used to collect annotations from crowdworkers.

| | Arabic | French | German | Japanese | Korean | Portuguese | Russian | Spanish | Turkish |
|---|---|---|---|---|---|---|---|---|---|
| accusation | 87 | 105 | 120 | 84 | 56 | 100 | 137 | 140 | 61 |
| non-accusation | 113 | 95 | 80 | 116 | 144 | 100 | 63 | 60 | 139 |

Table 4: Number of instances labelled as accusations (**Acc.**) and non-accusations (**Non-acc.**) by annotators per language.

### A.2 LLM Annotations

In the following, we show the prompt used for soliciting annotations from GPT-3.5 to annotate our training datasets. The placeholder [language] is replaced by the respective language, and [tweet] is replaced by the actual tweet to be annotated:

> Given the tweet below in [language], determine whether the user who wrote it is accusing other user(s) of being bot(s). Classify this text as "Yes" if the user is accusing other user(s) of being bot(s), "No" if there is no accusation of being a bot, or "Unclear" if it cannot be determined easily. Pay attention to the negation statement and think about it step by step. Tweet: [tweet], Classification:

## B Appendix Methods

### B.1 Zero-Shot Setup

Table 5 details the pretrained NLI models used for zero-shot classification in the different languages. Table 6 shows for each language the templates used as the hypothesis in the zero-shot setup, and Table 7 shows the candidate labels.

### B.2 Multilingual BERT Setup

In the following, we make transparent the hyperparameters used for the fine-tuning of the pre-trained multilingual language model. This hyperparameter setup as well as the optimization algorithm, at the same time, serve as the default setup for the fine-tuning of every other model introduced above.

To fine-tune the pre-trained model to the accusation detection task, we add a dropout and a classification layer on top of the base architecture, using a 128 token input context, a dropout rate of 0.3, a learning rate of 2e-5, a batch size of 32, and an early stopping regime that interrupts training if the performance on a held-out evaluation set does not improve for five consecutive iterations. The Adam algorithm (Kingma and Ba, 2017) is used for optimization with $\beta = (0.9, 0.999)$ and $\epsilon = 10^{-8}$, individually adjusting the learning rates for each parameter to accommodate for low- and high-gradient parameters simultaneously. Due to resource constraints, we did not conduct any hyperparameter tuning but rather relied on a default constellation of parameters.

### B.3 Language-Specific Classifiers

Table 8 details the pre-trained language models user for developing the language-specific classifiers.

### B.4 Context Clustering

The prompt used to label the found clusters based on their most significant tokens is the following, with [language] and [keywords] being replaced by the respective language as well as the most significant tokens of the cluster:

> I have clustered tweets in [language] and extracted the keywords of each cluster. Given one cluster below, if you are asked to classify it as one of the classes: automated behavior, polarizing debates, insults, and others. Which class would you assign it to and why? In addition, please translate all words into English. Return the results in json format: {{"class": "", "reason": "", "translations": ""}} List of keywords: [keywords], Class:

## C Appendix Results

Figure 5 shows the toxicity over time of the original tweets, i.e., the tweets preceding the bot accusations, across different languages. Tables 9 to 17 show the ten nearest neighbors to the (language-specific) term bot over time and for each included language.

| Language | Model |
|---|---|
| Arabic | MoritzLaurer/mDeBERTa-v3-base-xnli-multilingual-nli-2mil7 |
| French | MoritzLaurer/mDeBERTa-v3-base-xnli-multilingual-nli-2mil7 |
| German | MoritzLaurer/mDeBERTa-v3-base-xnli-multilingual-nli-2mil7 |
| Japanese | Formzu/bert-base-japanese-jsnli |
| Korean | muhammadravi251001/fine-tuned-KoreanNLI-KorNLI-with-xlm-roberta-large |
| Portuguese | MoritzLaurer/mDeBERTa-v3-base-xnli-multilingual-nli-2mil7 |
| Russian | MoritzLaurer/mDeBERTa-v3-base-xnli-multilingual-nli-2mil7 |
| Spanish | MoritzLaurer/mDeBERTa-v3-base-xnli-multilingual-nli-2mil7 |
| Turkish | MoritzLaurer/mDeBERTa-v3-base-xnli-multilingual-nli-2mil7 |

Table 5: Pretrained NLI models used for zero-shot classification in different languages.

| Language | Template Hypothesis |
|---|---|
| Arabic | عن يتحدث النص هذا {} |
| French | Ce texte parle de {}. |
| German | Dieser Text handelt von {}. |
| Japanese | このテキストは{}についてのものです。 |
| Korean | 이 텍스트는 {} 에 관한 것입니다. |
| Portuguese | Este texto é sobre {}. |
| Russian | Этот текст о {}. |
| Spanish | Este texto trata sobre {}. |
| Turkish | Bu metin {} hakkında. |

Table 6: Templates used for the hypothesis in zero-shot classification in different languages. All templates translate to the English *This text is about {}*.

| Language | Template Accusation | Template Non-accusation |
|---|---|---|
| Arabic | روبوت بأنه المستخدم اتهام | روبوت بأنه المستخدم اتهام |
| French | ne pas accuser l'utilisateur d'être bot | accuser l'utilisateur d'être bot |
| German | den Benutzer nicht beschuldigen, Bot zu sein | den Benutzer beschuldigen, Bot zu sein |
| Japanese | ユーザーをボットとして非難しない | ユーザーをボットとして非難する |
| Korean | 사용자를 봇으로 비난하지 않음 | 사용자를 봇으로 비난함 |
| Portuguese | não acusar o usuário de ser robô | acusar o usuário de ser robô |
| Russian | не обвинять пользователя в том, что он бот | обвинять пользователя в том, что он бот |
| Spanish | no acusar al usuario de ser bot | acusar al usuario de ser bot |
| Turkish | kullanıcının bot olmadığını iddia etmek | kullanıcının bot olduğunu iddia etmek |

Table 7: Templates used for the candidate labels in zero-shot classification in different languages. All templates translate to the English *accusing user of being bot* and *not accusing user of being bot.*

| Language | Pre-trained Model |
|---|---|
| Arabic | Davlan/xlm-roberta-base-finetuned-arabic |
| French | dbmdz/bert-base-french-europeana-cased |
| German | dbmdz/bert-base-german-cased |
| Japanese | cl-tohoku/bert-base-japanese-v3 |
| Korean | KoichiYasuoka/roberta-base-korean-hanja |
| Portuguese | neuralmind/bert-base-portuguese-cased |
| Russian | bert-base-multilingual-cased |
| Spanish | dccuchile/bert-base-spanish-wwm-uncased |
| Turkish | burakaytan/roberta-base-turkish-uncased |

Table 8: Pre-trained models for language-specific classifiers.

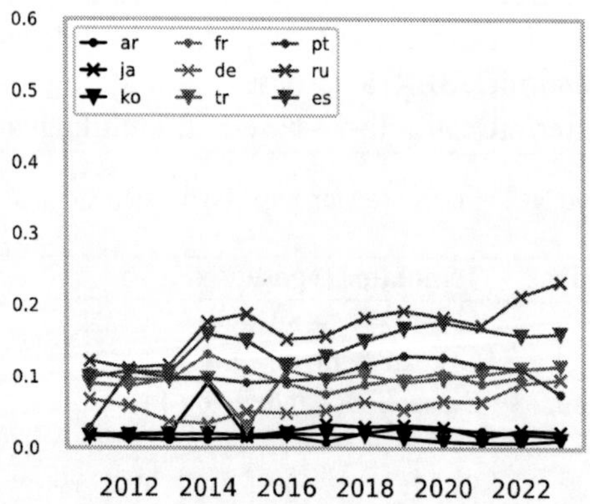


Figure 5: Development of toxicity scores for original tweets in different languages. The toxicity levels of the tweets preceding the bot accusations are generally lower and less volatile across the included languages. Strikingly, the increase in bot accusation toxicity after 2018 for languages from Group 2 is not paralleled by a similar increase in the original tweets of these languages.

| Year | Terms Arabic (English Translations) |
|---|---|
| 2011-2016 | الله (God), تحديث (update) , حسابك (account) , الرسمي (official), ممكن (possible), اخوي (brother), البرنامج (program) , تويت (tweet) , الحساب (account) , برنامج (program) |
| 2017-2018 | كه (electricity), وهمي (fake) , البوت (bot) , تويت (tweet) , حساب (account) , انسان (human), ياخي (brother), الله (God), راسك (head), تويتر (Twitter) , ابيض (white), لازم (necessary) |
| 2019 | حساب (account) , تلعب (play), البوت (bot) , تويتر (Twitter) , عادي (normal), شكلك (look), نوب (noob) , ياخي (brother), طول (length), الله (God), واضح (clear), الناس (people) |
| 2020 | تلعب (play), الله (God), شكلك (look), اصلا (originally), اللعبه (game), رد (reply) , حقير (despicable) , شخص (person), عادي (normal), وهمي (fake) , انسان (human) |
| 2021 | شخص (person), يرد (responds) , حساب (account) , بشري (human), وهمي (fake) , لاعق (licker), الله (God), يجاوب (answers), حقيقي (real), بصراحة (frankly), اشك (doubt), شريحة (slice) |
| 2022-2023 | يرد (responds) , بيس (base), كلمة (word), شخص (person), الله (God), حساب (account) , انسان (human), الحساب (account) , يكتب (writes), طبيعي (natural) العسكر (military) تويتر (Twitter) |

Table 9: Nearest neighbors to the term بوت (bot) in the Arabic word embedding space.

| Year | Terms French (English Translations) |
|---|---|
| 2011-2016 | compte (account) , mots(words), spam (spam) , répondre (respond) , temps (time), monde (world), fake (fake) , regarde (look), robot (robot) vraiment (really) |
| 2017 | compte (account) , temps (time), phrase (sentence), probablement (probably), programmé (programmed) , fake (fake) , écrit (writes), réponse (response) , troll (troll) |
| 2018 | propagande (propaganda) , compte (account) , russe (Russian) , temps (time), photo (photo), merde (shit) , répond(responds) , mec (guy), croire (believe), voir (see) |
| 2019 | compte (account) , petit (small), cas (case), troll (troll) , temps (time), vraiment (really), humain (human), russe (Russian) , bonne (good), jamais (never) répondre (respond) |
| 2020 | compte (account) , troll (troll) , temps (time), profil (profile) , message (message) , humain (human), vraiment (really), répondre (respond) , vrai (true), fake (fake) |
| 2021 | troll (troll) , compte (account) , vie (life), france (France) , cas (case), humain (human), propagande (propaganda) , monde (world), répondre (respond) , chose (thing) |
| 2022-2023 | compte (account) , troll (troll) , vraiment (really), créé (created), merde (shit) , profil (profile) , répondre (respond) , fake (fake) , bloquer(block) , gros (big) |

Table 10: Nearest neighbors to the term bot in the French word embedding space.

| Year | Terms German (English Translations) |
|---|---|
| 2011-2016 | automatisch (automatic) , einfach (easy), tweet , wort (word), programmiert (programmed) , account , schreibt (writes), reagiert (reacts), denke (think), wahrscheinlich (probably) |
| 2017 | account , twitter , einfach (easy), schreiben (write), tweets , glaub (believe), follower , langsam (slow), fragen (ask), hashtag , dummer (stupid) , offensichtlich (obvious), doof (dumb) |
| 2018 | hör (listen), aufstehen (get up), missbrauchen (abuse) , einfach (easy), fake , account , profil (profile) , antworten(answer), tweet , troll , völlig (completely), dummer (stupid) , nazi |
| 2019 | antworten (answer), troll , einfach (easy), gesellschaft (society), aktiv (active), account , melden (report), beleidigen (insult) , arbeitest (work), tweet , jederzeit (anytime) frage (question) |
| 2020 | troll , einfach (easy), account , leute (people), trump , fleisch (meat), blut (blood), tweets , profil (profile) automatischen (automatic) follower , russischer (Russian) , dumm (stupid) |
| 2021 | troll , account , fake, tweets , leute (people), person (person), twitter , propaganda , schreibt (writes), follower , profil (profile) leben (life), antworten (answer), russischer (Russian) |
| 2022-2023 | ukraine , einfach (easy), putin , twitter , russland (Russia) , account , propaganda , profil (profile) , eigentlich (actually), russischer (Russian) , antworten (answer), schreiben (write) |

Table 11: Nearest neighbors to the term bot in the German word embedding space.

| Year | Japanese Terms (English Translations) |
|---|---|
| 2011-2016 | ツイート (tweet), 人 (person), アカウント (account), 発言 (statement), 笑 (laugh), ブロック (block), フォロー (follow), 反応 (response), ボット (bot), 思っ (thought) |
| 2017 | アプリ (app), ウェブサイト (website), 突然 (suddenly), 体感 (body sensation), デジタル (digital), 力 (power), 証明 (proof), 問題 (problem), 基礎 (foundation) |
| 2018 | 問題 (problem), 笑 (laugh), 損ない (harmless), 数学 (mathematics), 同じ (same), 人 (person), アカウント (account), 自動 (automatic), 返信 (reply), 思っ (thought), 意味 (meaning) |
| 2019 | だろう (probably), 同じ (same), 人 (person), 質問 (question), まし (better), 自動 (automatic), 名前 (name), 思う (think), ツイート (tweet), でしょう (probably), 変 (strange), ガチ (serious) |
| 2020 | ブロック (block), 無能 (incompetent), ジャンル (genre), 突っ (thrust), 推薦 (recommendation), 首 (neck), 込ん (crowded), ツイート (tweet), 迷惑 (nuisance), アカウント (account) |
| 2021 | 自動 (automatic), ツイート (tweet), まし (better), たぶん (probably), 名前 (name), しれ (know), 垢 (account), 思っ (thought), 業者 (dealer) 思う (think), 人 (person), フォロー (follow) |
| 2022-2023 | アカウント (account), ブロック (block), 人 (person), ツイート (tweet), 詐欺 (fraud), ありがとう (thank you), だろう (probably), ござい (polite), 思う (think), ボット (bot) |

Table 12: Nearest neighbors to the term ボット (bot) in the Japanese word embedding space.

| Year | Korean Terms (English Translations) |
|---|---|
| 2011-2016 | 진짜 (real), 사진 (photo), 패러디 (parody), 아뇨 (no), 자동 (automatic), 저건 (that is) |
| 2017 | 계정 (account), 진짜 (real), 생각 (thought), 사진 (photo), 다른 (different), 사람 (person), 블락 (block), 정보 (information), 세상 (world), 독촉 (urge), 트윗 (tweet), 사실 (fact) |
| 2018-2018 | 계정 (account), 사람 (person), 트위터 (Twitter), 진짜 (real), 생각 (thought), 자동 (automatic), 사실 (fact), 팔로 (follow), 알티 (retweet), 정보 (information) |
| 2019 | 진짜 (real), 사람 (person), 아마 (probably), 계정 (account), 생각 (thought), 정도 (degree), 트윗 (tweet), 사실 (fact), 되어 (become), 존나 (damn), 신음 (groan), 얘기 (talk) |
| 2020-2020 | 사람 (person), 진짜 (real), 계정 (account), 트윗 (tweet), 생각 (thought), 마음 (mind), 알티 (retweet), 얘기 (talk), 자동 (automatic), 있는 (existing), 트위터 (Twitter) |
| 2021 | 진짜 (real), 사람 (person), 계정 (account), 트윗 (tweet), 트위터 (Twitter), 아마 (probably), 생각 (thought), 마음 (mind), 가요 (song), 봇임 (a bot), 자동 (automatic) |
| 2022-2023 | 진짜 (real), 사람 (person), 트윗 (tweet), 계정 (account), 정도 (degree), 아마 (probably), 사실 (fact), 알티 (retweet), 자동 (automatic), 생각 (thought), 있는 (existing) |

Table 13: Nearest neighbors to the term 봇 (bot) in the Korean word embedding space.

| Year | Portuguese Terms (English Translations) |
|---|---|
| 2011-2016 | manda (send), puta (whore), lixo (trash), block (block), tweets (tweets), merda (shit), boca (mouth), achar (find), responde (responds), frase (phrase) |
| 2017 | mundo (world), pessoa (person), fica (stay), milhões (millions), cara (guy), fake (fake), ruim (bad), merda (shit), começando (starting), safado (naughty) |
| 2018 | cara (guy), perfil (profile), fake (fake), pessoa (person), mulher (woman), news (news), conta (account), twitter (Twitter), merda (shit), falar (speak), seguidores (followers) |
| 2019 | perfil (profile), cara (guy), governo (government), conta (account), falar (speak), merda (shit), tweet (tweet), fake (fake), twitter (Twitter), foto (photo), fala (speech) |
| 2020 | merda (shit), fala (speak), caralho (fuck), lixo (trash), ninguém (nobody), fica (stay), foto (photo), gado (cattle), presidente (president), cara (guy), imbecil (imbecile) |
| 2021 | gado (cattle), pessoa (person), merda (shit), conta (account), imbecil (imbecile), cara (guy), tweet (tweet), fala (speech), foto (photo), falando (speaking) |
| 2022-2023 | caralho (fuck), desgraçado (wretched), lula (Lula), bozo (idiot), block (block), fica (stay), país (country), merda (shit), ninguém (nobody), humano (human), lixo (trash) |

Table 14: Nearest neighbors to the term bot in the Portuguese word embedding space.

| Year | Russian Terms (English Translations) |
|---|---|
| 2011-2016 | бан (ban), судя (judging), россии (Russia), тупой (stupid), хуй (dick), пишет (writes), реально (really), дебил (idiot), платят (pay), людей (people) |
| 2017 | вероятно (probably), истории (stories), скажите (tell), обама (Obama), понятия (concepts), запись (record), президентом (president), черт (damn), идиот (idiot) |
| 2018 | тупой (stupid), внимания (attention), идиот (idiot), страшная (terrible), бан (ban), ум (mind), орать (yell), нахуй (fuck off), сша (USA), терять (lose) |
| 2019 | заплатил (paid), россии (Russia), понятно (clear), тупой (stupid), судя (judging), путин (Putin), реально (really), followers (followers), тупая (stupid), бан (ban) |
| 2020 | россии (Russia), идиот (idiot), мнение (opinion), судя (judging), понятно (clear), тупой (stupid), знает (knows), пишет (writes), хуй (dick), типичный (typical) |
| 2021 | россии (Russia), людей (people), судя (judging), идиот (idiot), тупой (stupid), слова (words), смысла (sense), ответ (answer), пишет (writes), страны (countries) |
| 2022-2023 | людей (people), россии (Russia), тупой (stupid), судя (judging), идиот (idiot), путин (Putin), дебил (idiot), русские (Russians), реально (really), пишет (writes) |

Table 15: Nearest neighbors to the term бот(bot) in the Russian word embedding space.

| Year | Spanish Terms (English Translations) |
|---|---|
| 2011-2016 | troll (troll), real (real), peña (crowd), seguidores (followers), tweets (tweets), hola (hello), foto (photo), alguien (someone), puto (fucking), programado (programmed) |
| 2017 | gobierno (government), alguien (someone), seguidores (followers), gente (people), ignorante (ignorant), foto (photo), troll (troll), perfil (profile), pobre (poor) |
| 2018 | pobre (poor), mierda (shit), troll (troll), seguro (sure), tuits (tweets), años (years), vida (life), pagado (paid), ignorante (ignorant), argumentos (arguments) |
| 2019 | publicaciones (publications), año (year), siguiendo (following), denuncia (report), unió (joined), granja (farm), boca (mouth), socialista (socialist), familia (family) |
| 2020 | procede (proceeds), morro (kid), inmediato (immediate), interese (interest), instante (instant), power (power), masivo (massive), metiche (nosy), orgánico (organic) |
| 2022-2023 | boludo (idiot), míseros (miserable), ladillas (crabs, pulgas (fleas), servido (served), seguidos (followed), masivo (massive), entrando (entering), inmediato (immediate) |

Table 16: Nearest neighbors to the term bot in the Spanish word embedding space.

| Year | Turkish Terms (English Translations) |
|---|---|
| 2011-2016 | salak (idiot), belli (obvious), hesapsın (account), bak (look), adamsın (man), muhtemelen (probably), düşünüyorum (thinking), piç (bastard), galiba (apparently) |
| 2017 | hesabı (account), robot (robot), kardeşim (brother), belli (obvious), sağol (thanks), takipçi (follower), sahte (fake), gerçek (real), botsun (bot), otomatik (automatic) |
| 2018 | beyinsiz (brainless), şaka (joke), sıralı (orderly), hesap (account), güzel (beautiful), çocuğu (child), kardeş (brother), cevap (answer), fav (favourite), botsun (bot) |
| 2019 | hesaptır (account), hemen (immediately), salak (stupid), bak (look), insan (human), orospu (whore), takipçi (follower), botsun (bot), güzel (beautiful), tweet (tweet) |
| 2020 | botsun (bot), sıstem (system), bayanısın (lady), hesap (account), yorum (comment), bak (look), sanalcı (virtualist), troll (troll), adam (man), muhtemelen (probably) |
| 2021 | botsun (bot), hesap (account), troll (troll), aynı (same), büyük (big), boş (empty), insan (human), takip (follow), adam (man), vatan (homeland), belli (clear), salak (fool), |
| 2022-2023 | botsun (bot), hesap (account), sahte (fake), troll (troll), belli (obvious), yalan (lie), tane (piece), insan (human) cevap (reply), takip (follow), gerçek (real), profil (profile) |

Table 17: Nearest neighbors to the term bot in the Turkish word embedding space.

# Operationalising the Hermeneutic Grouping Process in Corpus-assisted Discourse Studies

**Philipp Heinrich and Stephanie Evert**

Chair of Computational Corpus Linguistics
Friedrich-Alexander-Universität Erlangen-Nürnberg
Bismarckstr. 6, 91054 Erlangen, Germany

philipp.heinrich@fau.de stephanie.evert@fau.de

## Abstract

We propose a framework for quantitative-qualitative research in corpus-assisted discourse studies (CADS), which operationalises the central process of manually forming groups of related words and phrases in terms of "discoursemes" and their constellations. We introduce an open-source implementation of this framework in the form of a REST API based on Corpus Workbench. Going through the workflow of a collocation analysis for *fleeing* and related terms in the German Federal Parliament, the paper gives details about the underlying algorithms, with available parameters and further possible choices. We also address multi-word units (which are often disregarded by CADS tools), a semantic map visualisation of collocations, and how to compute assocations between discoursemes.

## 1 Introduction and Related Work

Corpus-assisted discourse studies (CADS) (Baker, 2006; Baker et al., 2008; Mautner, 2009) are a highly effective approach for exploring and understanding socio-political discourse, often building on a theoretical background rooted in critical discourse analysis (Fairclough, 2015). CADS research focuses on interpreting, explaining, and critiquing discourses surrounding socially contentious issues, intricate historical phenomena, and dominant narratives (Wodak and Meyer, 2015, 11). Typical examples of the themes explored in CADS include socio-economic concerns like austerity (Griebel et al., 2020), global challenges such as climate change (Grundmann and Krishnamurthy, 2010; Wang and Huan, 2023), and political ideologies such as right-wing or nationalistic perspectives (Baker and McEnery, 2005; Gabrielatos and Baker, 2008; Wodak, 2015, 2018).

CADS research usually relies on "low-level" corpus-linguistic techniques such as concordancing as well as keyword and collocation analyses (Baker, 2006). They are complemented by a hermeneutic interpretation of the observations that takes the wider socio-pragmatic context into account, but which is also influenced (more or less explicitly) by the intuitions and preconceptions of researchers. The use of corpora aims to mitigate such biases and the cherry-picking of examples that support them. A typical CADS investigation starts with a detailed examination of keywords and collocates (Baker, 2006; Baker et al., 2008). Keywords are lemmata[1] that occur with significantly higher frequency in a target corpus than in a reference corpus and indicate either important topics of the discourse (for a target corpus related to the theme of the study) or characteristic framings used by certain groups of actors (e.g. for right-wing vs. left-wing newspapers). Collocates are lemmata that are statistically associated (i.e. tend to co-occur) with a particular node lemma (or set of lemmata). They might indicate, e.g., the salient framings and evaluations associated with a certain topic indicated by the node lemmata (e.g. *refugee, displaced person*). Tentative interpretations obtained from this "distant reading" of the corpora are then confirmed and refined by "close reading" of concordances for individual lemmata, displaying their corpus occurrences in a compact tabular format with left and right context.

Relevant methodological research in corpus linguistics has focused on identifying suitable association measures and other parameter settings for the identification and ranking of keyword and collocation candidates (Stubbs, 1995; Hardie, 2014; Evert et al., 2017; Evert, 2022). However, it has been

[1]Analyses are typically carried out on the basis of lemmata rather than word forms. In most European languages beside English, different inflected forms of the same lemma are often selected due to syntactic constraints and do not to indicate different discourse-specific meanings. We thus refer to lemmata throughout our contribution; analyses can of course also be carried out on the basis of word forms or other annotation layers (such as POS-disambiguated lemmata or semantic tags).



*Proceedings of the 58th Annual Meeting of the Association for Computational Linguistics*, pages 33–44
July 5–10, 2020. 

established that there is no single "best" measure (Evert, 2008), leading researchers to advocate for the integration of multiple perspectives provided by different algorithms and parameter configurations (Gries, 2019, 2021).

A crucial step in CADS is the manual grouping of related keywords and collocations, which are then interpreted in terms of discursive patterns (topics, discursive strategies, positions or fragments (cf. Jäger, 2015, 80)). This "meso level" of discourse analysis (Fairclough, 2015, 58) thus forms the bridge between linguistic and discursive patterns. Most CADS research relies on off-the-shelf concordancing tools (such as CQPweb, AntConc, and #LancsBox) or SaaS platforms (such as SketchEngine and english-corpora.org), which are limited in the parameters of quantitative analysis such as choice of association measure (depending on the specific tool used) and present keywords and collocations as tables ranked by association score (making it difficult to recognise discursive patterns among them). The grouping process invariably happens outside the concordancing tools, using spreadsheet software or pen and paper.

Our aim is to improve the quantitative-qualitative interface in CADS research by (i) introducing an operationalisation of the grouping process in terms of "discoursemes" (see Section 2) and (ii) providing better software tools that integrate discoursemes into quantitative corpus analysis. We thus stay very close to established and successful practice in CADS, which at its core induces groupings and discursive patterns from the observed data in a corpus-driven fashion. This is markedly different from other ongoing research that might also contribute to the future of CADS. One strand focuses on machine learning techniques leveraging human "ground truth" annotations to detect functional properties of texts (or text segments) such as emotion (Wegge and Klinger, 2023) or sarcasm (Plepi et al., 2023). With the advent of large language models, another line of research is now conerned with zero-shot detection of topics (Navarretta and Hansen, 2023) or narratives (Heinrich et al., 2024).

In this contribution, we show both the possibilities of a discourseme-based operationalisation of CADS analyses and the technical challenges that come along with it, together with recommendations for best practices. Since "design and capabilities" of tools are essential to making sense of linguistic data (Anthony, 2013, 141), and off-the-shelf concordancing tools such as CQPweb (Hardie, 2012) do not provide any reasonable functionality to support the grouping process, we offer an open-source REST API for CADS research implemented in Python[2] with a corresponding OpenAPI Specification[3]. It builds on CWB (Evert and Hardie, 2011) for corpus storage, whose corpus query processor CQP (Evert and The CWB Development Team, 2022) allows efficient querying of large tokenised corpora, retrieving pairs of corpus positions for match and matchend of the query, respectively.

The API provides an extensive set of features designed to facilitate CADS analyses, including:

- classic CADS features such as CQP queries, concordancing (including various filtering and sorting techniques), query breakdown (including distribution across meta data), meta data management (using information stored in structural attributes in CWB), subcorpus creation, and collocation and keyword analysis;
- visualisation of collocation and keyword profiles via semantic maps (cf. Figure 1); and
- endpoints for managing discoursemes and discourseme constellations.

Here, we concentrate on the workflow of defining discoursemes via the result table of a collocation analysis and the technical challenges of its implementation (Section 3). Some reasonable discoursemes are given as illustrative examples. Note that the API can be accessed via HTTPS and thus allows analysts to combine an interactive graphical user interface (GUI) with low-level API calls when forming discoursemes, then use other tools such as R for further quantitative analyses of the discoursemes and their constellations (see Section 4 for a brief discussion).

## 2 Discoursemes and Constellations

Let us start from the example of a collocation analysis in a CADS investigation. In order to define the node of the collocation analysis, a researcher will manually select a set of lemmata and/or lemma sequences that identify a topic of interest such as refugees (e.g. *refugee* and *displaced person*). They will then scan the table of collocations (or multiple tables obtained with different parameter settings) to spot groups of related words that reflect common

[2]`https://github.com/ausgerechnet/cwb-cads`

[3]See the interactive documentation on our own production server at `https://corpora.linguistik.uni-erlangen.de/cwb-cads/docs`.

discursive patterns associated with the topic. For example, collocates like *Syria* and *Lybia* indicate debates about the refugees' origin, while *displacement*, *expulsion*, and *famine* indicate "push factors" of migration. The collocates in a group tend to be semantically related, but this is not always the case. The key criterion is whether they express the same meaning aspect within the discourse (as the example of *famine* shows).

Our approach to overcoming the current limitations of CADS practice rests on understanding this central grouping step as the formation of *discoursemes*, which we define as (minimal) units of lexical meaning in the context of a given discourse. Our goal here is to provide an operational concept that has a clear hermeneutic definition (unit of meaning in the context of a discourse) but can also be approximated via lists of lemmata and thus identified automatically in corpora, forming a link between qualitative and quantitative methods. We enclose references to discoursemes in angle brackets, e.g. ⟨origin⟩ and ⟨push factors⟩ for the groups mentioned above. The node of the collocation analysis is also understood as a discourseme ⟨refugees⟩, which just happens to be defined a priori by the researcher rather than via grouping collocations.

It is worth pointing out that not all occurrences of a lemma will always belong to the corresponding discourseme. For instance, the lemma *flood* will typically be assigned to the metaphor discourseme ⟨flood of people⟩ in a migration context, but its occurrence in *displaced families are uprooted again by severe floods* does not belong to the discourseme. Our operationalisation of discoursemes as manually formed groups of lemmata must thus be considered an approximation, since there will be false positives (occurrences of these items that do not in fact belong to the discourseme) and false negatives (occurrences of the discourseme that are realised through other linguistic expressions that are not frequent enough to show up among the keywords and collocations).

Our approach also recognises explicitly that discursive patterns do not arise from individual discoursemes (as the qualitative interpretation in traditional CADS might suggest), but rather from *constellations* of discoursemes. The discourseme ⟨flood of people⟩ mentioned above might comprise lemmata like *flood*, *surge*, or *pour into*, but they only evoke the discursive pattern "migrants as a flood of people" when used in conjunction with ⟨refugees⟩, ⟨migration⟩ or a similar discourseme. Such constellations are often implicit in CADS studies: e.g. groups of collocates form discoursemes that co-occur in a constellation with the node discourseme of the collocation analysis. We make this explicit in our approach, where the node of a collocation analysis is always a discourseme. It is noteworthy that discourseme constellations provide a partial solution to the lack of (discourse-specific) word sense disambiguation discussed above, due to the mutual disambiguation of discoursemes within a constellation (e.g. *displacement* is unlikely to refer to a car engine when used in conjunction with the discourseme ⟨migration⟩).

Our proposed operationalisation in terms of discoursemes and discourseme constellations offers several important advantages for future CADS research:

1. The quantitative-qualitative bridge at the meso level of discourse analysis becomes more formalised and reproducible. Listing discoursemes (as sets of lemmata and lemma sequences) and their constellations can be regarded as a form of research documentation.
2. Discoursemes can be fed back into quantitative analyses and visualisations. We exemplify the usefulness of this in our case study below.
3. Discoursemes can be used as a starting point for further analysis steps, e.g. as node of a collocation analysis.
4. Discoursemes need not be based on a single keyword/collocation analysis, but can incrementally grow during a study, taking different corpora and perspectives into account.
5. Statistical distributions of discoursemes can be determined (mostly) automatically, giving useful indications of the statistical distribution of discursive patterns (indicated by discourseme constellations).

## 3 Working with Discoursemes

As a running example, we will look into GermaParl[4], a corpus of all debates of the German federal parliament. Our goal is to describe discoursemes (via lists of lemmata) and to combine them into constellations that approximate discursive patterns, e.g. the framing of refugees as human beings in need for protection or questioning the legitimacy of seeking asylum.

Discoursemes can be created from the results of a collocation analysis, which puts them in a con-

[4] `https://zenodo.org/records/10421773`

stellation with the node discourseme of the analysis. We focus on the discourse around the discourseme ⟨fleeing⟩ (our "topic discourseme") in legislative period 19 (LP19), and on the parliamentary groups *Bündins90/Die Grünen* (GRUENE, a left-leaning environmentalist party) and *Alternative für Deutschland* (AfD, a right-wing populist party). However, we understand discourseme formation as an iterative process in which (i) different parameter settings for the same analysis can be used (e.g. different association measures or context definitions), and (ii) multiple analyses can be carried out (e.g. for different node discoursemes or (sub-)corpora). We concentrate on the formation of discoursemes via collocation analysis here. The API also supports an approach via keyword analysis (with a somewhat easier implementation). Of course, both approaches can be combined in a single study.

As mentioned above, discourseme descriptions for a given corpus are usually obtained by manually selecting lemmata from an $n$-best list of keywords or collocations, but they can also include multi-word units. Frequency counts for discoursemes are obtained in the same way as for individual lemmata, i.e. by counting all their occurrences in the corpus; some special precautions are necessary if a discourseme contains multi-word units (see Section 3.2). Such frequency counts are the basis for discourseme assocations (Section 3.6) as well as for further quantiative analyses.

The topic discourseme plays a special role in that it has to be defined a priori, and researchers have to take care not to miss relevant lemmata (or introduce false positives). For the example at hand, a manually curated list of lemmata is used based on the CQP query

`[lemma=".*flucht.*" %cd]`[5]

Additional candidates can be suggested via semantic similarity search in word embeddings (Mikolov et al., 2013), which is supported by the API.

### 3.1 Collocations

Our first step is a collcation analysis for the topic discourseme ⟨fleeing⟩ as node. Co-occurrences are determined for all unigram lemmata in the specified context around the node discourseme; see Appendix A for a discussion of context types and their definition. In our API, we allow context specification by a mix of surface and textual co-occurrence. For the case study at hand we include all corpus positions up to $w = 10$ tokens around the node discourseme, but only in the same sentence.

Evert (2004, 68: fn. 23) recommends that the node itself should be removed from the co-occurrence context, as each of its instances would count as a co-occurrence with itself, inevitably leading to a very high (and spurious) association score. However, we argue here that the situation is different in CADS because the same lemma can belong to multiple discoursemes. Removing all the occurrences of all lemmata of the node discourseme from the context might inadvertently discard instances of other discoursemes. It is thus better, and technically easier, to work with the full context including the node. In order not to confuse analysts, the API masks the lemmata of the node discourseme by default, so they are not displayed in the semantic map visualisation (cf. Section 3.4).

Following contingency table notation (see Table 4 in Appendix A), we refer to the number of instances of a collocate within the context as $O_{11}$ (with $R_1$ being the number of corpus positions in the context) and to the number of instances outside of the context as $O_{21}$ (with $R_2$ the number of corpus positions in the remainder of the corpus). Note that this directly translates to keyword analyses, where $O_{11}$ corresponds to the number of occurrences in the target corpus and $O_{21}$ to the number of occurrences in the reference corpus. Since there is no "best" association measure, the API offers selection from a wide range of association measures.[6] We recommend starting with a measure that combines statistical significance with effect size, such as a log-likelihood-filtered odds-ratio or conservative log ratio (LRC) (Evert, 2022); see Appendix A for more details.

### 3.2 Multi-word units

The API allows the manual definition of multi-word units (MWUs) as lemma sequences.[7] MWUs can either form discoursemes by themselves or be included in a discourseme alongside unigrams and other MWUs. MWU matches span several corpus positions and may thus (partially) overlap with cor-

[5] This CQP query uses a regular expression to find all lemmata that contain the substring *flucht*; `%cd` tells CQP to perform a case-insensitive search and ignore diacratics.

[6] As implemented in the Python module `https://pypi.org/project/association-measures/`.

[7] As with the suggestion of similar items, the API can easily be extended to automatically suggest MWU candidates, e.g. by means of named-entity recognition.

pus positions of other lemmata within the same or in other discoursemes. Internally, all discourseme descriptions are translated into CQP queries and we set CQP's matching strategy to *longest* in order to count corpus positions at most once. As an example, consider the *Bundesamt für Migration und Flüchtlinge* (the German Federal Office for Migration and Refugees, BAMF). If this MWU were to be included in a discourseme description also comprising the unigram *Flüchtlinge*, only occurrences of *Flüchtlinge* that are not included in the MWU would be considered as additional matches.

Furthermore, MWUs can overlap partially with the context. For co-occurrence counts of discoursemes, we thus have to define how partial overlaps are counted. A simple approach would be to assume a co-occurrence for any partial overlap, i.e. if at least the start or the end token of the match span is included in the context (and we do in fact retrieve concordance lines for all these cases when discourseme constellations are inspected). However, to ensure mathematical consistency, we only count discoursemes as co-occurrences (towards $O_{11}$) if they are completely within the context, and all other occurrences as outside the context (towards $O_{21}$).

Alternatively, the API also allows to count partial overlaps as co-occurrences. To ensure mathematical consistency in this case, we have to obtain counts on token level, which means that a single occurrence of a MWU increases the frequency count ($O_{11}$ or $O_{21}$) usually by more than one. This makes MWUs more sensitive to detection by association measures based on statistical significance, but leaves effect-size measures such as odds-ratio and the recommended LRC largely unaffected.

### 3.3 The choice of reference frequencies

Typically, reference frequencies $O_{21}$ and $O_{22}$ for collocation analyses are gained from the remainder of the corpus, i.e. all corpus positions that are not included in the context. Other approaches are possible, however, and these alternatives are especially important when working with subcorpora.

Table 1 shows assocation scores for collocates of the discourseme ⟨fleeing⟩ in the subcorpus of debates by the AfD in LP19, subject to different reference frequencies. It lists the top-20 candidates when compared against the entire remaining corpus (column "cf. GermaParl") and displays their reference frequency counts ($O_{21}$), association scores, and ranks when compared to other reference frequencies.[8]

Which frequency comparison is the most reasonable one? The three comparisons answer slightly different questions about the discourse around ⟨fleeing⟩ of AfD in LP19:

1. a comparison with the full corpus yields the collocation profile of ⟨fleeing⟩ as used by AfD in LP19,
2. a comparison with LP19 yields collocations of ⟨fleeing⟩ as used by AfD, against the background of the general discourse in LP19, and
3. a comparison with AfD in LP19 yields collocations of ⟨fleeing⟩ against the background of the overall AfD discourse in LP 19.[9]

As our goal is a collocation analysis for the discourseme ⟨fleeing⟩ (rather than, say, a keyword analysis for AfD or LP19), it may seem straightforward to prefer the third option. However, the very telling label *Mittelmeermigrant* ('mediterranean migrant') was coined by AfD in LP19 in the context of ⟨fleeing⟩ and does not occur anywhere else in the corpus. Due to its low frequency ($O_{11} = 2$) its association to ⟨fleeing⟩ is not significant within the small AfD-LP19 subcorpus, but is much more remarkable when compared against the entire corpus. For this reason, our API allows users to choose between the first and the third option.

### 3.4 Visualising collocation profiles

As has been pointed out above, the choice of association measure has a profound impact on collocational profiles (see Appendix A for a brief discussion). Although it is convenient to rely on a single measure, different association measures often provide complementary perspectives that need to be combined in order to capture the full picture. Some researchers have thus argued for a multidimensional visualisation of collocation profiles (Gries, 2019, 397ff), similar to the topographic maps in Figures 2 and 3 (Appendix A). Such maps can aid in understanding the different properties of association measures and provide a visual representation of the statistical profiles of collocates. However, the main task in CADS analyses is grouping

[8]We do not remove "stop words" from collocation profiles because punctuation marks, prepositions, etc. can be important for certain discourses. Our approach via semantic maps makes it easy for analysts to ignore such stop words.

[9]We do not include a comparison with the complete AfD subcorpus (across all periods) in this list for the simple reason that AfD only entered the federal parliament in LP19. Newer LP are not included in our version of GermaParl, so subcorpus AfD would be identical to AfD-LP19.

| item | cf. GermaParl | | | | cf. LP19 | | | | cf. AfD-19 | | | |
|---|---|---|---|---|---|---|---|---|---|---|---|---|
| | rank | O11 | O21 | LRC | rank | O11 | O21 | LRC | rank | O11 | O21 | LRC |
| Deutschsprachförderung | 1 | 5 | 17 | 6.95 | 4 | 5 | 15 | 3.50 | 10 | 5 | 6 | 1.38 |
| Globale | 2 | 18 | 669 | 6.89 | 1 | 18 | 298 | 4.43 | 2 | 18 | 52 | 3.65 |
| Migration | 3 | 31 | 2781 | 6.25 | 3 | 31 | 1390 | 3.64 | 3 | 31 | 262 | 2.86 |
| Migrant | 4 | 16 | 2423 | 4.70 | 8 | 16 | 781 | 2.72 | 25 | 16 | 378 | 0.61 |
| BAMF | 5 | 8 | 718 | 4.04 | 28 | 8 | 453 | 1.09 | 19 | 8 | 56 | 0.88 |
| Gesundheitsfonds | 6 | 9 | 1047 | 3.97 | 2 | 9 | 91 | 3.82 | 6 | 9 | 28 | 2.24 |
| UNRWA | 7 | 4 | 60 | 3.94 | 17 | 4 | 21 | 1.75 | – | 4 | 11 | **0** |
| berufsbezogen | 8 | 5 | 170 | 3.83 | 7 | 5 | 22 | 3.02 | 14 | 5 | 7 | 1.23 |
| 2015 | 9 | 18 | 6777 | 3.56 | 11 | 18 | 1368 | 2.26 | 12 | 18 | 291 | 1.32 |
| sogenannter | 10 | 54 | 44544 | 3.48 | 5 | 54 | 4105 | 3.31 | 5 | 54 | 902 | 2.34 |
| Asylbewerber | 11 | 13 | 4151 | 3.28 | 6 | 13 | 347 | 3.24 | 11 | 13 | 144 | 1.33 |
| Mittelmeermigrant | 12 | 2 | 0 | 3.17 | – | 2 | 0 | **0** | – | 2 | 0 | **0** |
| Wirtschaftsmigrant | 13 | 3 | 24 | 3.05 | – | 3 | 19 | **0** | – | 3 | 17 | **0** |
| syrisch | 14 | 9 | 1998 | 3.04 | 19 | 9 | 435 | 1.62 | 17 | 9 | 77 | 0.91 |
| Bundesamt | 15 | 16 | 9439 | 2.74 | 10 | 16 | 921 | 2.48 | 4 | 16 | 87 | 2.65 |
| Pakt | 16 | 13 | 6289 | 2.68 | 13 | 13 | 863 | 1.94 | 9 | 13 | 131 | 1.46 |
| Erdogan | 17 | 7 | 1348 | 2.55 | 54 | 7 | 642 | 0.02 | – | 7 | 146 | **0** |
| Heimatland | 18 | 8 | 2119 | 2.48 | 12 | 8 | 241 | 1.99 | 18 | 8 | 55 | 0.90 |
| “ | 19 | 48 | 75571 | 2.47 | 49 | 48 | 31305 | 0.14 | – | 48 | 5063 | **0** |
| Aufnahmegesellschaft | 20 | 3 | 40 | 2.36 | 30 | 3 | 7 | 0.98 | – | 3 | 4 | **0** |

Table 1: Excerpt of collocation rankings of discourseme ⟨fleeing⟩ in AfD-19 subject to different reference frequencies. There are $R_1 = 13{,}344$ tokens in the context $W$ (⟨fleeing⟩) in AfD-19; the reference corpora (excluding $W$) contain $R_2 = 271{,}064{,}105$ (GermaParl), $R_2 = 22{,}274{,}643$ (LP19), and $R_2 = 2{,}531{,}322$ (AfD-19) tokens, respectively. The table lists the top-20 collocates cf. GermaParl as ranked by conservative log-ratio (LRC).

collocates based on their discourse-specific semantics, not according to similarities in their frequency distribution or contingency tables.

A better way of supporting the manual grouping step is to visualise collocates in a semantic map, i.e. a two-dimensional projection that arranges collocates by their semantic similarity according to high-dimensional word embeddings. Although general semantic similarity is not the only criterion that discoursemes are based on (cf. the example of ⟨push factors⟩ above, which includes both *famine* and *expulsion*), most of the lemmata in a discourseme tend to be semantically similar in practice. A semantic map is therefore an excellent starting point for the grouping process. Our API combines the semantic map coordinates with the score of the selected association measure, which can be visualised by font size or other means (cf. Figure 1).

We use embeddings trained out-of-domain on German Wikipedia here. In principle, we could train embeddings on the corpus at hand to increase representativeness of the target domain. However, GermaParl is comparatively small with ca. 270 million tokens (compared to billions of tokens of Wikipedia) and CADS analyses are often carried out on much smaller corproa. To our knowledge there is no well-established way to fine-tune pre-trained embeddings on an in-domain corpus (except to train from scratch on the combined data). A further alternative is the use of context-sensitive embeddings, yielding a different representation for each occurrence of the same lemma depending on its context. Since the semantic map is a type-level visualisation, a global representation would have to be obtained, e.g. by averaging over all individual token embeddings in the target corpus. Note that administrators can easily prepare and deploy such global context-sensitive embeddings, giving a high degree of flexibility to the API.

For the two-dimensional projection, we use $t$-distributed stochastic neighbour embedding (van der Maaten and Hinton, 2008) by default, but other techniques can also be selected; the API e.g. offers uniform manifold approximation and projection as an alternative (McInnes et al., 2018).

### 3.5 Comparing collocation profiles

The semantic map in Figure 1 also allows for a qualitative comparison of collocation profiles. We can e.g. observe on the right-hand side of Figure 1 that GRUENE talks about the ⟨risk⟩ that refugees are taking (*Lebensgefahr*, ‘risk of death’) whereas *angeblich* (‘alleged(ly)’), *sogenannt* (‘so-called’), and the use of quotation marks indicates that the

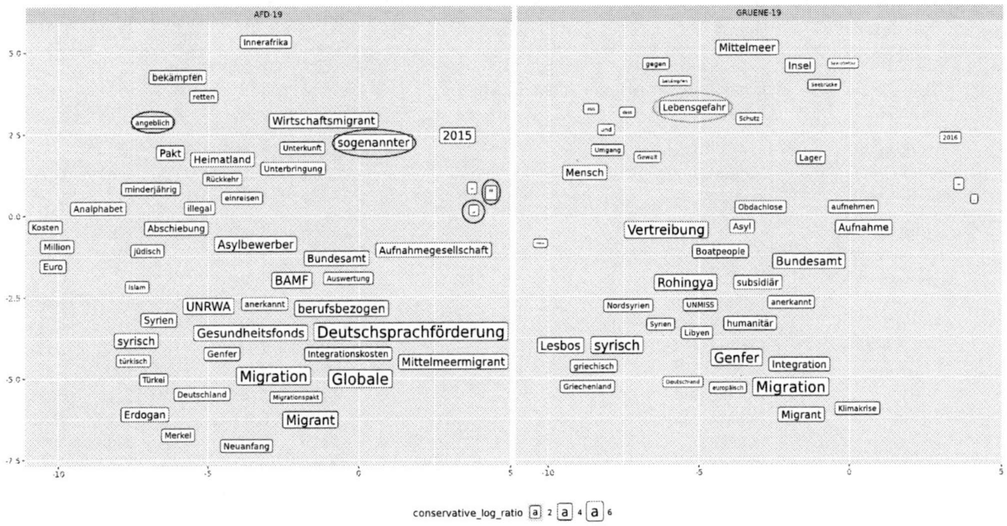


Figure 1: Semantic map visualisation of the collocation profiles of discourseme ⟨fleeing⟩ in two subcorpora (left panel: AfD in LP19, right panel: GRUENE in LP19). Both profiles are cf. GermaParl.

AfD is doubtful about the official narrative. Such qualitative comparisons of collocation profiles are often very fruitful in CADS studies. We argue that semantic maps are highly effective for this purpose: collocates appear at the same coordinates in both panels of Figure 1 rather than at entirely different ranks in two $n$-best lists, aiding in a direct visual comparison.

For a quantitative comparison of two given collocation profiles (or keyword lists), several approaches are available. One possibility is rank-biased overlap (Webber et al., 2010):

$$\text{rbo}(P_1, P_2; p) = (1-p) \sum_{d=1}^{\infty} p^{d-1} A(d)$$

where $A(d)$ is the proportion of shared lemmata in the top $d$ ranks of profiles $P_1$ and $P_2$, and the sensitivity parameter $p$ controls the depth of the comparison. We are planning to support such quantitative comparisons in a future version of the API.

Furthermore, we plan to include a quantitative method for analysing collocation profiles over time that aims to find disruptions in the usage of words ("usage fluctuation analysis", UFA) (McEnery et al., 2019, 418). In UFA, a corpus must be partioned into overlapping sliding windows across time; subsequently, the resulting profiles are iteratively compared providing a scalar value, and finally a statistical regression model is estimated to detect outliers in the corresponding time series.[10]

### 3.6 Discourseme associations

In order to identify discourseme constellations, it is quite straightforward to look at pairwise co-occurrences of discoursemes and their assocation strength. For this purpose, one discourseme is taken as the node of a collocation analysis and the co-occurrences of all lemmata and lemma sequences from the other discourseme are added up. This is reasonable because items from the same discourseme do not overlap, which is ensured by our query-based matching (cf. Section 3.2). Focussing iteratively on each discourseme in the database, pairwise associations between all discoursemes can be calculated, yielding a network structure with discoursemes as nodes and discourseme associations as edges.

As an illustration, Table 2 shows association scores between ⟨fleeing⟩ and a tentative (and incomplete) set of discoursemes created from its collocation profiles in the subcorpora GRUENE-LP19 and AfD-LP19 (cf. GermaParl). Because of the way the discoursemes were formed, all entries in the table are relevant constellations with ⟨fleeing⟩. The API yields both a global association score for each discourseme and individual scores for its lem-

[10] McEnery et al. (2019) use Gwet's AC1 (Gwet, 2001) to compare profiles. The formula is similar to the Cohen's Kappa but incorporates a different method for estimating the probability of chance agreement, which helps mitigate the issues associated with marginal imbalances.

| discourseme | lemma (sequence) | GRUENE-19 O11 | GRUENE-19 O21 | GRUENE-19 LRC | AfD-19 O11 | AfD-19 O21 | AfD-19 LRC |
|---|---|---|---|---|---|---|---|
| ⟨BAMF⟩ | | 19 | 1235 | 7.44 | 24 | 1230 | 7.50 |
| —″— | Bundesamt für Migration und Flüchtling | 16 | 512 | 8.08 | 16 | 512 | 7.64 |
| —″— | BAMF | 3 | 723 | 1.62 | 8 | 718 | 5.25 |
| ⟨migration⟩ | | 36 | 5215 | 6.68 | 47 | 5204 | 6.75 |
| —″— | Migration | 28 | 2784 | 7.02 | 31 | 2781 | 6.79 |
| —″— | Migrant | 8 | 2431 | 4.17 | 16 | 2423 | 5.55 |
| ⟨origin⟩ | | 39 | 18268 | 5.03 | 44 | 18263 | 4.82 |
| —″— | syrisch | 14 | 1993 | 5.73 | 9 | 1998 | 4.04 |
| —″— | Boatpeople | 2 | 4 | 5.66 | 0 | 6 | 0.00 |
| —″— | Rohingya | 5 | 208 | 5.65 | 1 | 212 | 0.00 |
| —″— | Nordsyrien | 3 | 120 | 3.94 | 0 | 123 | 0.00 |
| —″— | Libyen | 6 | 2938 | 2.56 | 1 | 2943 | 0.00 |
| —″— | Syrien | 7 | 6066 | 2.06 | 11 | 6062 | 3.03 |
| —″— | Heimatland | 0 | 2127 | 0.00 | 8 | 2119 | 3.58 |
| —″— | Innerafrika | 0 | 5 | 0.00 | 2 | 3 | 5.51 |
| —″— | Islam | 0 | 1439 | 0.00 | 5 | 1434 | 2.44 |
| —″— | jüdisch | 2 | 3368 | 0.00 | 7 | 3363 | 2.47 |
| ⟨push⟩ | | 17 | 2939 | 5.95 | 8 | 2948 | 3.60 |
| —″— | Vertreibung | 17 | 2912 | 5.87 | 5 | 2924 | 1.91 |
| —″— | Wirtschaftsmigrant | 0 | 27 | 0.00 | 3 | 24 | 6.53 |
| ⟨route⟩ | | 32 | 31146 | 3.88 | 31 | 31147 | 3.37 |
| —″— | Lesbos | 4 | 98 | 5.87 | 0 | 102 | 0.00 |
| —″— | Mittelmeer | 8 | 2246 | 4.02 | 3 | 2251 | 0.00 |
| —″— | Lager | 7 | 4475 | 2.59 | 2 | 4480 | 0.00 |
| —″— | Griechenland | 8 | 8095 | 2.17 | 7 | 8096 | 1.29 |
| —″— | Mittelmeermigrant | 0 | 2 | 0.00 | 2 | 0 | 7.44 |
| —″— | Türkei | 5 | 15155 | 0.00 | 12 | 15148 | 2.01 |
| —″— | einreisen | 0 | 1075 | 0.00 | 5 | 1070 | 2.97 |
| ⟨asylum⟩ | | 8 | 7131 | 2.77 | 16 | 7123 | 4.09 |
| —″— | Asyl | 7 | 2968 | 3.48 | 3 | 2972 | 0.00 |
| —″— | Asylbewerber | 1 | 4163 | 0.00 | 13 | 4151 | 4.28 |
| ⟨accommodation⟩ | | 46 | 60400 | 3.62 | 40 | 60406 | 2.91 |
| —″— | Aufnahme | 12 | 8419 | 3.32 | 8 | 8423 | 1.70 |
| —″— | Integration | 15 | 14882 | 3.08 | 8 | 14889 | 0.88 |
| —″— | aufnehmen | 15 | 31725 | 1.98 | 8 | 31732 | 0.00 |
| —″— | Aufnahmegesellschaft | 0 | 43 | 0.00 | 3 | 40 | 5.29 |
| —″— | Unterbringung | 2 | 3011 | 0.00 | 7 | 3006 | 2.76 |
| —″— | Unterkunft | 2 | 2320 | 0.00 | 6 | 2316 | 2.60 |
| ⟨collaboration⟩ | | 6 | 13962 | 0.93 | 36 | 13932 | 4.83 |
| —″— | Seebrücke | 2 | 14 | 4.32 | 0 | 16 | 0.00 |
| —″— | Erdogan | 1 | 1354 | 0.00 | 7 | 1348 | 3.84 |
| —″— | Globale Flüchtlingsforum | 0 | 16 | 0.00 | 1 | 15 | 0.00 |
| —″— | Migrationspakt | 0 | 138 | 0.00 | 3 | 135 | 3.45 |
| —″— | Pakt | 0 | 6302 | 0.00 | 13 | 6289 | 3.47 |
| —″— | UNRWA | 0 | 64 | 0.00 | 4 | 60 | 6.06 |
| —″— | türkisch | 3 | 6074 | 0.00 | 8 | 6069 | 2.11 |
| ⟨help⟩ | | 26 | 49256 | 2.80 | 26 | 49256 | 2.36 |
| —″— | Seenotretter | 2 | 16 | 4.24 | 0 | 18 | 0.00 |
| —″— | subsidiär | 5 | 823 | 3.79 | 2 | 826 | 0.00 |
| —″— | UNMISS | 4 | 673 | 3.12 | 0 | 677 | 0.00 |
| —″— | Schutz | 14 | 42054 | 1.38 | 11 | 42057 | 0.30 |
| —″— | berufsbezogen Deutschsprachförderung | 0 | 20 | 0.00 | 5 | 15 | 8.89 |
| —″— | retten | 1 | 5670 | 0.00 | 8 | 5663 | 2.24 |
| ⟨risk⟩ | | 4 | 340 | 4.84 | – | – | – |
| —″— | Lebensgefahr | 4 | 340 | 4.84 | – | – | – |
| ⟨doubt⟩ | | – | – | – | 65 | 58177 | 3.86 |
| —″— | angeblich | – | – | – | 11 | 13633 | 2.13 |
| —″— | sogenannter | – | – | – | 54 | 44544 | 3.87 |

Table 2: Tentative (and incomplete) discourseme formation for collocations of ⟨fleeing⟩ in two subcorpora ($R_1 =$ 9,830, $R_2 =$ 271,067,619 in GRUENE-19 and $R_1 =$ 13,344, $R_2 =$ 271,064,105 in AfD-19). Both scores of individual lemmata and lemma sequences and global discourseme scores are provided.

mata and lemma sequences. The discourseme associations provide a bird's-eye view on the distribution across subcorpora: we can e.g. see that the ⟨BAMF⟩ (the German Federal Office for Migration and Refugees) plays a role for both GRUENE and AfD, whereas ⟨collaboration⟩ is clearly only associated with AfD. Associations for individual items give a more detailed view, revealing e.g. that although ⟨accommodation⟩ is associated with both parliamentary groups, AfD has a particularly high association for *Aufnahmegesellschaft* ('receiving society'), which might prompt us to reconsider the inclusion of this lemma in the discourseme.

In our approach, discoursemes are usually created and extended iteratively by working with different parameter settings and in different subcorpora. This also has an impact on discourseme associations, cf. Table 3. Working solely on a collocation profile of ⟨fleeing⟩ in the subcorpus of GRUENE in LP19, for instance, would not have brought up the lemmata *Unterbringung* ('accommodation') und *Unterkunft* ('lodging') for the discourseme ⟨accommodation⟩. Inclusion of these lemmata does however change its association with ⟨fleeing⟩, increasing the LRC score from 3.00 to 3.11, even though the two additional lemmata are not significant by themselves (with an LRC of 0).

| item | O11 | O21 | LRC |
|---|---|---|---|
| ⟨accommodation⟩ | 27 | 40144 | 3.00 |
| ... Aufnahme | 12 | 8419 | 3.32 |
| ... aufnehmen | 15 | 31725 | 1.98 |
| ⟨accommodation⟩ | 31 | 45475 | 3.11 |
| ... Aufnahme | 12 | 8419 | 3.32 |
| ... aufnehmen | 15 | 31725 | 1.98 |
| ... Unterbringung | 2 | 3011 | 0.00 |
| ... Unterkunft | 2 | 2320 | 0.00 |

Table 3: Two alternative definitions for discourseme ⟨accommodation⟩. Frequencies taken from subcorpus GRUENE in LP19 cf. GermaParl ($R_1$ = 9,830, $R_2$ = 271,067,619).

## 4 Working with the API

As outlined in the introduction, interaction with the API is possible both from dedicated GUIs and through low-level API calls e.g. from widespread languages such as Python or R. Both interaction methods operate on the same discourseme database, ensuring consistency across tools while giving users the freedom to select the most convenient option for their analysis.

Typically, a graphical frontend is ideal for tasks such as defining the topic discourseme, forming discoursemes based on collocation profiles or keyords, and examining concordance lines of discoursemes or individual lemmata. We have already experimented with a prototype frontend[11] and are currently developing an improved version, which can be found in the `cwb-cads` repository linked above. Development of the new frontend, implemented in React, focusses on flexible selection of semantic maps, more straightforward definitions of MWUs, and efficient recalculations.

For operations such as analysing the distribution of discoursemes or discourseme networks across metadata variables, or exporting discourseme descriptions and individual concordance lines for research documentation, API calls are more suitable. Manuals for working with the API are available in the `cwb-cads` repository.

## 5 Conclusion and Future Work

We have presented a CWB-based REST API that aims to provide convenient methods for CADS researchers, offering a variety of parameter choices to enable customised and comprehensive research. We have outlined the available parameters and provided guidelines on making reasonable selections.

A significant contribution of our work is the conceptual and technical framework for working with manually defined semantic groups ("discoursemes"). The paper includes details on the calculation of discourseme scores and how to tackle the challenges associated with multi-word units (MWUs) and overlapping discoursemes.

It is worth mentioning that our approach necessarily shares the same limited perspective on discourse as classic CADS. Working on word or lemma types means neglecting word-sense or discourse-specific disambiguation. However, this is somewhat mitigated by the fact that discoursemes are mutually disambiguated within constellations.

We plan to expand the API by adding more parameters to its endpoints, further increasing flexibility. Most importantly, while the current implementation only supports pairwise associations of discoursemes, we aim to visualise these associations as discourseme networks.

[11] `https://github.com/fau-klue/mmda-toolkit`

## Acknowledgements

This work has been funded by the Deutsche Forschungsgemeinschaft (DFG, German Research Foundation), project no. 466328567.

## References

Laurence Anthony. 2013. A critical look at software tools in corpus linguistics. *Linguistic Research*, 30:141–161.

Paul Baker. 2006. *Using Corpora in Discourse Analysis*. Continuum, London.

Paul Baker, Costas Gabrielatos, Majid KhosraviNik, Michał Krzyżanowski, Tony McEnery, and Ruth Wodak. 2008. A useful methodological synergy? Combining critical discourse analysis and corpus linguistics to examine discourses of refugees and asylum seekers in the UK press. *Discourse & Society*, 19(3):273–306.

Paul Baker and Tony McEnery. 2005. A corpus-based approach to discourses of refugees and asylum seekers in UN and newspaper texts. *Journal of Language and Politics*, 4(2):197–226.

Stefan Evert. 2004. *The Statistics of Word Cooccurrences: Word Pairs and Collocations*. Ph.D. thesis, Institut für maschinelle Sprachverarbeitung, University of Stuttgart.

Stefan Evert. 2008. Corpora and collocations. In Anke Lüdeling and Merja Kytö, editors, *Corpus Linguistics. An International Handbook*, chapter 58, pages 1212–1248. Mouton de Gruyter, Berlin, New York.

Stefan Evert. 2009. 58. corpora and collocations. In Anke Lüdeling and Merja Kytö, editors, *Volume 2*, pages 1212–1248. De Gruyter Mouton, Berlin, New York.

Stefan Evert and Andrew Hardie. 2011. Twenty-first century corpus workbench: Updating a query architecture for the new millennium. In *Proceedings of the Corpus Linguistics 2011 Conference*, Birmingham, UK.

Stefan Evert and The CWB Development Team. 2022. *The IMS Open Corpus Workbench (CWB) CQP Interface and Query Language Tutorial*. CWB Version 3.5.

Stefan Evert, Peter Uhrig, Sabine Bartsch, and Tobias Proisl. 2017. E-view-alation – a large-scale evaluation study of association measures for collocation identification. In *Electronic lexicography in the 21st century. Proceedings of the eLex 2017 conference*, pages 531–549, Leiden, The Netherlands.

Stephanie Evert. 2022. Measuring keyness. In *Digital Humanities 2022*, pages 202 – 205.

Norman Fairclough. 2015. *Language and Power*, 3 edition. Routledge, Oxon.

Costas Gabrielatos and Paul Baker. 2008. Fleeing, sneaking, flooding: A corpus analysis of discursive constructions of refugees and asylum seekers in the uk press, 1996-2005. *Journal of English Linguistics*, 36(1):5–38.

Tim Griebel, Stefan Evert, and Philipp Heinrich, editors. 2020. *Multimodal Approaches to Media Discourses: Reconstructing the Age of Austerity in the United Kingdom*. Routledge, London.

Stefan Th. Gries. 2019. 15 years of collostructions: Some long overdue additions/corrections (to/of actually all sorts of corpus-linguistics measures). *International Journal of Corpus Linguistics*, 24(3):385–412.

Stefan Th. Gries. 2021. A new approach to (key) keywords analysis: Using frequency, and now also dispersion. *Research in Corpus Linguistics*, 9(2):1–33.

Reiner Grundmann and Ramesh Krishnamurthy. 2010. The discourse of climate change: a corpus-based approach. *Critical Approaches to Discourse Analysis Across Disciplines*, 4(2):125–146.

Kilem Gwet. 2001. *Handbook of Inter-Rater Reliability: How to Estimate the Level of Agreement Between Two or Multiple Raters*. STATAXIS Publishing Company, Gaithersburg, MD.

Andrew Hardie. 2012. CQPweb – combining power, flexibility and usability in a corpus analysis tool. *International Journal of Corpus Linguistics*, 17(3):380–409.

Andrew Hardie. 2014. A single statistical technique for keywords, lockwords, and collocations. Internal CASS working paper no. 1, unpublished.

Philipp Heinrich, Andreas Blombach, Bao Minh Doan Dang, Leonardo Zilio, Linda Havenstein, Nathan Dykes, Stephanie Evert, and Fabian Schäfer. 2024. Automatic Identification of COVID-19-Related Conspiracy Narratives in German Telegram Channels and Chats. In *Proceedings of the 2024 Joint International Conference on Computational Linguistics, Language Resources and Evaluation (LREC-COLING 2024)*, page 1932–1943, Turin, Italy.

Siegfried Jäger. 2015. *Kritische Diskursanalyse: Eine Einführung*. UNRAST.

Gerlinde Mautner. 2009. Corpora and critical discourse analysis. In Paul Baker, editor, *Contemporary Corpus Linguistics*, pages 32–46. Continuum, London/New York.

Tony McEnery, Vaclav Brezina, and Helen Baker. 2019. Usage Fluctuation Analysis: A new way of analysing shifts in historical discourse. *International Journal of Corpus Linguistics*, 24(4):413–444.

Leland McInnes, John Healy, and James Melville. 2018. Umap: Uniform manifold approximation and projection for dimension reduction. *ArXiv e-prints*.

Tomas Mikolov, Kai Chen, Greg Corrado, and Jeffrey Dean. 2013. Efficient estimation of word representations in vector space. *Preprint*, arXiv:1301.3781.

Costanza Navarretta and Dorte H. Hansen. 2023. According to BERTopic, what do Danish parties debate on when they address energy and environment? In *Proceedings of the 3rd Workshop on Computational Linguistics for the Political and Social Sciences*, pages 59–68, Ingolstadt, Germany. Association for Computational Lingustics.

Joan Plepi, Magdalena Buski, and Lucie Flek. 2023. Personalized intended and perceived sarcasm detection on Twitter. In *Proceedings of the 3rd Workshop on Computational Linguistics for the Political and Social Sciences*, pages 8–18, Ingolstadt, Germany. Association for Computational Lingustics.

Michael Stubbs. 1995. Collocations and semantic profiles: On the cause of the trouble with quantitative studies. *Functions of Language*, 1:23–55.

Laurens van der Maaten and Geoffrey Hinton. 2008. Visualizing data using t-SNE. *Journal of machine learning research*, 9(Nov):2579–2605.

Guofeng Wang and Changpeng Huan. 2023. Negotiating climate change in public discourse: insights from critical discourse studies. *Critical Discourse Studies*, 21(2):133–145.

William Webber, Alistair Moffat, and Justin Zobel. 2010. A similarity measure for indefinite rankings. *ACM Trans. Inf. Syst.*, 28:20.

Maximilian Wegge and Roman Klinger. 2023. Automatic emotion experiencer recognition. In *Proceedings of the 3rd Workshop on Computational Linguistics for the Political and Social Sciences*, pages 1–7, Ingolstadt, Germany. Association for Computational Lingustics.

Ruth Wodak. 2015. *The Politics of Fear: What Right-Wing Populist Discourses Mean*. SAGE, London.

Ruth Wodak. 2018. *Discourse and European Integration*, volume 86 of *KFG Working Paper Series*. Freie Universität Berlin, FB Politik- und Sozialwissenschaften, Otto-Suhr-Institut für Politikwissenschaft Kolleg-Forschergruppe "The Transformative Power of Europe", Berlin.

Ruth Wodak and Michael Meyer. 2015. *Methods of Critical Discourse Studies*, chapter Critical discourse studies: history, agenda, theory and methodology. Sage.

# A Parameters in Collocation Analyses

Context settings and the choice of association measure can have a huge influence on the outcome of a collocation analysis. Evert (2009) distinguishes three types of co-occurrence:

1. surface co-occurrence – where one counts up to $w$ tokens in any direction (asymmetrical windows are obviously possible),
2. textual co-occurrence – using the whole sentence, paragraph, post, etc. as context,
3. syntactic co-occurrence – which we will ignore here because it presupposes reliable syntactic annotation and does not generalise for various parts of speech that can be included in discoursemes.

As mentioned above, the API supports a combination of surface and textual co-occurrences, defining context via a window span $w$ and a structural context break (e.g. texts, paragraphs, or sentences). For small context windows $w$, collocates are e.g. often part of multi-word expressions rather than indicating discourseme constellations. Confining the context to individual texts is especially important for corpora with small "natural" text units such as tweets. A large shortcoming of CQPweb is that the context of a collocation analysis cannot be confined to individual texts (or sentences), and collocation analyses on Twitter corpora are thus oftentime misleading (since the context often includes the last or first couple of tokens of different tweets).

Given a well-defined context, all occurrences of (unigram) types can be directly classified as being inside or outside the context.[12] In "contingency table notation", these numbers are named $O_{11}$ and $O_{21}$, respectively, with $O_{12}$ the remaining number of corpus positions within the context and $O_{22}$ the remaining number of corpus positions outside the context.

Statistical association measures allow the calculation of a single scalar value to quantify the association, either in terms of the effect size or in terms of statistical significance – or by some other heuristic (e.g. motivated by information theory). Straightforward measures are the ratio of relative frequencies (measuring the effect size) or log-likelihood ratio (measuring statistical significance). Note that effect-size measures are biased

[12]This works similar for keyword analyses, where $O_{11}$ is the number of occurrences in the target corpus and $O_{21}$ the number of occurrences in the reference corpus; $R_1$ and $R_2$ being the respective sizes of the corpora.

|  | $w_2$ | $\neg w_2$ |  |
|---|---|---|---|
| $W(\langle d \rangle)$ | $O_{11}$ | $O_{12}$ | $= R_1$ |
| $\neg W(\langle d \rangle)$ | $O_{21}$ | $O_{22}$ | $= R_2$ |
|  | $= C_1$ | $= C_2$ | $= N$ |

Table 4: Contingency table notation: For a focus discourseme $\langle d \rangle$ and a given lemma $w_2$, all lemmata in the corpus are categorised according to whether they appear within the context $W$ of $\langle d \rangle$ or its complement (rows), and whether they are a realisation of $w_2$ or not (columns). The row marginals are named $R_1$ and $R_2$, the column marginals $C_1$ and $C_2$, respectively; the total number of tokens in the corpus is $N$.

to low-frequency terms. The association measure presented by Evert (2022) and recommended in this paper combines effect size and statistical significance: it is the binary logarithm of the lower bound of the confidence interval of relative risk.

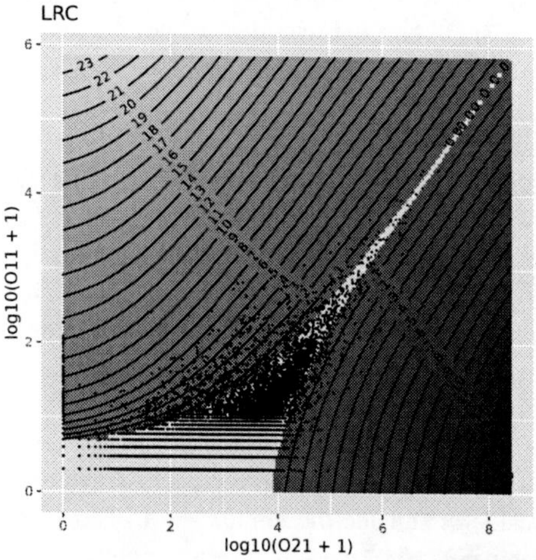


Figure 2: Topographic map for collocation profile of discourseme ⟨fleeing⟩ in GermaParl using conservative log-ratio as association measure.

As mentioned above, a wide variety of association measures are implemented in the Python package `association-measures`. This package also allows the creation of *topographic maps*, which visualise association measures in form of contour plots above a two-dimensional plane spanned by (the logarithm of) the number of occurrences in the target (the cotext) and the reference corpus (the remaining corpus). Figure 2 and Figure 3 show such topographic maps for the collocation profile of discourseme ⟨fleeing⟩ in GermaParl subject to two different association measures ($R_1 = 725{,}839$, $R_2 = 270{,}351{,}610$). Each point represents a collocation candidate of discourseme ⟨fleeing⟩ (which are identical in both figures).

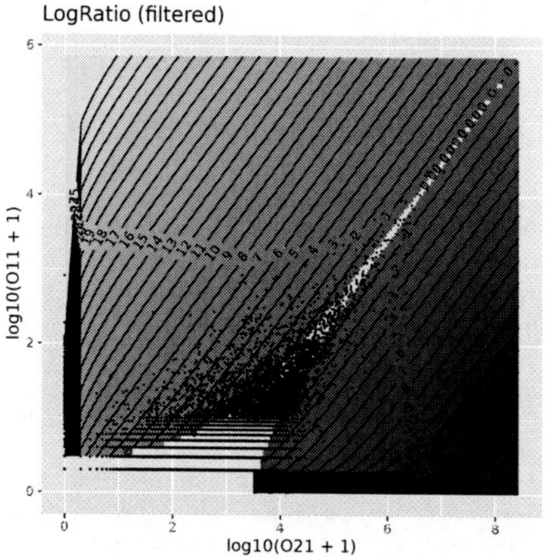


Figure 3: Topographic map for collocation profile of discourseme ⟨fleeing⟩ in GermaParl using log-ratio filtered by log-likelihood as association measure ($\alpha = 99.9\%$)

Both conservative log-ratio and log-ratio filtered by log-likelihood-ratio combine effect size and statistical significance: candidates are ranked high (upper left corner) if they appear frequently and relatively more frequently in the context than outside. Note that the two measures differ mainly in their decision for low-frequency candidates, where it is debatable how much statistical evidence is needed to support some observable effect.

# A Few Hypocrites: Few-Shot Learning and Subtype Definitions for Detecting Hypocrisy Accusations in Online Climate Change Debates

**Paulina Garcia Corral[1], Avishai Green[2], Hendrik Meyer[3*]**
**Anke Stoll[4], Xiaoyue Yan[5], Myrthe Reuver[6]**
[1] Data Science Lab, Hertie School [2] Hebrew University of Jerusalem [3] University of Hamburg
[4] Ilmenau University of Technology [5] University of Zurich [6] Vrije Universiteit Amsterdam
[1] corral@hertie-school.org, [2] avishai.green@mail.huji.ac.il
[3]hendrik.meyer-1@uni-hamburg.de
* The first three authors contributed equally, and are shared first authors.

## Abstract

The climate crisis is a salient issue in online discussions, and hypocrisy accusations are a central rhetorical element in these debates. However, for large-scale text analysis, *hypocrisy accusation detection* is an understudied tool, most often defined as a smaller subtask of fallacious argument detection. In this paper, we define hypocrisy accusation detection as an independent task in NLP, and identify different relevant subtypes of hypocrisy accusations. Our Climate Hypocrisy Accusation Corpus (CHAC) consists of 420 Reddit climate debate comments, expert-annotated into two different types of hypocrisy accusations: personal versus political hypocrisy. We evaluate few-shot in-context learning with 6 shots and 3 instruction-tuned Large Language Models (LLMs) for detecting hypocrisy accusations in this dataset. Results indicate that the GPT-4o and Llama-3 models in particular show promise in detecting hypocrisy accusations (F1 reaching 0.68, while previous work shows F1 of 0.44). However, context matters for a complex semantic concept such as hypocrisy accusations, and we find models struggle especially at identifying political hypocrisy accusations compared to personal moral hypocrisy. Our study contributes new insights in hypocrisy detection and climate change discourse, and is a stepping stone for large-scale analysis of hypocrisy accusation in online climate debates.

## 1 Introduction

Perhaps no accusation is more commonly lobbied in political discourse as that of hypocrisy (Collins, 2018; Thompson, 2004). Allegations of hypocrisy, defined by the Oxford English Dictionary as the assumption "of a false appearance of virtue or goodness" (OED, 2024) and understood in practice as an incongruity between behavior and publicly expressed beliefs (Furia, 2009), are so ubiquitous as to lead Hannah Arendt to describe politics itself as a "never ending fight to ferret out hypocrites" (Arendt, 2006). Making such an accusation of one's rival is effective, as hypocrisy is widely and deeply loathed, with research showing that perceived hypocrisy negatively affects voters' opinions of politicians above and beyond other underlying scandals (Bhatti et al., 2013; Laurent et al., 2014; Grover and Hasel, 2015). It may also seem, in a polarized political landscape, like the only rhetorical tool available. When political opponents lack shared standards, moral persuasion becomes near-impossible, and what is left is undermining one's opponent with "the revelation that… [he or she] is not living up to his own professed ideal" (Shklar, 1984) . While discourse on political hypocrisy dates centuries back, it has only intensified online, buoyed by social media's amplification of polarization (Allcott et al., 2020) and valorization of authenticity (Hallinan et al., 2021).

An arena of online discourse in which the hypocrisy charge is especially pertinent is that of debates around climate change, where hypocrisy accusations have been shown to be central to increasingly polarized, cross-ideological online interactions (Brüggemann and Meyer, 2023). An example of such an online hypocrisy accusation is a Reddit commenter describing COP26, an international political climate conference in 2020, as *"the biggest hypocrisy in the world"* [because the politicians are] *"arriving in their private jets."* Hypocrisy accusations have been found to drive polarization in online climate debates (Falkenberg et al., 2022), facilitating not cross-camp deliberation but rather segregation into opposing ideological camps (Meyer et al., 2023) and affective polarization (Tyagi et al., 2020). Being able to analyze (online) debates about climate policy, focusing on hypocrisy accusations can help us better measure the use of hypocrisy in such debates.

Detecting accusations of hypocrisy is understudied in computational text analysis and Natural Language Processing (NLP). Usually, hypocrisy is only



*Proceedings of the 58th Annual Meeting of the Association for Computational Linguistics*, pages 45–60
July 5–10, 2020. ©2020 Association for Computational Linguistics

included as part of broader logical fallacy detection tasks, as in Habernal et al. (2018). However, hypocrisy accusations are a distinct phenomenon: Linguistically, they often contain contrastive conjunctions between clauses to highlight inconsistencies. Semantically, their identification relies on context to understand contradictions.

Earlier work (see Section 2) reports good performance on detecting *logical fallacies* in general, but it is noticeable in the literature that hypocrisy accusation are a difficult and sometimes neglected phenomenon in state-of-the-art NLP. Alhindi et al. (2022) report relatively low performance of 0.43 in macro-F1 for detecting *whataboutism*, a hypocrisy-related fallacy – and only 0.21 in macro-F1 for all fallacies in climate debates. Recently, Piskorski et al. (2023) report a performance of RoBERTa-XLM multilingual detection of the *whataboutism* concept with an F1 of 0.06. However, this concept consists of only 0.05% of their fallacy dataset.

Due to a lack of attention to the specific *hypocrisy accusation* construct, there is a scarcity of data annotated for hypocrisy detection as well as little research of nuances in this construct, such as different types of hypocrisy accusations. Yet hypocrisy allegations are varied, and we believe an account of different kinds will afford a better understanding of the online debate and the performance of models detecting such accusations.

Our contributions to the literature are:
(1) We, unlike previous work, analyze **hypocrisy accusation detection as an individual and nuanced task** particularly relevant for analyzing online climate discourse;
(2) We are also, to our knowledge, the first to define **different types of hypocrisy** accusation for computational analysis, where we differentiate personal moral hypocrisy from political hypocrisy;
(3) Additionally, we release a **dataset**: the Climate Hypocrisy Accusation Corpus (CHAC), with 420 comments annotated by social scientists for the different types of hypocrisy accusations;
(4) We **analyze the potential of Large Language Models** as hypocrisy accusation detectors and evaluate LLMs with the various hypocrisy constructions we find in our data. We note where models struggle with the task, as a building block for future hypocrisy accusation analyses.

This paper is as organized as follows: Section 2 describes previous research on measuring social science constructs using LLMs, including hypocrisy detection. Section 3 introduces our dataset: the different types of hypocrisy, our annotation process, and corpus statistics. We describe our experiments to evaluate the capabilities of different instruction-tuned models on this dataset in Section 4, and present results of these experiments in Section 5. We then reflect on our results and the complexity of our task (Section 6), and conclude our work in Section 7.

## 2 Background

Large Language Models (LLMs) are models trained on predicting sequences of text. These models are trained in human preferences and instructions, and can perform in-context learning: with a natural language prompt or instruction, these models are able to do tasks such as classifying text examples on a new construct (Brown et al., 2020).

### 2.1 Promise and Limits of LLMs for Social Science Construct Detection

LLMs show great promise for detecting complex social science constructs in text. Recent comparative analyses highlight their exceptional performance and adaptability across numerous NLP tasks, including but not limited to sentiment analysis, offensive language detection, intent recognition, fake news classification, stance detection, and document classification (Fields et al., 2024). Alizadeh et al. (2024) compared the performance of open-source LLMs in text classification tasks typical for political science research, employing both zero-shot and fine-tuned LLMs for tasks including stance, topic, and relevance classification on news articles and tweets. They concluded that fine-tuning enhances the performance of open-source LLMs, making it preferable to few-shot training with a relatively modest quantity of annotated text. Törnberg (2023) explored the utility of GPT models for annotating political Twitter messages and found that ChatGPT-4o achieved higher accuracy, reliability, and either equal or lower bias compared to human classifiers. It also excelled in annotations requiring contextual reasoning and inference of authorial intent.

However, these models show some potential limitations. Plaza-del Arco et al. (2023) have found LLMs using in-context learning to outperform other NLP models in detecting complex social constructs such as sexist comments and misogynist hate, though they do report prompt brittleness – resulting in less stability of construct detection over slightly different prompt formulations. Additionally, humans remain better than LLMs at editing and improving difficult examples for model training, e.g. in sexist language detection (Sen et al., 2023). This indicates that LLMs are promising for the annotation and detection of social science construct in text, but also show some limitations in subtle understanding of the underlying construct.

### 2.2 Fallacies and Hypocrisy Accusations

Hypocrisy accusations are a subtle construct, but are not often the main topic in research using state-of-the-art NLP. Habernal et al. (2018) identify fallacies as unfair arguments in debates, 'deceptions in disguise' whose conceptualization goes back to Aristotle (Aristotle, 1909). Their work locates hypocrisy accusations as a subtype of *ad hominem* fallacy, and find a convolutional neutral network is able to detect *ad hominem* fallacies with 0.81 accuracy. Sahai et al. (2021) mention hypocrisy accusations as a common fallacy in online debate, but do not include it as one of the eight fallacy types they detect with neural models with 0.76 accuracy.

Hypocrisy has also been part of other types of tasks. Piskorski et al. (2023) introduce a multilingual dataset with an annotated hypocrisy accusation concept as part of a 'persuasion techniques task'. They also introduce an XLM-RoBERTa model as a baseline. One of the topics in their dataset is the climate change debate. Their appendix reports a performance of the *whataboutism* concept of 0.25% precision, with extremely low recall (0.034%) leading to an F1 of 0.06. However, this concept is only 0.05% of the entire dataset.

More recently, fallacy detection has also been explored with LLMs. The Logical Fallacy Understanding Dataset (LFUD) (Li et al., 2024) was created to evaluate LLMs' capability of logical fallacy understanding. The authors show how this dataset can be fine-tuned to obtain significantly enhanced performance on logical reasoning. On a limited set of logical fallacies (*Against the Person, Appeal to Authority, Appeal to Popularity, Appeal to Emotion, Hasty Generalization, Questionable Cause, and Red Herring*), GPT-4o achieves an accuracy of 0.79, and when used in cases that exclude invalid or unidentified instances, an accuracy of 0.90 (Lim and Perrault, 2024). Additionally, Valdovinos (2023) created a real-time fallacy detection for events such as presidential debates online, which integrates audio transcription models with four fallacy classification models. However, there is no category of hypocrisy accusations in these previous LLM works, nor do they focus on climate debates.

Alhindi et al. (2023) apply LLMs for detecting fallacies in online climate debates, using five existing fallacy datasets as well a new dataset constructed specifically for the task. Their experimental set-up consists of fine-tuning different sizes of the T5 LLM model on five fallacy datasets with different fallacies (and different topics of debate, from COVID-19 to the climate) before using in-context learning with prompts for detecting fallacies in the target dataset. Using this training scheme, they are able to detect *whataboutism* in one dataset with 0.44 accuracy. Their climate dataset contains no hypocrisy class, and sees an average performance of 0.21 in macro-F1 over nine other fallacies. They acknowledge that context is essential for understanding both the climate debate and *whataboutism*.

Thus, hypocrisy accusations have so far not received sufficient attention in either dataset creation or model development. Yet hypocrisy accusation detection is a complex task in its own right, with both semantic and logical context needed for success, and complexity added by several social language factors such as irony and sarcasm. Additionally, earlier results lack a careful evaluation of which different types of hypocrisy accusations can be detected. In our dataset and experiments, we intend to fill this gap by presenting a specialized climate hypocrisy accusation dataset, and an analysis of the performance of currently popular LLMs in detecting hypocrisy accusations.

## 3 Data

We present a dataset based on the English-language *Reddit European Sustainability Initiatives* corpus released by Reuver et al. (2024). This corpus consists of 2,073 sustainability discussions from between 2017 and 2022 on the Reddit.com subcommunities (Proferes et al., 2021) called *europe*, *europeanunion*, and *europes*, with 46,285 comments. Nearly half (922) of these discussions have at least one comment.

We focus on the comments in this dataset, as they constitute active discourse between users on the identified discussion topics, which are relevant for hypocrisy accusations. This means that our unit of analysis is a comment, which can contain a single or multiple sentences.

### 3.1 Data Sample and Annotation Process

Our sample selection involves two main strategies. We divided the data into two groups: 1) instances were hypocrisy was explicitly mentioned, by using the regex pattern `hypocr*`, and 2) the remaining data. Subsequently, we randomly selected 300 samples from each group, and consolidated them into a single dataset with 600 samples. The sampling strategy was done due to the relative rarity of the explicit hypocrisy mentions.

The six expert annotators were the authors of this study, all experts in political science, environmental communication science, or (computational) linguistics, which allowed for thorough, high-quality annotations. All participated in a test round to test the annotation scheme and make comments and adjustments. After flagged issues were solved, we then proceeded to annotate the final dataset.

Each expert annotated half of the final dataset, which yielded 3 annotations per sample. This sample size also aligns with existing literature, which suggests that a dataset of this magnitude is generally sufficient for few-shot learning tasks, offering a balanced measure of model performance with respect to human annotation capabilities.

#### 3.1.1 Annotation Scheme

We devised a nested annotation scheme to identify instances of hypocrisy allegations within statements (Q1), and when these are detected, the type of accusation (Q2). First, hypocrisy allegations are coded binarily: *Hypocrisy Accusation/ No accusation.* A statement is considered an allegation of hypocrisy when it does at least one of the following:

- Includes a direct hypocrisy accusation, such as calling someone a hypocrite or describing their actions as hypocritical (e.g., "COP26 is the biggest hypocrisy in the world, arriving in their private jets")
- Highlights a clear inconsistency or contradiction between someone's actions and their stated values, usually in a way which is negatively morally coded (e.g., "Leonardo DiCaprio simply doesn't get it, protecting marine animals and flying private jets at the same time")
- Employs a rhetorical device such as questioning or invoking hypothetical scenarios to indirectly accuse someone of hypocrisy (e.g., "Shouldn't you consider your own actions before instructing us on what needs to be done?")

The codebook further specifies that allegations can target individuals, institutions, or collectives. Second-hand accusations (e.g., "Lucy Dracus said that Obama is a hypocrite") do not constitute an accusation. Allegations can also be expressed through phrases or sayings synonymous with hypocrisy, such as "double standard" or "one rule for thee, another for me".

In cases in which a hypocrisy accusation was detected (Q1 answered positively), the annotator proceeded to identify the type of hypocrisy (Q2). The categorization into hypocrisy types draws from Gunster's typology (Gunster et al., 2018) of climate hypocrisy discourses, which lays out a distinction between types focused on individual (individual-lifestyle outrage and personal reflective discourse) versus institutional (institutional cynicism and calls to action) behavior. Operationalizing these distinctions, we lay out the following categorization:

A) **Personal moral hypocrisy (PMH)**: a gap between personal behavior and professed beliefs.

   *Example:* "You claim to care about climate change, yet you eat beef."

B) **Political hypocrisy (PH)**: a discrepancy between professed beliefs, values, or ideology and policy or political action.

   *Example:* "You talk about the importance of climate change but oppose nuclear power."

   *Note:* this category also includes inconsistencies between different policy positions.

C) **Neither**: We apply this when we cannot decide between A and B, when there are reasons to choose both, or when we think that neither A or B fit.

When determining the type of hypocrisy, the primary consideration is the content of the targeted action, statement or position. For instance, consumer choices typically indicate personal moral hypocrisy, while explicitly political action such as voting or protesting indicates political hypocrisy. If the content is unclear, the type of actor being accused can guide the decision: accusations against nations or

| Label | N |
|---|---|
| Personal Moral Hypocrisy | 35 |
| Political Hypocrisy | 35 |
| Neither | 2 |
| No accusation | 221 |

Table 1: Count summary label distributions of the labelled dataset

governments are usually political, whereas accusations against private citizens are typically personal. Accusations against specific politicians can be either, depending on the content of the allegation.

### 3.2 Climate Hypocrisy Accusations Corpus

Our *Climate Hypocrisy Accusations Corpus* (CHAC) corpus consists of 420 labeled comments. We calculate an inter-annotator agreement score of Fleiss' $\kappa$: 0.512, indicating a reasonable level of consensus among the annotators. We use majority voting to assign labels to each comment. There are 293 comments with a majority-class assigned label (the rest did not have a majority label). However, we keep the comments without majority consensus and release it with our dataset, as recent calls for perspectivism (Röttger et al., 2022; Romberg, 2022) have highlighted the importance of looking beyond majority consensus when it comes to complex social and argumentative concepts. The distribution of labels is summarized in Table 1. The source-code of the analysis[1] as well as our corpus[2] is available online, released for non-commercial use only under CC-BY-NC licence.

## 4 Experimental Approach

Our experiments are a first attempt at using the *Climate Hypocrisy Accusations Corpus* to measure the capabilities of different currently popular and high-performing LLMs in detecting hypocrisy accusations. We use few-shot prompting, also known as in-context learning. (Brown et al., 2020). Previous research has shown that for complex social constructs, few-shot out performs zero-shot (Alhindi et al., 2023).

### 4.1 Model Selection

Our experiments compare two families of high-performing and currently popular LLMs that have shown promise on complex social tasks. We use two GPT series models (Brown et al., 2020) and one LLama series model (Touvron et al., 2023).

We also purposefully chose one more closed and one more open family of models in terms of development and model access. LLama models (Meta AI) do not require payment, and its development team has openly released most of its code and training procedure, while GPT (OpenAI) does require payment and is less open in its architecture. However, almost no currently released LLM by a large technology company is fully open in its release of code, training data, and analysis (see Liesenfeld et al. (2023) for comparing aspects of 'opennness' when it comes to LLMs).[3]

### 4.2 Prompt and Shot Selection

We opt for a six-shot learning approach to provide the model with two robust examples per category. This provides sufficient context for each classification type without risk of overfitting. This also allows to have some control over the output format, avoiding complex parsing and streamlining the analysis of the results.

We use an iterative prompt design process using the GPT-4o as our base model. We base our prompt on classification formats present in our literature review on fallacy detection. The examples we choose to include in the prompt are not in the test set and are selected to maximize model learning capabilities. This includes hypocrisy examples with complex constructions, reported speech, and rhetorical questions. We also include reasoning in our prompt, as previous literature found reasoning increases model performance, even if it is not reliably correct (Ye and Durrett, 2022).[4]

## 5 Results

We report our results on the dataset of 293 majority-annotated instances from our *Climate Hypocrisy Accusation Corpus*. To ensure consistency and accuracy in our analysis, we use a systematic parsing process for the strings generated by each model. We standardize the formatting of the outputs to eliminate any discrepancies in punctuation, capitalization, and spacing, using regex patterns to detect and correct common formatting issues, as well as custom scripts designed to handle unique idiosyncrasies of each model's outputs.

[1] `https://github.com/pgarco/few-hypo`

[2] In `https://huggingface.co/datasets/Myrthe/RedditEuropeanSustainabilityInitiatives`

[3] Full model description in Appendix A and A.3.

[4] Full prompt is in Appendix A.2

| | Acc | Prec | Recall | F1 |
|---|---|---|---|---|
| LLama-3 | 0.75 | 0.72 | 0.71 | 0.67 |
| GPT-3.5 | 0.83 | 0.55 | 0.49 | 0.51 |
| GPT-4o | 0.75 | 0.74 | 0.72 | 0.68 |

Table 2: Classification results on the 293 examples labelled for hypocrisy. Results of LLama-3, GPT-3.5, and GPT-4o in accuracy, precision, and recall.

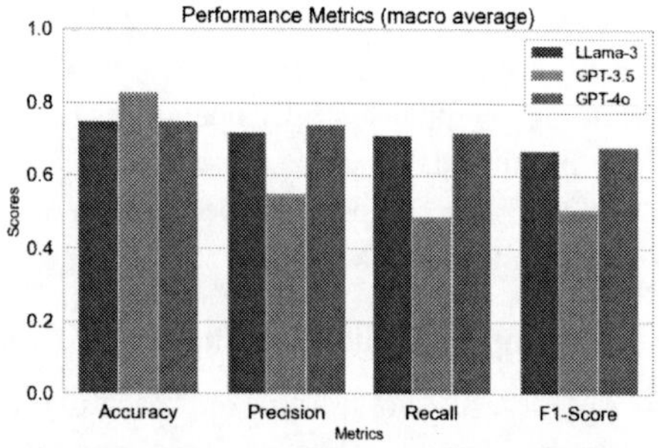


Figure 1: Bar graph comparing result metrics of LLM performance, from left to right we see LLama-3 (blue), GPT-3.5 (orange), and GPT-4o (green), grouped by accuracy (first group), precision (second group), recall (third group), and F1-score (last group).

### 5.1 Overall Results

The classification results can be seen in Table 2 and Figure 1. LLama-3 and GPT-4o both perform relatively well, significantly outperforming GPT-3.5 overall. In terms of accuracy, all models make predictions that are correct at least 75% of the time, with GPT-3.5 actually leading the way (83%). However, this high accuracy in GPT-3.5 appears to be an artefact of the imbalance between categories. As Table 6 and Figure 2 show, the "No accusation" label is far more prevalent than the other categories, and GPT-3.5 does a better job at predicting it, while GPT-4o and LLama-3 under-predict this class but are better in detecting the two hypocrisy classes.

### 5.2 Sub-class Prediction

The important difference between the models lies in the prediction of the two hypocrisy classes, reflected in both precision and recall. While GPT-3.5 managed both tasks roughly half of the time, LLama-3 and GPT-4o both succeeded at both tasks above 70% of the time.

Results of the sub-class predictions are visible in Table 3 for GPT-4o , Table 4 for GPT-3.5, and Table 5 for Llama-3. All models perform worse when identifying both Personal Moral Hypocrisy (PMH) (F1 scores between 0.67 and 0.63) and Political Hypocrisy (PH) (F1 scores between 0.46 and 0.54) than in identifying "no accusation" (0.91). All over-predict the different subtype labels, and are worst at identifying accusations not falling under either subtype, though these accusations are very rare. Overall, LLama-3 and GPT-4o respectively have nearly-identical macro-averaged F1 scores of 0.67 and 0.68 over all classes.

We view these scores as a good benchmark for complex hypocrisy accusation detection. The LLama-3 and GPT-4o models show potential for identification of hypocrisy accusations and classification of specific hypocrisy types.

| | precision | recall | f1-score | support |
|---|---|---|---|---|
| No accusation | 0.98 | 0.73 | 0.84 | 221 |
| Personal Moral Hypocrisy | 0.60 | 0.74 | 0.67 | 35 |
| Political Hypocrisy | 0.38 | 0.91 | 0.54 | 35 |
| Neither | 1.00 | 0.50 | 0.67 | 2 |
| accuracy | | | 0.75 | 293 |
| macro avg | 0.74 | 0.72 | 0.68 | 293 |
| weighted avg | 0.87 | 0.75 | 0.78 | 293 |

Table 3: Multiclass classification results for GPT-4o on the 293 examples with a majority label for hypocrisy acccusations

| | precision | recall | f1-score | support |
|---|---|---|---|---|
| No accusation | 0.87 | 0.95 | 0.91 | 221 |
| Personal Moral Hypocrisy | 0.71 | 0.63 | 0.67 | 35 |
| Political Hypocrisy | 0.62 | 0.37 | 0.46 | 35 |
| Neither | 0.00 | 0.00 | 0.00 | 2 |
| accuracy | | | 0.83 | 293 |
| macro avg | 0.55 | 0.49 | 0.51 | 293 |
| weighted avg | 0.82 | 0.83 | 0.82 | 293 |

Table 4: Multiclass classification results for GPT-3.5-turbo-1025 on the 293 examples with a majority label for hypocrisy acccusations.

| | precision | recall | f1-score | support |
|---|---|---|---|---|
| No accusation | 0.97 | 0.74 | 0.84 | 221 |
| Personal Moral Hypocrisy | 0.50 | 0.86 | 0.63 | 35 |
| Political Hypocrisy | 0.41 | 0.74 | 0.53 | 35 |
| Neither | 1.00 | 0.50 | 0.67 | 2 |
| accuracy | | | 0.75 | 293 |
| macro avg | 0.72 | 0.71 | 0.67 | 293 |
| weighted avg | 0.85 | 0.75 | 0.77 | 293 |

Table 5: Multiclass classification results for Llama-3-70b-chat-hf on the 293 examples with a majority label for hypocrisy acccusations.

| Label | GPT-3.5 | GPT-4o | LLama-3 | CHAC |
|---|---|---|---|---|
| Personal Moral Hypocrisy | 31 | 43 | 60 | 35 |
| Political Hypocrisy | 21 | 84 | 64 | 35 |
| Neither | 2 | 1 | 1 | 2 |
| No accusation | 239 | 165 | 168 | 221 |

Table 6: Distribution of Class Prediction on the 293 examples with a majority label for hypocrisy acccusations.

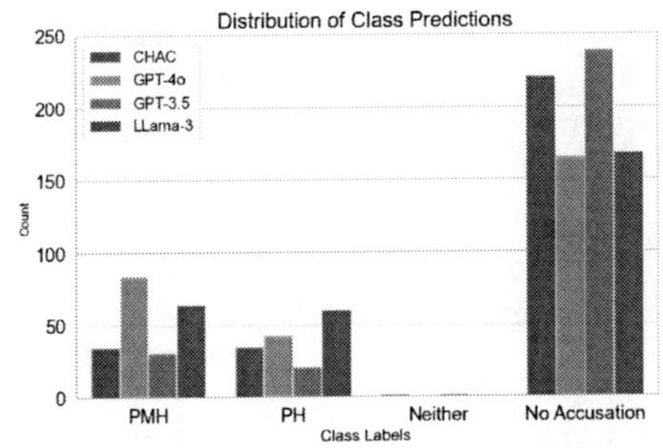


Figure 2: Bar graph comparing prediction and real labels distribution: from left to right we see CHAC dataset (blue), GPT-4o (orange), GPT-3.5 (green) and Llama-3 (red) grouped by class label: PMH (first group), PH (second group), Neither (third group), and No accusation (last group).

### 5.3 Error Analysis

We perform an error analysis to see whether there are error patterns relating to model type in hypocrisy accusation detection. Overall, we do not find a connection between error type and model family. Each model makes distinct errors.[5]

Broadly, we see three types of error in our results. Firstly, the LLMs predict False Positives, which we refer to as **hypocrisy accusation hallucinations**, often accompanied by a false reasoning in the explanation of the labelling decision generated by the model. A second common error is misclassification of subtype: a correct identification of an accusation, but an incorrect classification of the accusation type. Less common are False Negatives, where a hypocrisy accusation is not found where there is one. Below we discuss each type of error in the different models.

**False Positives: Accusation Hallucination** While all models sometimes identify hypocrisy accusations where there are none, we find different patterns between the models. GPT-4o and LLama-3 overpredict accusations where there are none, predicting 59 and 58 false positives, respectively. GPT-3.5, meanwhile, hallucinated accusations far less, with only 12 cases of false positives.

Further investigating false positives, we find the cases of hypocrisy accusation hallucination that include the regex pattern `hypocr*` to determine if the presence of the *mention* of hypocrisy could explain the models' over-prediction. Not every mention of the word hypocrisy actually contains a hypocrisy accusation, but it may be a common confusion for models. We find that 37 out of 59 (62%) of GPT-4o's false positives contain the pattern `hypocr*`. For the Llama-3 model, 31 cases (52%), and for the GPT-3.5 errors only 9 cases out of 28 (32%) match the regex pattern. Thus, we observe that GPT-3.5 is better at distinguishing a hypocrisy *accusation* from the *mention* of hypocrisy than other models. See the example below.[6]

> *"What will happen is when it is declared a national emergency, the right will call the left hypocrites for only caring because it was Trump. When in reality, the right's emergency is a baseless claim and climate change is* fucking *real."*
>
> Human label: **Not an accusation**
>
> Llama-3 predicted label: **Political Hypocrisy**
>
> Error: This is a case of the model classifying a second-hand accusation (and a hypothetical one at that) as a hypocrisy allegation. We would not wish to classify this as an allegation: the comment is reporting on this purported accusation in order to refute it.

> *"By that logic basically everyone who wants to stop climate change is a hypocrite."*
>
> Human label: **Not an accusation**
>
> GPT-4o predicted label: **Personal Moral Hypocrisy**
>
> Error: We understand this comment to mention a hypocrisy accusation critically, presumably responding to a hypocrisy allegation by pointing out how its reasoning leads to a conclusion that is *prima facie* absurd. The GPT-4o model seemed to simply take the comment at face value, reasoning that "The commenter is suggesting that anyone who advocates for stopping climate change is a hypocrite". This points to the complexity of understanding nuanced concepts such as irony or sarcasm.

[5]Confusion Matrices for all models are in Appendix B.

[6]Appendix C has examples of the different types of errors.

**False Negatives** GPT-3.5 misclassifies 28 comments as false negatives – not correctly identifying an accusation. False negatives, then, are the main source of errors for GPT-3.5.

We again look into whether there are any confusions between the *mention* of the word 'hypocrisy' and an *accusation* of hypocrisy. We find that GPT-4o did not label any comment that contains the regex pattern `hypocr*` as *not* being accusations when these were positive cases, while for Llama-3 we find 3 cases of such false negatives.

GPT-3.5 labeled 16 false negative comments containing the pattern. This indicates that GPT-3.5 is not relying on the presence of `hypocr*` related words to label comments, compared to the two other larger models, which is a surprising finding. However, as we see, this did not lead to a better overall performance for GPT-3.5 in detection hypocrisy accusations.

**Subtype Misclassification** Aside from confusing non-accusations with accusations, the models also show confusion in the subtypes of hypocrisy. We find that these errors are not consistent across models. In the case of *Personal* hypocrisy being labeled as *Political*, the biggest confusion comes from GPT-4o (22%). While Llama-3 has the opposite error: *Political* is labeled as *Personal* (17%). Again, our findings indicate that the smaller model, GPT-3.5, does not confuse types of hypocrisy as much, with only 4 instances of *Political* predicted as *Personal*, and one single case of the opposite. While GPT-3.5 under-predicted the hypocrisy accusations (having more false negatives), it was better at distinguishing between the hypocrisy classes once they were labeled as accusations.

> *"It's James Shaw, the biggest hypocrite out there when it comes to travel. Don't expect a realistic response."*
>
> Human label: **Personal Moral Hypocrisy**
>
> GPT-4o predicted label: **Political Hypocrisy**
>
> Error: The model appears to conclude that James Shaw, the former New Zealand Minister for Climate Change, is a political figure. However, we have noted that accusations against specific politicians can be personal or political depending on their content, and would classify personal travel as a consumer choice and thus an example of personal hypocrisy. However, we recognize this is something of a gray area, and that the model and human coders disagree on it.

We want to find the source of confusion of classes, and investigate if the mention of political figures or events leads to mislabeling. A qualitative analysis reveals that all subtype misclassification cases for GPT-4o include references to political figures or events. In this case, correct annotation of subtype (political hypocrisy or not) requires the model to establish whether the comment has a political context. The errors in LLama-3 and GPT-3.5 of identifying *Political Hypocrisy* as *Personal Moral Hypocrisy* all have references to political figures or events. All four subtype errors by GPT-3.5 are a subset of the error cases made by LLama-3. However, we cannot conclude that references to political figures or events are the source of subclass error, but it is possible that the model is unable to correctly identify mentions as political.

In summary, our error analysis shows some interesting patterns. GPT-3.5, our least successful model overall, is conservative in labelling comments as hypocrisy accusations, but therefore also has less false positives than the other models. We furthermore find this model is less confused by the mention of the word 'hypocrisy'. The other two models, LLama-3 and GPT4o, are better at labelling comments, but also confuse the two subtypes of hypocrisy more. Overall, political hypocrisy seems hard to identify for all models, and the models struggle with identifying a political context from the mention of political actors.

## 6 Discussion

Our results provide more insight into the complexities of the hypocrisy accusation as a construct. Specifically, we find different model strengths (see Section 6.1) and specifics of different types of hypocrisy accusations (Section 6.2).

### 6.1 Model Difference

Our results indicate that the most recent models, including GPT-4o, are considerably better than the earlier GPT3.5. This indicates that the current development of instruction-tuned models is one where improvement also means being better at detecting and annotating a complex construct like hypocrisy accusations. Newer models seem to be better at identifying nuanced context. One possible reason for this may be more recently updated training data e.g. new politicians or political events, required to fully understand hypocrisy accusations. However, due to lack of model training transparency, this cannot be verified.

Additionally, the acceptable results of both LLama-3 and GPT-4o are worth considering in light of the former being more open source and freely available, and the latter a more closed model requiring payment. Given their similar performance, the more open model offers clear advantages to researchers in social science. More open models are better for science: these are more reproducible, understandable and allow researchers to not be dependent on paying a third party (Liesenfeld et al., 2023). While none of our tested models are completely open in all aspects (training data, code, and openly accessible), it is useful for social scientists to know that Llama is a LLM that is easily accessible, able to analyze a complex construct such as a climate hypocrisy accusation, and not requiring third-party payment.

### 6.2 Results in the Context of Other Research

The results also suggest that hypocrisy detection, as most logical fallacies, is a complex task. A pattern-matching approach would consider mentions of 'hypocrite' as positive cases, but – as our experiments illustrate – such accusations also occur indirectly, and their detection is complicated by reported speech, sarcasm, rhetorical questions, and other devices in online debates. We observe that using LLM in-context prompting, detection of hypocrisy accusations achieves decent results. However, compared to other classification tasks for social science constructs (Lim and Perrault, 2024), using LLMs to classify accusations of hypocrisy is below expected model capabilities.

Our results (Macro F1 = 0.68 for GPT-4o ) see a performance gap with the fallacy detection on other fallacies reported in earlier work, e.g. F1 = 0.76 for fallacy accusation detection in Sahai et al. (2021), and 0.81 in Habernal et al. (2018) for detecting *ad hominem* attacks. However, these earlier papers did not distinguish hypocrisy accusations from other fallacies, and this narrowing of the concept could lead to more difficulty for our models.

Other literature also reports a more mixed performance of LLMs (especially when compared to fine-tuned Transformer models) for fallacy detection. Ruiz-Dolz and Lawrence (2023) report a F1 score of 0.79 by a fine-tuned Roberta model for two fallacy argument datasets with classes such as *ad hominem attacks* and *appeal to majority*, and in contrast a 0.56 F1 score for GPT-4o on these datasets. This paper also reports a lower performance of GPT-4o on the *ad hominem* fallacy class. Potentially, this could be because of a connection to hypocrisy accusations, which (as we have established) are difficult, and are often forms of *ad hominem* arguments, criticizing the rival personally instead of their positions.

Our results indicate that hypocrisy accusation is an interesting concept that deserves its own task, as well as benchmark datasets outside of more common fallacy datasets. Moreover, these results prove the usefulness of breaking down complex constructs into sub-categories: we found that detecting the hypocrisy/no hypocrisy distinction is relatively easy (e.g., reaching F1 > 0.80 for all models), while the subclass Political Hypocrisy is much harder to detect, showing F1s <= 0.50s for all models. The subclass that may be especially relevant for political analysis, attacks on political actions or views, is not well-detected by LLMs.

## 7 Conclusions

Hypocrisy accusations are central to increasingly polarized, cross-ideological online interactions. Despite recent research on detecting argument fallacies, hypocrisy accusations remain under-researched and are often a small sub-class in argument fallacy datasets. We define hypocrisy accusation detection as an individual NLP task and create an annotation scheme where we identify subclasses of hypocrisy accusation: personal moral hypocrisy versus political hypocrisy. We present a dataset, the *Climate Hypocrisy Accusation Corpus* (CHAC), consisting of 420 reddit comments, annotated by six experts. Using our dataset, we compare three different instruction-tuned models (GPT-4o , GPT-3.5, and Llama-3) in a six-shot setting for detecting hypocrisy accusations. The different models have different strengths, but overall perform with a macro F1 class of around 0.80, and show that Llama, as a more open model than the GPT-family and one not requiring payment, can perform on par for hypocrisy accusation detection with the less open GPT model that requires payment. LLMs are capable of detecting accusations with a binary distinction, but we identify room for improvement when it comes to the different accusation types. Models are somewhat worse at detecting political hypocrisy than personal moral hypocrisy, which could have implications for social science research.

## Limitations

As with all research, this paper has some limitations. We identify four sources of limitations.

**Data Annotation** First, the data annotation process could have led to higher inter-annotator agreement score, which, research has shown, is detrimental to achieving high results in computational modelling. However, considering this is a complex theoretical construct, we are satisfied with this first limited result.

**Debate Context** Second, the validity of the results should be understood as pertaining especially to climate change discourse; As we have described in the paper, hypocrisy relies on the understanding of a contrast between two events, usually a professed belief and an action. These actions and beliefs often need to be understood in context in order to be understood as (allegedly) inconsistent. Hence, we expect identification of hypocrisy accusations to be somewhat dependent on an understanding of both the factual reality of a topic as well as the social context in which it is discussed. This paper analyzes the climate change debate, and the tool's relevance to other fields requires further study and, potentially, training.

**Geographical, Linguistic, and Cultural Context** Additionally, we acknowledge that our paper is focused on European debates around climate change, in a single high-resource language, English (Bender, 2019). The results we find depend on the data the models were trained on, and as such we expect that non-European debates and debates in low-resource languages will probably produce results that are not as high.

**Political Context** Lastly, LLMs are not without its issues for social science analysis: these models display political worldviews (Ceron et al., 2024). When analyzing different political contexts (e.g. one more conservative than European climate debates), the results could therefore differ. While adding these results is beyond the scope of the current paper, it is important to keep this in mind for future work.

## Ethics Statement

The data used in this project was scraped from Reddit in December 2022 with the PushShift API, before Reddit's PushShift API restrictions were enforced in April 2023, ensuring compliance with the platform's terms of service at the time. We remove any personal identifying information such as usernames from the data. We also ensure the data is released for non-commercial use only. This is also in-line with Reddit users' concern of their data being used for training commercial LLMs or other technology.

Furthermore, some comments reflect personal opinions that are not in-line with the established scientific consensus on climate change. While these opinions are valuable for understanding public sentiment and discourse, we do not endorse any misinformation or scientifically inaccurate statements present in the dataset. Our goal is to analyze these discussions to better understand the dynamics of public discourse on climate change, promoting more effective strategies to engage with the public, address misconceptions, and promote scientifically accurate information.

## Acknowledgements

The dataset used in this research was funded by a research voucher grant for the project *Reasons for online (dis)trust in sustainable initiatives* awarded to Myrthe Reuver and Ana Isabel Lopes by the Network Institute at the Vrije Universiteit Amsterdam. Myrthe Reuver was also funded by the Netherlands Organisation for Scientific Research (NWO) through the *Rethinking News Algorithms* project (grant nr: 406.D1.19.073). Paulina Garcia Corral was funded by the DFG (EXC number 2055 – Project number 390715649, SCRIPTS).

A preliminary version of this paper was presented at the hackathon at the International Communication Association (ICA) 2023 conference in Toronto, where this project was initiatied and where all authors participated, and another preliminary version was presented at CompText 2024 in Amsterdam. We would like to thank the ICA hackathon organizers and participants as well as all reviewers, whose comments improved this paper.

We used Github Copilot and ChatGPT to assist in writing our experimental code, and editing code snippets for data processing and data analysis. We used ChatGPT to assist in writing sections of this manuscript. This assistance, in accordance with the ACL Ethics Policy, was solely in dealing with the language of the paper rather than in producing new content or new ideas. All final writing is ultimately done by the authors, who are responsible for it.

## References


2024. Oxford english dictionary. Accessed June 19, 2024.

Tariq Alhindi, Tuhin Chakrabarty, Elena Musi, and Smaranda Muresan. 2022. Multitask instruction-based prompting for fallacy recognition. In *Proceedings of the 2022 Conference on Empirical Methods in Natural Language Processing*, pages 8172–8187, Abu Dhabi, United Arab Emirates. Association for Computational Linguistics.

Tariq Alhindi, Tuhin Chakrabarty, Elena Musi, and Smaranda Muresan. 2023. Multitask instruction-based prompting for fallacy recognition. *arXiv Preprint arXiv:2301.09992*.

Meysam Alizadeh, Maël Kubli, Zeynab Samei, Shirin Dehghani, Mohammadmasiha Zahedivafa, Juan Diego Bermeo, Maria Korobeynikova, and Fabrizio Gilardi. 2024. Open-source llms for text annotation: A practical guide for model setting and fine-tuning.

Hunt Allcott, Luca Braghieri, Sarah Eichmeyer, and Matthew Gentzkow. 2020. The welfare effects of social media. *American Economic Review*, 110(3):629–76.

Hannah Arendt. 2006. *On Revolution*. Penguin.

Aristotle. 1909. *The Rhetoric of Aristotle: A Translation*. Cambridge University Press, Cambridge [Cambridgeshire].

Emily Bender. 2019. The# benderrule: On naming the languages we study and why it matters. *The Gradient*, 14:34.

Yosef Bhatti, Kasper M. Hansen, and Asmus Leth Olsen. 2013. Political hypocrisy: The effect of political scandals on candidate evaluations. *Acta Politica*, 48(4):408–28.

Tom Brown, Benjamin Mann, Nick Ryder, Melanie Subbiah, Jared D Kaplan, Prafulla Dhariwal, Arvind Neelakantan, Pranav Shyam, Girish Sastry, Amanda Askell, et al. 2020. Language models are few-shot learners. *Advances in neural information processing systems*, 33:1877–1901.

Michael Brüggemann and Hendrik Meyer. 2023. When debates break apart: discursive polarization as a multi-dimensional divergence emerging in and through communication. *Communication Theory*, 33(2-3):132–142.

Tanise Ceron, Neele Falk, Ana Barić, Dmitry Nikolaev, and Sebastian Padó. 2024. Beyond prompt brittleness: Evaluating the reliability and consistency of political worldviews in llms. *arXiv preprint arXiv:2402.17649*.

Timothy P. Collins. 2018. *Hypocrisy in American Political Attitudes*. Springer International Publishing, Cham.

Max Falkenberg, Alessandro Galeazzi, Maddalena Torricelli, Niccolò Di Marco, Francesca Larosa, Madalina Sas, Amin Mekacher, Warren Pearce, Fabiana Zollo, and Walter Quattrociocchi. 2022. Growing polarization around climate change on social media. *Nature Climate Change*, 12(12):1114–21.

John Fields, Kevin Chovanec, and Praveen Madiraju. 2024. A survey of text classification with transformers: How wide? how large? how long? how accurate? how expensive? how safe? *IEEE Access*, 12:6518–6531.

Peter A. Furia. 2009. Democratic citizenship and the hypocrisy of leaders. *Polity*, 41(1):113–133.

Steven L. Grover and Marcus C. Hasel. 2015. How leaders recover (or not) from publicized sex scandals. *Journal of Business Ethics*, 129(1):177–94.

Shane Gunster, Darren Fleet, Matthew Paterson, and Paul Saurette. 2018. 'why don't you act like you believe it?': Competing visions of climate hypocrisy. *Frontiers in Communication*, 3:49.

Ivan Habernal, Henning Wachsmuth, Iryna Gurevych, and Benno Stein. 2018. Before name-calling: Dynamics and triggers of ad hominem fallacies in web argumentation. *arXiv Preprint arXiv:1802.06613*.

Blake Hallinan, Bumsoo Kim, Rebecca Scharlach, and Tommaso Trillò. 2021. Mapping the transnational imaginary of social media genres. *New Media & Society*.

Sean M. Laurent, Brian A. M. Clark, Stephannie Walker, and Kimberly D. Wiseman. 2014. Punishing hypocrisy: The roles of hypocrisy and moral emotions in deciding culpability and punishment of criminal and civil moral transgressors. *Cognition and Emotion*, 28(1):59–83.

Yanda Li, Dixuan Wang, Jiaqing Liang, Guochao Jiang, Qianyu He, Yanghua Xiao, and Deqing Yang. 2024. Reason from fallacy: Enhancing large language models' logical reasoning through logical fallacy understanding.

Andreas Liesenfeld, Alianda Lopez, and Mark Dingemanse. 2023. Opening up chatgpt: Tracking openness, transparency, and accountability in instruction-tuned text generators. In *Proceedings of the 5th international conference on conversational user interfaces*, pages 1–6.

Gionnieve Lim and Simon T. Perrault. 2024. Evaluation of an llm in identifying logical fallacies: A call for rigor when adopting llms in hci research.

Meta. 2024. Introducing meta llama 3: The most capable openly available llm to date.

Hendrik Meyer, Amelia Katelin Peach, Lars Guenther, Hadas Emma Kedar, and Michael Brüggemann. 2023. Between calls for action and narratives of denial: Climate change attention structures on twitter. *Media and Communication*, 11(1):278–292.

Jakub Piskorski, Nicolas Stefanovitch, Nikolaos Nikolaidis, Giovanni Da San Martino, and Preslav Nakov. 2023. Multilingual multifaceted understanding of online news in terms of genre, framing, and persuasion techniques. In *Proceedings of the 61st Annual Meeting of the Association for Computational Linguistics (Volume 1: Long Papers)*, pages 3001–3022, Toronto, Canada. Association for Computational Linguistics.

Flor Miriam Plaza-del Arco, Debora Nozza, Dirk Hovy, et al. 2023. Respectful or toxic? using zero-shot learning with language models to detect hate speech. In *The 7th Workshop on Online Abuse and Harms (WOAH)*. Association for Computational Linguistics.

Nicholas Proferes, Naiyan Jones, Sarah Gilbert, Casey Fiesler, and Michael Zimmer. 2021. Studying reddit: A systematic overview of disciplines, approaches, methods, and ethics. *Social Media+ Society*, 7(2):20563051211019004.

Myrthe Reuver, Alessandra Polimeno, Antske Fokkens, and Ana Isabel Lopes. 2024. Topic-specific social science theory in stance detection: a proposal and interdisciplinary pilot study on sustainability initiatives. In *4th Workshop on Computational Linguistics for the Political and Social Sciences (CPSS), co-located with KONVENS*.

Julia Romberg. 2022. Is your perspective also my perspective? enriching prediction with subjectivity. In *Proceedings of the 9th Workshop on Argument Mining*, pages 115–125.

Paul Röttger, Bertie Vidgen, Dirk Hovy, and Janet Pierrehumbert. 2022. Two contrasting data annotation paradigms for subjective nlp tasks. In *Proceedings of the 2022 Conference of the North American Chapter of the Association for Computational Linguistics: Human Language Technologies*, pages 175–190.

Ramon Ruiz-Dolz and John Lawrence. 2023. Detecting argumentative fallacies in the wild: Problems and limitations of large language models. In *Proceedings of the 10th Workshop on Argument Mining*. Association for Computational Linguistics.

Saumya Yashmohini Sahai, Oana Balalau, and Roxana Horincar. 2021. Breaking down the invisible wall of informal fallacies in online discussions. In *ACL-IJCNLP 2021-Joint Conference of the 59th Annual Meeting of the Association for Computational Linguistics and the 11th International Joint Conference on Natural Language Processing*.

Indira Sen, Dennis Assenmacher, Mattia Samory, Isabelle Augenstein, Wil Aalst, and Claudia Wagner. 2023. People make better edits: Measuring the efficacy of llm-generated counterfactually augmented data for harmful language detection. In *Proceedings of the 2023 Conference on Empirical Methods in Natural Language Processing*, pages 10480–10504.

Judith N. Shklar. 1984. *Ordinary Vices*. Belknap Press of Harvard University Press.

Dennis F. Thompson, editor. 2004. *Restoring Responsibility: Ethics in Government, Business, and Healthcare*. Cambridge University Press, Cambridge.

Petter Törnberg. 2023. Chatgpt-4 outperforms experts and crowd workers in annotating political twitter messages with zero-shot learning. *ArXiv*, abs/2304.06588.

Hugo Touvron, Thibaut Lavril, Gautier Izacard, Xavier Martinet, Marie-Anne Lachaux, Timothée Lacroix, Baptiste Rozière, Naman Goyal, Eric Hambro, Faisal Azhar, et al. 2023. Llama: Open and efficient foundation language models. *arXiv preprint arXiv:2302.13971*.

Aman Tyagi, Joshua Uyheng, and Kathleen M. Carley. 2020. Affective polarization in online climate change discourse on twitter. In *2020 IEEE/ACM International Conference on Advances in Social Networks Analysis and Mining (ASONAM)*, pages 443–447.

Lino Valdovinos. 2023. Real-time fallacy detection. `https://github.com/latent-variable/Real_time_fallacy_detection`.

Xi Ye and Greg Durrett. 2022. The unreliability of explanations in few-shot prompting for textual reasoning. *Advances in neural information processing systems*, 35:30378–30392.

## Appendix

## A Implementation Details

### A.1 Model Details

- GPT-3.5-turbo-0125: This is an OpenAI GPT series (Brown et al., 2020) model, optimized for efficient and cost-effective performance in conversational AI tasks, providing advanced language understanding and generation capabilities. This is a closed-source model.
- GPT-4-turbo: An enhanced version of OpenAI's GPT-4, this model offers improved speed and performance for complex language processing tasks, making it ideal for both conversational agents and other sophisticated AI applications. This is a closed-source model.
- Llama-3-70b-instruct[7]: Developed by Meta AI (Meta, 2024), this is a language model with 70 billion parameters, designed for high-quality conversational AI, capable of understanding and generating human-like text in diverse contexts. This is a non-proprietary model, i.e., it does not require payment.

### A.2 Prompt

**System:**
You are an advanced classification AI. Your task is to labels Reddit comments following the instructions below:
*Instructions*
Accusations of hypocrisy are when someone accuses someone or something of being a hypocrite because of a moral contradiction between what they profess and their actions or words. Accusations of hypocrisy are sometimes direct such as "You are a hypocrite" and sometimes are understood via context, by highlighting a connoted inconsistency between what people profess or claim their believe and what people actually do. An example would be criticizing a celebrity for using a private jet while publicly claiming the need for climate action.
There are different types of hypocrisy accusations, such as accusing someone of personal moral hypocrisy or accusing someone of political hypocrisy. The primary consideration to decide the accusation type is the content of the targeted action, statement or position. For instance, consumer choices typically indicate personal moral hypocrisy, while explicit political action such as voting or protesting indicates political hypocrisy. If the content is unclear, the type of actor being accused can guide the decision: accusations against nations or governments are usually political, whereas accusations against private citizens are typically personal.
*Classification steps*
1. You will analyze a Reddit Comment and evaluate if there is an accusation of hypocrisy.
2. You will make sure to consider contextual factors, implications, and rhetorical devices to make sure things such as irony or double meaning are taken into account.
3. You will assign a label to the comment: "Not an accusation" or "Hypocrisy accusation".
4. If the label is "Hypocrisy accusation", then you will analyze what type of accusation it is:
1) "Personal moral hypocrisy": a gap between personal behavior and professed beliefs
2) "Political hypocrisy": a gap between professed beliefs, values, or ideology and policy or political action.
3) "Neither"
5. Then you will assign a second label to the hypocrisy accusations: "Personal moral hypocrisy", "Political hypocrisy" or "Neither".
Choose the most appropriate label, and remember to consider all the rhetorical devices.
**User:**
Label the next comment:
Not being vegan seems kinda hypocritical to me, if you're serious about climate change and have looked into it then you'd know that it's honestly the easiest way we can make a big impact as consumers. Vegan activists aren't hurting anyone or being violent. Meanwhile, farming is directly causing pain, suffering, and death to animals for profit. That's the real difference.
**Assistant:**
Label: Hypocrisy accusation - Personal moral hypocrisy
Reasoning: The commenter is directly stating that it is hypocritical to care about climate change and not be vegan. This identifies a perceived gap between the professed belief in fighting climate change and the personal behavior of not adopting a vegan lifestyle. The hypocrisy accusation here is based on an individual's personal moral stance

[7] https://huggingface.co/meta-llama/Meta-Llama-3-70B-Instruct

(caring about climate change) not aligning with their personal behavior (not being vegan).
**User:**
Label the next comment:
For real?? Are you saying their hypocrites because they protest carbon mining? I've seen the mines firsthand they're wrecking nature, displacing people, and demolishing villages just for that dirty, low-energy rock. Get it right, it's the most disgusting and destructive form of electricity generation ever.
**Assistant:**
Label: Not an accusation
Reasoning: The invocation of hypocrisy in the second sentence ("Hypocrites" because…?") is not itself an accusation, but a rhetorical questioning of such an allegation, one which the commenter subsequently answers negatively ("Smh", meaning "shaking my head", i.e. expressing incredulity at the accusation). The commenter goes on to express frustration and criticism towards the use of lignite for electricity generation, highlighting its environmental impact and the availability of other energy sources. Bottom line: the commenter is defending someone from a hypocrisy accusation.
**User:**
Label the next comment:
Climate activists think they're on a moral high horse, but they're just making life tougher for everyone else. We've got jobs to get to, and they claim they're saving the future but end up screwing up our daily commutes. No one feels sorry for them—that's not how you protest effectively.
**Assistant:**
Label: Hypocrisy accusation - Political hypocrisy
Reasoning: The commenter is accusing climate activists of claiming to care about the future of humanity while making daily life harder for others, specifically through disrupting commutes. This highlights a perceived inconsistency between their professed goal (caring for humanity's future) and their actions (disrupting daily life). The hypocrisy accusation is focused on the contradiction between the activists' political goal (caring about the future of humanity) not aligning with the direct results results their behavior (disrupting commutes and making life harder for others).
**User:**
Label the next comment:
Ugh, this "Green" parties are pathetic. They choose Brown coal over nuclear energy, but won't shut up about air pollution. Get a grip.
**Assistant:**
Label: Hypocrisy accusation - Political hypocrisy
Reasoning: The commenter is highlighting a (purported) inconsistency between what the Greens profess to care about (c̈rying around about air pollution)̈ and what they actually have done (p̈referred Brown coal over nuclear energy)̈. In addition, this alleged contrast carries a clear negative connotation (c̈rying around)̈. The inconsistency being alleged is between professed values (caring about air pollution) and political action (supporting coal over nuclear energy).
**User:**
Label the next comment:
I read only that he was accused of being not only a war criminal, but also a hypocrite.
**Assistant:**
Label: Not an accusation
Reasoning: While the comment does report on an explicit hypocrisy accusation, this is an instance of reported speech. We count only hypocrisy allegations made or endorsed by the commenter, not descriptions of accusations made by someone else.
**User:**
Label the next comment:
I agree that, if it's there, people need to use trains instead of flying.
However, what does it matter if it's hypocritical? Just because *they* are hypocrites and chose to fly, doesn't mean what they say is untrue. The world is complicated, grow up.
**Assistant:**
Label: Hypocrisy accusation - Personal moral hypocrisy
This comment it likely responding to a hypocrisy accusation. Even though the commenter seeks to defend the people in question from the criticism inherent in such an accusation, they do so by conceding that the hypocrisy allegation is likely true (j̈ust because they are hypocrites)̈ - even if they contend this is not in fact so bad. While hypocrisy allegations in general carry a negative connotation, this is an unusual case in which such an allegation is explicitly made (or conceded) while attempting to divorce it from the (usual expected) negative charge. The inconsistency being alleged in this allegation stems from personal lifestyle choices - choice of commute, i.e. not taking a train.
**User:**
Label the next comment: `REDDIT COMMENT`

### A.3 Training strategy, model parameters, and other resources

For data processing we used Pandas. To test our prompt and run inference we used the OpenAI API for the GPT models, OpenAI provides their own processing equipment and is not specified. For the Meta AI model, we used TogetherAI API for inference. We used 1 Nvidia A100 GPU for our experiment. We used all default model parameters and set the generation parameters to restrict creativity (temperature = 0, max_tokens=200, top_p=1, frequency_penalty=0, presence_penalty=0). To ensure reproducibility, each model's output was subjected to identical preprocessing and post-processing steps. To analyze classification results, we used the "classification_report" function from Scikit-learn.

## B Error Analysis Figures

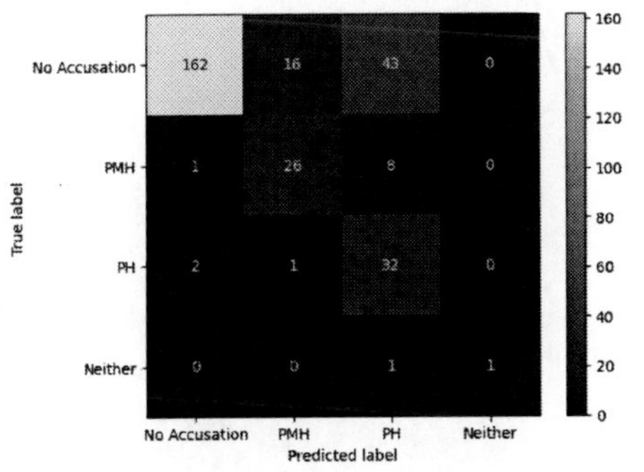


Figure 3: Confusion Matrix for predictions of GPT-4o .

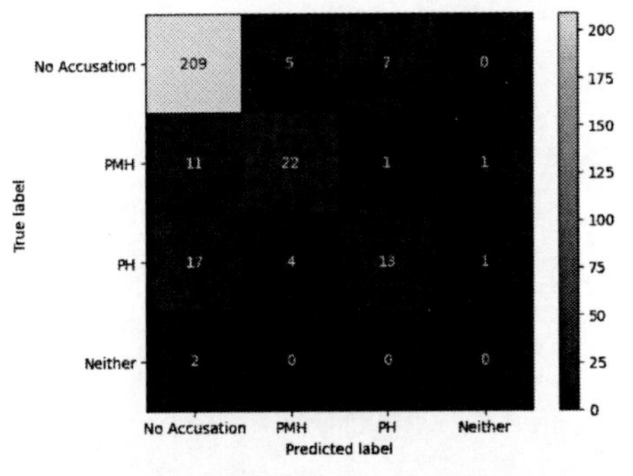


Figure 4: Confusion Matrix for predictions of GPT-3.5.

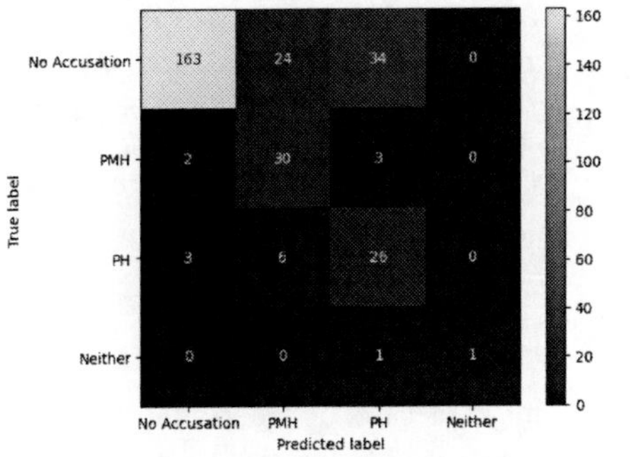


Figure 5: Confusion Matrix for predictions of Llama-3 70B.

## C Examples Error Analysis

### Examples of Misclassifications

1. *"It's James Shaw, the biggest hypocrite out there when it comes to travel. Don't expect a realistic response."*

   Human label: **Personal Moral Hypocrisy**

   GPT-4o predicted label: **Political Hypocrisy**

   The model appears to based its reasoning on the fact that James Shaw, the former New Zealand Minister for Climate Change, is a political figure. However, we have noted that accusations against specific politicians can be personal or political depending on their content, and would classify personal travel as a consumer choice and thus an example of personal hypocrisy. However, we recognize this is something of a gray area and the model and human coders disagree on it.

2. *"Conservatives are bollocks but let me tell you how good their policies actually are! Hypocrite much?"*

   Human label: **Political Hypocrisy**

   Llama-3 predicted label: **Personal Moral Hypocrisy**

   The comment points to a clear inconsistency between one's political belief (conservatives are bad) and action (praising their policies). However, the GPT-4o model appears to interpret on the fact that the accusation appears directly at another speaker as evidence it is a case personal moral hypocrisy.

### Examples of False Positives

1. *"What will happen is when it is declared a national emergency, the right will call the left hypocrites for only caring because it was Trump. When in reality, the right's emergency is a baseless claim and climate change is* fucking *real."*

   Human label: **Not an accusation**

   Llama-3 predicted label: **Political Hypocrisy**

   This is a case of the model classifying a second-hand accusation (and a hypothetical one at that) as a hypocrisy allegation. We would not wish to classify this as an allegation, especially as the comment is reporting on this purported accusation in order to refute it.

2. *"By that logic basically everyone who wants to stop climate change is a hypocrite."*

   Human label: **Not an accusation**

   GPT-4o predicted label: **Personal Moral Hypocrisy**

   While this comment makes an explicit suggestion of hypocrisy, we understand it to be doing so critically, presumably responding to a hypocrisy allegation by pointing out how its reasoning leads to a conclusion that is prima facie absurd. Two of the models concurred, but the GPT-4o model seemed to simply take the comment at face value, reasoning that "The commenter is suggesting that anyone who advocates for stopping climate change is a hypocrite". This points to the complexity of understanding nuanced concepts such as irony or sarcasm.

# Language Complexity in Populist Rhetoric

**Sergio E. Zanotto**[1], **Diego Frassinelli**[1,2], **Miriam Butt**[1]
[1]Department of Linguistics & Cluster of Excellence "The Politics of Inequality", University of Konstanz
[2]Center for Information and Language Processing, LMU Munich
{sergio.zanotto, diego.frassinelli, miriam.butt}@uni-konstanz.de

## Abstract

Research suggests that politicians labeled as populists tend to use simpler language than their mainstream opponents. Yet, the metrics traditionally employed to assess the complexity of their language do not show consistent and generalizable results across different datasets and languages. This inconsistencies raise questions about the claimed simplicity of populist discourse, suggesting that the issue may be more nuanced than it initially seemed. To address this topic, we analyze the linguistic profile of IMPAQTS, a dataset of transcribed Italian political speeches, to identify linguistic features differentiating populist and non-populist parties. Our methodology ensures comparability of political texts and combines various statistical analyses to reliably identify key linguistic characteristics to test our case study. Results show that the "simplistic" language features previously described in the literature are *not* robust predictors of populism. This suggests that the characteristics defining populist statements are highly dependent on the specific dataset and the language being analysed, thus limiting the conclusions drawn in previous research. In our study, various linguistic features statistically differentiate between populist and mainstream parties, indicating that populists tend to employ specific well-known rhetorical strategies more frequently; however, none of them strongly indicate that populist parties use simpler language.

## 1 Introduction

The concept of populism has gained a huge focus in social sciences, with different scholars attempting to systematically analyse the phenomenon to understand its core components (e.g., Huguet Cabot et al., 2021; Pérez-Curiel et al., 2021; Klamm et al., 2023). For instance, inspired by the *social identity theory* of Tajfel and Turner (2004), different studies have employed Natural Language Processing (NLP) techniques to studying social group appeals[1] in political texts (Huber, 2022; Licht and Sczepanski, 2023; Zanotto et al., 2024). Several studies have explored the rhetorical power of identity appeals to citizens and their effects on voting behavior (e.g., Strom, 1990; Wodak, 2012; Thau, 2019). This rhetorical power is evident especially when focusing on populist communication, where the tendency to appeal to "the people" is considered a universal component of all different realizations of populism (Canovan, 2004; Laclau, 2006). Populist parties divide society in two groups: "pure people" and "corrupt elite" and advocate for politics to represent the general will of the people (Mudde, 2004; Jagers and Walgrave, 2007). Therefore, language complexity becomes both an important characteristic of populist communication, as well as a tool for appealing to a broader public of ordinary people (Decadri and Boussalis, 2020; McDonnell and Ondelli, 2022). This assumption lies on the idea that "the people" are less-educated and therefore speak simpler. Simple language helps citizens to better understand political positions (Senninger, 2023), and scholars claim populists use it to convey their simplistic message and strengthen their positions as part of "the people" (Canovan, 1999; Zaslove, 2008; McDonnell and Ondelli, 2022). Thus, to describe populist language, different researchers have analysed political texts throughout syntactic and lexical features like readability scores, type-token ratio analysis, and dictionary approaches (Rooduijn and Pauwels, 2011; Bischof and Senninger, 2018), showing that populist parties generally employ simpler language than their mainstream opponents. However, different studies have highlighted very diverse patterns in the language of populism, questioning the validity of using lan-

[1]Social group appeals refer to strategies of communication that target specific groups based on shared characteristics, such as ethnicity, religion, socioeconomic status, or political affiliation (Huber, 2022).



*Proceedings of the 58th Annual Meeting of the Association for Computational Linguistics*, pages 61–80
July 5–10, 2020. ©2020 Association for Computational Linguistics

guage complexity as a distinguishing feature for populism. (Trotta et al., 2019; McDonnell and Ondelli, 2022).

In this paper, we investigate what are the distinctive features that set populist from non-populist parties apart. Compared to existing studies, our analysis focuses on speeches within the Italian political arena, extracted from the IMPAQTS corpus (Cominetti et al., 2022). We categorized the discourses in IMPAQTS as either populist or non-populist given the political affiliations of the speakers, as outlined in previous research such as Di Cocco and Monechi (2022). The categorization of populist and non-populist parties rely on the classification from "The PopuList 3.0" (Rooduijn et al., 2023).

Our main contributions are: (i) we challenge the prevailing notion that populism is characterized by simpler language; and (ii) we identify specific linguistic features that indicate a tendency in using well-known rhetorical strategies; (iii) we propose a systematic approach to empirically select linguistic features that differentiate populist and non-populist discourses in our dataset.

## 2 Related Work

Scholars investigate how populist politicians influence the public opinion via their discourses (Canovan, 2004; Laclau, 2006). Among the different definitions of *populism*, the division of society in two groups, namely the "pure people" and the "corrupt elite", is considered a universal feature of all populist parties (Mudde, 2004; Jagers and Walgrave, 2007). This is the definition we adopt in our research. Several studies measure populism in text by looking at *how* and *to whom* populists refer in their discourses (Jagers and Walgrave, 2007; Huguet Cabot et al., 2021; Klamm et al., 2023). In this way, they show how the indexing of people and the anti-establishment rhetoric are typical characteristics of populist communication. For instance, Rooduijn and Pauwels (2011) and Decadri and Boussalis (2020) conduct a semi-automatic content analysis using dictionaries of words related to populist rhetoric, such as *citizen, people, caste, elite*.

### 2.1 Language complexity

Even though the use of simple and accessible language is considered a tool for appealing to a broader audience of "ordinary people" (Decadri and Boussalis, 2020; McDonnell and Ondelli, 2022), to date, there is no agreement on which computational measures best describe how complex a language is (Ehret et al., 2021). The literature indicates that evaluating language complexity requires to analyze both syntactic and lexical information (Ehret et al., 2023). Consequently, focusing solely on textual complexity, often measured through readability scores, captures only one facet of it. Of the various definitions of language complexity available in the literature (Pallotti, 2015), we adopt the one from second language acquisition (SLA), especially the definition of *structural complexity* as “a formal property of texts and linguistic systems having to do with the number of their elements and their relational patterns” (Pallotti, 2015). Therefore, in order to estimate the complexity of a text, it is necessary to analyze it through its linguistic dimensions.

### 2.2 Complexity of political texts

Many studies rely on readability scores to assess the complexity of political texts (e.g., Spirling (2016); Bischof and Senninger (2018); Schoonvelde et al. (2019); Decadri and Boussalis (2020); Senninger (2023)). Readability scores are language specific and assess textual complexity by analyzing elements such as the number of words, sentences, and characters. For example, the Flesch-Kincaid readability tests (Kincaid et al., 1975) are tailored for English, using sentence length and syllable count. The Gulpease Index (Lucisano and Piemontese, 1988), used for Italian texts, considers the number of characters per word and words per sentence.

Given the criticisms regarding the validity of readability scores for measuring text complexity (see Chall (1996) for an extensive overview of these criticisms), alternative measures have been employed to quantify the textual complexity and the syntactic complexity of political discourses. These measures include the number of tokens in a document, as well as the length of its words, its sentences and its syntactic complexity (Tolochko and Boomgaarden, 2019; McDonnell and Ondelli, 2022). Syntactic complexity is typically analysed through syntactic depth or syntactic dependency (Tolochko and Boomgaarden, 2019). Syntactic depth considers the number of nested clauses or phrases within each sentence, while syntactic dependency measures the distance between a syntactic head and its farthest dependent for each sentence. They are used as a better fitting measures of language complexity for spoken language.

Another level of analysis pertains to lexical complexity, and it involves the use of type-token ratio, lexical density and the use of frequent words (e.g., Schoonvelde et al. (2019); Trotta et al. (2019); Takikawa and Sakamoto (2020); McDonnell and Ondelli (2022)). However, according to the literature, these features are not always significant across different studies in distinguishing populist and non-populist discourses (Trotta et al., 2019; McDonnell and Ondelli, 2022).

## 3 Data

In this section, we describe the dataset used for our analysis and we illustrate the criteria of classification of populist and non-populist parties.

**Dataset**
We use the IMPAQTS corpus (Cominetti et al., 2022) to identify linguistic features that distinguish between populist and non-populist parties. IMPAQTS is a corpus containing circa 1,500 transcripts of Italian political speeches from 1948 to 2023. We select this corpus as it is the biggest corpus available of multi-genre speeches of Italian politicians. The nature of these discourses is monological. There are six different genres of speech, namely rallies, parliamentary speeches, party meetings, face-to-face declarations, transmitted declarations, and new media declarations. We restrict our analysis to discourses from 1994 onwards, aligning with the emergence of the first populist parties in Italy (e.g., *Forza Italia*, "Forward Italy"). We further filter the data by keeping only 88 politicians having at least eight documents each. Thus, in our analyses we include 851 documents, 369 (43%) of which are labelled as populist. Table 2 in the Appendix reports the number of documents and tokens for each politician included in our analysis.

**Classification of populist parties**
We rely on "The PopuList 3.0" (Rooduijn et al., 2023) to extract the list of populist and non-populist parties for our feature analysis. The definition used to classify parties as populist relies on the Mudde (2004) identification of "The People" vs. "The Elitè" distinction and their view of politics as expression of the general will of the people. The classification of parties in "The PopuList 3.0" (Rooduijn et al., 2023) was conducted using an 'Expert-informed Qualitative Comparative Classification' (EiQCC). This method uses experts of political communication who qualitatively compare and classify political parties based on their expertise. Table 3 in the Appendix provides a list of Italian populist parties.

## 4 Methodology

Analyzing language involves dealing with several challenges, like the need for selecting among a vast number of features and the strong collinearity between different language features. In this section, we present the main features used in our analysis and the control features used to guarantee the comparability of the different texts. Then, we illustrate the feature selection procedure and the logistic regression models used to assess the statistical significance of the selected features.

### 4.1 Features Collection

In total, we collected 147 features from different linguistic levels of analysis. All features are included in the selection mechanism.

#### 4.1.1 Features derived from the literature

In our analysis, we include the six features mostly used in the literature to quantify language complexity in populist and non-populist parties.

**Raw text Parameters**
**Gulpease Index:** `G_index` (Lucisano and Piemontese, 1988) is the Italian measure for readability in text. This measure suggests that the higher the level of readability, the easier the text is.
**Characters per token:** `Char_per_Tok` are calculated with the "UD profiling" tool (Brunato et al., 2020) and represents the average length of words per document. The interpretation of this measure suggests that the longer the words in a text, the more complex the text is.

**Lexical Features**
**Lexical density:** `Lexical_density` is calculated using the "UD profiling" tool, and it consists in the number of content words divided by the total number of words. This measure indicates the degree of use of content words in a text, suggesting that the higher the degree, the more informative the text.
**Type-token ratio:** `Type_token_ratio` is calculated by counting the number of unique tokens and divide it by the total number of tokens. We include this feature to verify if populist texts tend to have a lower lexical diversity compared to non-populist texts.

**Word frequency:** `Word_frequency` is calculated using a frequency list[2] and, based on the way we calculated it, indicates that the greater the score, the less frequent words are used in a text.

**Syntactic measures**

**Syntactic depth:** the average maximal depth (`Avg_max_depth`) is calculated using the "UD profiling" tool. The intepretation of this measure indicates that the greater the average depth of syntactic trees in sentences, the more complex the text is.

#### 4.1.2 Other tested features

We extend our feature analysis by using the "UD profiling" tool for profiling the linguistic style of each text. Moreover, we include "Age of Acquisition" and "Concreteness" as plausible features in differentiating populist and non-populist rhetoric. Finally, we add a measures of people-centric and anti-elitè rhetoric as in Decadri and Boussalis (2020).

**UD Profiling's features:** UD Profiling's features are 141 features measured using the "UD profiling" tool. They can be grouped as follows: Raw Text Properties, Lexical Variety, Morphosyntactic Information, Verbal Predicate Structure, Global and Local Parse Tree Structures, Syntactic Relations, and Use of Subordination. A detailed list of the UD profiling's features can be found in Table 4 in the Appendix.

**Age of Acquisition:** `AoA` is calculated using the vocabulary in Montefinese et al. (2019). This parameter is calculated summing the age of acquisition of each word in the text and dividing it by the total number of tokens in the text. We include this feature to verify if populist texts tend to use simpler, earlier acquired words compared to non-populist texts.

**Concreteness:** `Concreteness` is calculated using the vocabulary in Gregori et al. (2020). This parameter is calculated summing the concreteness score of each word in the text and dividing it by the total number of tokens. We include this feature to verify if populist texts tend to use more concrete, tangible words compared to non-populist texts.

**People-centric and anti-elitè rhetoric**

**Populist words ratio:** The ratio of using populist words (`Populist_words_ratio`) is calculated using the dictionary approach in Decadri and Boussalis (2020), without distinguishing anti-elitism and people-centric rhetoric.[3] Table 5 in Appendix shows the seed words of the dictionary. We include this feature to verify if populists tend to use more people-centric and anti-elitè words compared to non-populists.

### 4.2 Control Features

We focus on the comparability of political texts and their metadata to guarantee a reliable analysis of their linguistic components. By using control features in our regression analyses, we account for potential confounding variables, thereby enhancing the accuracy and comparability of our modeling study. For each political text, it is fundamental to control for the following metadata extracted from the IMPAQTS corpus:

**Time:** `Decade` includes span of 10 years from the 1994 until 2023.

**Genre:** `Type` consists of 6 different genres of transcribed speeches. The institutional setting varies among the speeches (e.g. Rallies vs Parliamentary speeches), making them clearly different from a theoretical perspective.

**Author:** `Author` refers to the politician that acts as the speaker of the speech.

**Topic(s):** `Topic` is the main argument of one document. We apply a Latent Dirichlet Allocation (LDA) (Blei et al., 2003) to identify the dominant topic of each text (see Table 9 in the Appendix for further details).

**Author's role:** `Is_Majority` refers to the government/opposition role of the speaker's party during the date of the document.

**Author's political party:** `Political_Party` refers to the affiliation's party of the author at the date of the speech.

**Transcriber:** `Transcriber` refers to the person who transcribed the speech. It does not apply to written texts.

[2]https://invokeit.wordpress.com/frequency-word-lists

[3]Populist rhetoric is typically divided into two components: anti-elitism and people-centric rhetoric (refer to Section 2). We aggregate these components to focus on the general level of populist rhetoric.

### 4.3 Study: Populism Classification

We focus on the multifaceted concept of populism as a case study for profiling political texts and verifying different communication strategies, given a politician affiliation with populist parties. In our analysis, the classification of a document as populist relies on the author's political party. A score of 1 is given to parties classified as populist, 0 viceversa. For details on the classification of parties as populists see Section 3.

We streamlined a methodological framework that enhances the reliability of linguistic profile analyses within political texts. All codes are accessible at `https://github.com/Sergio-E-Zanotto/language_complexity_populism`.

#### 4.3.1 Data Pre-Processing

To obtain a balanced corpus, we selected 88 authors represented by at least eight texts (refer to Section 3). Given that different features come with very different scales, we pre-process our data by standardizing all the numerical variables.

#### 4.3.2 Feature Selection

We apply LASSO regression (Least Absolute Shrinkage and Selection Operator) (Tibshirani, 1996) to automatically identify the most relevant linguistic measures among all our 147 features. LASSO is a logistic regression method that includes a penalty term, which is the absolute value of the magnitude of the coefficients. This penalty term encourages the reduction of less important feature coefficients to zero, thereby performing feature selection and regularization to enhance the prediction accuracy and interpretability of the model. We automatically scored the penalty term $\lambda$ (0.199) to address collinearity issues through our feature selection process. After each logistic regression, we apply the Variance Inflation Factor (VIF) to ensure that no collinearity remains.

#### 4.3.3 Features Analysis

In our analysis, we utilize logistic regression to identify the statistically significant features that differentiate populist and non-populist discourses. First, we test only the features derived from the literature to assess their importance in distinguishing populists and non-populists discourses (see Section 4.1.1). Subsequently, we consider all features for our analysis and we select the top 15 predictors[4] that the feature selection process indicated as the most important in distinguishing between populist and non-populist discourses (refer to Section 4.3.2). First, we analyse the features with a logistic model to verify differences among populist and non-populist parties, without accounting for the communication style of each individual politician or any possible effect of the process of transcriptions. Second, we utilize a general mixed-effects model to add author and transcriber effects as random structure. All the regressions include control features (see Section 4.2).

## 5 Results

### 5.1 Features analysis on Populism

Table 1 reports the mean value of each linguistic feature for populist and non-populists parties and their difference (populist−non-populist). It also indicates which predictors reach significance according to the logistic regression (GLM) and the mixed-effects logistic regression (GLMER) models. Respectively, Table 6 and Table 7 in the Appendix report all the details of our statistical analyses.

According to the GLM model, `Lexical_Density` is the only feature derived from the literature that is significant in classifying populism, and it shows how populists utilize a slightly higher number of content words. We can appreciate from our selection of features how the degree of proper nouns (`Upos_dist_PROPN`) is significantly higher in populist texts. Additionally, populist texts show a higher ratio of populist words (`Populist_words_ratio`) and a higher number of second-person singular verbs (`Verbs_num_pers_dist_Sing2`). Furthermore, the percentage of verbal roots (`Verbal_root_perc`) is slightly lower in populist texts. The distribution of determiners and predeterminers (`Dep_dist_det_predet`) is also notably higher in populist texts. In Italian, this relation is used for the lemmas *tutto* ('all'), *entrambi* ('both'), and *ambedue* ('both'), when they appear in front of another determiner. We can also see that the degree of adjectives (`Upos_dist_ADJ`) is significantly lower in populist texts.

[4] We selected the top 15 features, which represent approximately 10% of the total features, to focus on the most impactful predictors while maintaining a manageable number of variables for the analysis. The features that are not significant are not reported in the paper.

| Predictor | Populist | Non-Populist | Difference | Significance | |
|---|---|---|---|---|---|
| | | | | GLM | GLMER |
| G_index | 52.063 | 52.037 | 0.026 | | |
| Char_per_tok | 4.703 | 4.705 | -0.002 | | |
| Type_token_ratio | 0.406 | 0.408 | -0.002 | | |
| Word_frequency | 0.596 | 0.602 | 0.006 | | |
| Avg_max_depth | 5.629 | 5.812 | -0.183 | | |
| Lexical_density | 0.471 | 0.469 | 0.002 | ** | |
| Upos_dist_PROPN | 2.744 | 2.237 | 0.507 | *** | |
| Dep_dist_det_predet | 0.225 | 0.180 | 0.045 | *** | |
| Populist_words_ratio | 0.008 | 0.007 | 0.001 | *** | |
| Verbs_num_pers_dist_Sing2 | 2.066 | 1.584 | 0.482 | ** | |
| Verbal_root_perc | 84.680 | 86.418 | -1.738 | * | |
| Verbs_mood_dist_Cnd | 1.177 | 1.487 | -0.310 | * | ** |
| Verbs_form_dist_Fin | 43.163 | 45.105 | -1.942 | *** | ** |
| Upos_dist_ADJ | 5.241 | 5.580 | -0.339 | *** | |
| Subordinate_dist_4 | 1.255 | 0.951 | 0.304 | * | * |
| Verb_edges_dist_1 | 14.129 | 13.508 | 0.621 | * | ** |

Table 1: Comparison of linguistic predictors between *Populist* and *Non-Populist* groups along with their differences (Populist-Non-Populist). Statistical significance * $p < 0.05$, ** $p < 0.01$, *** $p < 0.001$.

The GLMER model that includes author and transcriber effects shows that most of those features lose significance, and neither features derived from the literature nor populist words remains robust predictors of populism. We can attribute such change to the high variance in the author group (see Table 7 in the Appendix). However, a few features remain robust and indicate distinct patterns in populist language. Specifically, populists use fewer conditionals (`Verbs_mood_dist_Cnd`) and fewer finite verbs (`Verbs_form_dist_Fin`) than non-populists. Additionally, they tend to use more verbs with valency 1 (`Verb_edges_dist_1`) and employ subordinate clauses in chains of four (`Subordinate_dist_4`).

Moreover, when comparing models with random effects, the model informed with our automatically selected features performs better in terms of AIC (Akaike Information Criterion) than the one informed by the features derived from the literature (see Table 8 in the Appendix).

## 6 Discussion

Our analysis of multiple linguistic features yields several insights. First, traditional language complexity features identified in populism research do not robustly transfer to our data, often failing to distinguish populist discourse effectively. This suggests that the characteristics defining populist statements are highly dependent on the specific dataset and the language analysed, thus limiting the general conclusions drawn in previous research. Second, our feature selection revealed interesting trends when comparing populist vs. non-populist parties, particularly the well-known difference in the use of populist words. According to the literature, populists often emphasize a dichotomy between "the people" and "the elite" to rally support (Mudde, 2004). The most significant features also indicate a much wider use of proper nouns and quantifiers such as "all" and "both" as predeterminers by populist parties. This could imply a tendency to make absolute statements and to generalize broadly, reinforcing the populist narrative of representing the entire population against a unified elite, as exemplified in our corpus by sentence (1).

(1) [...] *perché non pensate a tutti gli italiani, pensate solo ad alcuni di essi* [...]
'[...] because you don't think about all Italians, you only think about some of them[...]'

Moreover, lexical density is significant in showing that populists use more content words. However, while populists use fewer adjectives, they tend to use proper nouns and second-person singular verbs more consistently. This might suggest a focus on specific individuals or groups and direct engagement with the audience, respectively. Additionally, populists use fewer verbal roots to structure their sentences, potentially indicating a reliance on more direct and straightforward statements.

When controlling for authors' effects, all these features lose significance, indicating huge variance in politicians' communication styles. Only four features remain significant after accounting for authors' effects. In IMPAQTS, we observe a trend among populist parties to use conditional verbs less frequently, potentially indicating a preference for stronger epistemic modality. For example, in our corpus, non-populists might prefer statements that convey less epistemic strength, as exemplified by sentence (2), which clearly conveys less certainty compared to a straightforward statement like 'we want to say something'.

(2) *E vorremmo, vorremmo poter dire una cosa:* [...]
'an we would, we would want to say something: [...]'

We also observe that populists use fewer finite verbs, implying a greater use of non-finite verbal forms. We notice a consistent use of nominalizations with non-finite verbs as the syntactic head of noun phrases, as exemplified by sentence (3). In adult speech, nominalization facilitates abstractness, which creates a sense of detachment and allows events to be presented as undeniable facts (Bello, 2016).

(3) *So bene che conoscere la regola dell'ascolto e del rispetto in democrazia non è cosa condivisa da tutti.*
'I know well that knowing the rule of respect in democracy is not something shared by everyone.'

Furthermore, nominalizations can be seen as a form of valency reduction in the formation of predicates (Mackenzie, 1985). We observe that populists tend to employ more verbs with a valency of 1, meaning verbs with only a single dependency link, either with an argument or a modifier. This strengthens the interpretation that populists seek to present events as undeniable, as exemplified in the corpus by sentence (4).

(4) [...] *la gente vuole tornare a contare,* [...] *a contare, a decidere, accogliere chi vuole accogliere, espellere chi vuole espellere* [...]
'[...] people want to matter again, [...] to matter, to decide, to welcome those they want to welcome, to expel those they want to expel [...]'

Finally, the use of subordinate clauses in chains of four shows a tendency for populists to employ repetitions in their sentences, as in sentence (5). This technique emphasizes the key points and creates a memorable rhythm, akin to the well-known rhetorical strategy known as the "rule of three" (Barry, 2018).

(5) *perché voi lo sapete, io credo nel consiglio comunale, credo nei dibattiti consiliari, credo che questo sia un fulcro forte della democrazia.*
'because you know, I believe in the city council, I believe in council debates, I believe that this is a strong cornerstone of democracy.'

Overall, our models do not strongly suggest that populist parties use simpler language than their mainstream rivals. We argue that substantial differences can be found in the simplicity of the conveyed content, more than in the simplicity of the language used to convey it, as discussed in McDonnell and Ondelli (2022). Instead, our results suggest that populists adhere more to specific, well-known rhetorical strategies, making populism a communication strategy that is common to very diverse parties and politicians. Indeed, in our corpus, sentence (6) is the perfect example of a combination of the above characteristics. The use of copular "be" conveys a stronger epistemic modality and affirms the undeniability of the stated facts, while the repetitions in the sentence help to emphasize key points and create a memorable rhythm.

(6) *La crisi non c'è, la crisi non esiste, c'è il pessimismo e non date retta al pessimismo.*
'there is no crisis, the crisis does not exist, there is pessimism and do not listen to pessimism.'

## 7 Conclusion and Future Work

In our analysis of the linguistic characteristics of Italian political speeches, we implemented a detailed methodology to ensure the comparability of texts and utilized a feature selection process to explore linguistic differences among populists and non-populists parties. Our study reveals that traditionally employed features of language complexity derived from the literature do not show statistical significance in distinguish populist and non-populist discourse in the IMPAQTS corpus. This inconsistency underscores the importance of context and corpus specificity in linguistic analyses, cautioning against overgeneralizing findings.

Moreover, while we observed an increased occurrence of populist rhetoric —characterized by themes of people-centrism and anti-elitism— in speeches from aggregating populist parties, this did not coincide with simpler language use. Especially, most of these features were not robust to the individuality of speakers communication style within our dataset. We highlight the tendency of populists' speaker to employ specific, well-known rhetorical strategies in their speeches. However, our research highlights again the need for nuanced analysis that considers the diverse characteristics of the corpus being studied.

Building on this foundation, future research will aim to enhance the granularity of populism annotation in textual data, following approaches like those outlined by Klamm et al. (2023). Additionally, examining other features of political communication, such as emotional content as suggested by Huguet Cabot et al. (2021), may offer deeper insights into the nuances of populist rhetoric across different authors and political parties. This direction promises to refine our understanding of the linguistic strategies employed within political discourse.

## 8 Limitations

One limitation of our study involves the nature of the corpus analyzed. The controls within IMPAQTS present challenges due to their unbalanced nature, making it difficult to aggregate the results. For example, this imbalance may potentially favor more frequent genres, such as parliamentary speeches, over smaller ones. Despite this, the significance of incorporating controls to enhance the robustness of our findings remains undisputed.

## References


Patrick Barry. 2018. The rule of three. *Legal Communications and Rhetoric: JALWD*, 15:247.

Iria Bello. 2016. Cognitive implications of nominalizations in the advancement of scientific discourse. *International Journal of English Studies*, 16(2):1–23.

Daniel Bischof and Roman Senninger. 2018. Simple politics for the people? Complexity in campaign messages and political knowledge. *European Journal of Political Research*, 57(2):473–495.

David M Blei, Andrew Y Ng, and Michael I Jordan. 2003. Latent dirichlet allocation. *Journal of Machine Learning Research*, 3(Jan):993–1022.

Dominique Brunato, Andrea Cimino, Felice Dell'Orletta, Giulia Venturi, and Simonetta Montemagni. 2020. Profiling-UD: a tool for linguistic profiling of texts. In *Proceedings of the Twelfth Language Resources and Evaluation Conference*, pages 7145–7151, Marseille, France.

Margaret Canovan. 1999. Trust the people! Populism and the two faces of democracy. *Political Studies*, 47(1):2–16.

Margaret Canovan. 2004. Populism for political theorists? *Journal of Political ideologies*, 9(3):241–252.

Jeanne S Chall. 1996. Varying approaches to readability measurement. *Revue qué Bécoise de linguistique*, 25(1):23–40.

Federica Cominetti, Lorenzo Gregori, Edoardo Lombardi Vallauri, and Alessandro Panunzi. 2022. Impaqts: un corpus di discorsi politici italiani annotato per gli impliciti linguistici. In *Corpora e Studi linguistici. Atti del LIV Congresso della Società di Linguistica Italiana (Online, 8–10 settembre 2021), a cura di Emanuela Cresti e Massimo Moneglia. Milano, Officinaventuno*, pages 151–164.

Silvia Decadri and Constantine Boussalis. 2020. Populism, party membership, and language complexity in the italian chamber of deputies. *Journal of Elections, Public Opinion and Parties*, 30(4):484–503.

Jessica Di Cocco and Bernardo Monechi. 2022. How populist are parties? Measuring degrees of populism in party manifestos using supervised machine learning. *Political Analysis*, 30(3):311–327.

Katharina Ehret, Aleksandrs Berdicevskis, Christian Bentz, and Alice Blumenthal-Dramé. 2023. Measuring language complexity: challenges and opportunities. *Linguistics Vanguard*, 9(s1):1–8.

Katharina Ehret, Alice Blumenthal-Dramé, Christian Bentz, and Aleksandrs Berdicevskis. 2021. Meaning and measures: Interpreting and evaluating complexity metrics. *Frontiers in Communication*, 6:640510.

Lorenzo Gregori, Maria Montefinese, Daniele P Radicioni, Andrea Amelio Ravelli, and Rossella Varvara. 2020. CONCRETEXT@EVALITA2020: The concreteness in context task. In *Proceedings of the 7th Evaluation Campaign of Natural Language Processing and Speech Tools for Italian (EVALITA 2020)*. CEUR.org.

Lena Maria Huber. 2022. Beyond policy: the use of social group appeals in party communication. *Political Communication*, 39(3):293–310.

Pere-Lluís Huguet Cabot, David Abadi, Agneta Fischer, and Ekaterina Shutova. 2021. Us vs. them: A dataset of populist attitudes, news bias and emotions. In *Proceedings of the 16th Conference of the European Chapter of the Association for Computational Linguistics: Main Volume*, pages 1921–1945, Online. Association for Computational Linguistics.

Jan Jagers and Stefaan Walgrave. 2007. Populism as political communication style: An empirical study of political parties' discourse in Belgium. *European Journal of Political Research*, 46(3):319–345.

J Peter Kincaid, Robert P Fishburne Jr, Richard L Rogers, and Brad S Chissom. 1975. Derivation of new readability formulas (automated readability index, fog count and flesch reading ease formula) for navy enlisted personnel. *Tech. Rep.*

Christopher Klamm, Ines Rehbein, and Simone Paolo Ponzetto. 2023. Our kind of people? Detecting populist references in political debates. In *Findings of the Association for Computational Linguistics: EACL 2023*, pages 1227–1243, Dubrovnik, Croatia. Association for Computational Linguistics.

Ernesto Laclau. 2006. On populist reason. *Tijdschrift Voor Filosofie*, 68(4):832–835.

Hauke Licht and Ronja Sczepanski. 2023. Who are they talking about? detecting mentions of social groups in political texts with supervised learning. OSF Preprints, 20 June 2023.

Pietro Lucisano and Maria Emanuela Piemontese. 1988. Gulpease: una formula per la predizione della leggibilita di testi in lingua italiana. *Scuola e Città*, pages 110–124.

J Lachlan Mackenzie. 1985. Nominalization and valency reduction. *Predicates and Terms in Functional Grammar. Dordrecht: Foris*, pages 31–51.

Duncan McDonnell and Stefano Ondelli. 2022. The language of right-wing populist leaders: Not so simple. *Perspectives on Politics*, 20(3):828–841.

Maria Montefinese, David Vinson, Gabriella Vigliocco, and Ettore Ambrosini. 2019. Italian age of acquisition norms for a large set of words (itaoa). *Frontiers in Psychology*, 10:278.

Cas Mudde. 2004. The populist zeitgeist. *Government and Opposition*, 39(4):541–563.

Gabriele Pallotti. 2015. A simple view of linguistic complexity. *Second Language Research*, 31(1):117–134.

Concha Pérez-Curiel, Rubén Rivas-de Roca, and Mar García-Gordillo. 2021. Impact of Trump's digital rhetoric on the us elections: A view from worldwide far-right populism. *Social Sciences*, 10(5):152.

Matthijs Rooduijn and Teun Pauwels. 2011. Measuring populism: Comparing two methods of content analysis. *West European Politics*, 34(6):1272–1283.

Matthijs Rooduijn, Andrea LP Pirro, Daphne Halikiopoulou, Caterina Froio, Stijn Van Kessel, Sarah L De Lange, Cas Mudde, and Paul Taggart. 2023. The populist: A database of populist, far-left, and far-right parties using expert-informed qualitative comparative classification (eiqcc). *British Journal of Political Science*, pages 1–10.

Martijn Schoonvelde, Anna Brosius, Gijs Schumacher, and Bert N Bakker. 2019. Liberals lecture, conservatives communicate: Analyzing complexity and ideology in 381,609 political speeches. *PloS One*, 14(2):e0208450.

Roman Senninger. 2023. What makes policy complex? *Political Science Research and Methods*, 11(4):913–920.

Arthur Spirling. 2016. Democratization and linguistic complexity: The effect of franchise extension on parliamentary discourse, 1832–1915. *The Journal of Politics*, 78(1):120–136.

Kaare Strom. 1990. A behavioral theory of competitive political parties. *American journal of political science*, pages 565–598.

Henri Tajfel and John C. Turner. 2004. The social identity theory of intergroup behavior. In *Political Psychology*, pages 276–293. Psychology Press.

Hiroki Takikawa and Takuto Sakamoto. 2020. The moral–emotional foundations of political discourse: a comparative analysis of the speech records of the us and the japanese legislatures. *Quality & Quantity*, 54:547–566.

Mads Thau. 2019. How political parties use group-based appeals: Evidence from britain 1964–2015. *Political Studies*, 67(1):63–82.

Robert Tibshirani. 1996. Regression shrinkage and selection via the lasso. *Journal of the Royal Statistical Society Series B: Statistical Methodology*, 58(1):267–288.

Petro Tolochko and Hajo G Boomgaarden. 2019. Determining political text complexity: Conceptualizations, measurements, and application. *International Journal of Communication*, 13:21.

Daniela Trotta, Sara Tonelli, Alessio Palmero Aprosio, and Elia Annibale. 2019. Annotation and analysis of the polimodal corpus of political interviews. In *Proceedings of the Sixth Italian Conference on Computational Linguistics (CLiC-it 2019)*.

Ruth Wodak. 2012. Language, power and identity. *Language Teaching*, 45(2):215–233.

Sergio E. Zanotto, Qi Yu, Miriam Butt, and Diego Frassinelli. 2024. GRIT: A dataset of group reference recognition in Italian. In *Proceedings of the 2024 Joint International Conference on Computational Linguistics, Language Resources and Evaluation (LREC-COLING 2024)*, pages 7963–7970, Torino, Italia. ELRA and ICCL.

Andrej Zaslove. 2008. Here to stay? Populism as a new party type. *European Review*, 16(3):319–336.

# A Appendix

Table 2 presents the list of politicians analyzed with the number of documents and tokens available (see Section 3); Table 3 shows the list of populist parties used for our classification (see Section 3); Table 4 reports the list of all features extracted using the profiling UD's tool (Brunato et al., 2020); Table 5 provides the list of seed words of the dictionary in Decadri and Boussalis (2020) used to calculate the rate of populist words in each discourse (see Section 4.1.2).

## A.1 Statistical Model Details

Furthermore, we provide all the details about the logistic regression analyses as presented in Section 5.1. Tables 6 presents the logistic regression (GLM) analysis on the most used features from the literature for analyzing language complexity in political texts and the significant features extracted by our feature selection procedure (see Section 4.3.2). Table 7 presents the mixed-effects logistic regression model (GLMER), accounting for possible author effects and transcriber effects. Controls are present in all regressions (see 4.2 for the detailed list of controls). Subsequently, Table 8 presents the comparison between mixed-effects models for the predictors derived from the literature and the automatically selected predictors (see Section 5).

## A.2 Topic Analysis

In our analysis, we categorized each document based on its most prominent topic. To capture changes over time, we calculated topics at 10-year intervals. We score the optimal number of topics that better represents documents for each decade with the coherence model from Gensim python library[5]. The optimal number of topics per decade are: {'1990-1999': 3, '2000-2009': 8, '2010-2019': 7, '2020-2023': 9}. We employed Latent Dirichlet Allocation (LDA) to identify the most relevant topics for each decade, defined by the three most relevant key terms associated with each topic. Table 9 presents the topics identified for each decade, along with their corresponding key terms.

[5]https://radimrehurek.com/gensim/models/coherencemodel.html

| Author | Documents | Tokens |
|---|---|---|
| Luigi di Maio | 11 | 24630 |
| Alessandra Mussolini | 10 | 8195 |
| Alessandro Di Battista | 10 | 19524 |
| Alfonso Bonafede | 10 | 12696 |
| Andrea Orlando | 10 | 17292 |
| Angelino Alfano | 10 | 15026 |
| Anna Finocchiaro | 10 | 13005 |
| Antonio di Pietro | 10 | 12846 |
| Beppe Sala | 10 | 11263 |
| Carlo Calenda | 10 | 15466 |
| Claudio Scajola | 10 | 12120 |
| Daniele Capezzone | 10 | 13179 |
| Danilo Toninelli | 10 | 15469 |
| Dario Franceschini | 10 | 15720 |
| Debora Serracchiani | 10 | 15332 |
| Enrico Letta | 10 | 15742 |
| Eugenia Maria Roccella | 10 | 10600 |
| Fabrizio Cicchitto | 10 | 10462 |
| Francesco Storace | 10 | 13034 |
| Graziano Delrio | 10 | 14478 |
| Guglielmo Epifani | 10 | 16558 |
| Ignazio La Russa | 10 | 15546 |
| Ignazio Marino | 10 | 12134 |
| Irene Pivetti | 10 | 11958 |
| Italo Bocchino | 10 | 14805 |
| Laura Boldrini | 10 | 18068 |
| Letizia Moratti | 10 | 12979 |
| Luca Zaia | 10 | 19435 |
| Lucia Borgonzoni | 10 | 13854 |
| Luigi De Magistris | 10 | 16978 |
| Mara Carfagna | 10 | 12016 |
| Maria Elena Boschi | 10 | 16155 |
| Maria E. Alberti Casellati | 10 | 9563 |
| Mariastella Gelmini | 10 | 14552 |
| Matteo Orfini | 10 | 15194 |
| Maurizio Gasparri | 10 | 15211 |
| Maurizio Lupi | 10 | 15725 |
| Monica Cirinnà | 10 | 11682 |
| Nichi Vendola | 10 | 12965 |
| Nicola Fratoianni | 10 | 12166 |
| Nicola Zingaretti | 10 | 15390 |
| Oliviero Diliberto | 10 | 13556 |
| Paola Binetti | 10 | 11190 |
| Paola Taverna | 10 | 13409 |
| Paolo Ferrero | 10 | 13692 |
| Paolo Gentiloni | 10 | 16652 |
| Pier Luigi Bersani | 10 | 15914 |
| Pietro Grasso | 10 | 15898 |
| Renata Polverini | 10 | 12067 |
| Renato Brunetta | 10 | 12338 |
| Renato Schifani | 10 | 14527 |
| Roberta Lombardi | 10 | 12941 |
| Roberto Calderoli | 10 | 17480 |
| Roberto Castelli | 10 | 12849 |
| Roberto Fico | 10 | 11659 |
| Roberto Speranza | 10 | 13798 |
| Rocco Buttiglione | 10 | 11621 |
| Romano Prodi | 10 | 15343 |
| Rosy Bindi | 10 | 9892 |
| Sandro Bondi | 10 | 12449 |
| Sergio Cofferati | 10 | 9920 |
| Stefania Prestigiacomo | 10 | 8810 |
| Vincenzo De Luca | 10 | 15305 |
| Virginia Raggi | 10 | 15337 |
| Walter Veltroni | 10 | 18349 |
| Clemente Mastella | 9 | 16888 |
| Daniela Santanchè | 9 | 11394 |
| Fausto Bertinotti | 9 | 14338 |
| Giorgia Meloni | 9 | 18375 |
| Lamberto Dini | 9 | 11351 |
| Mario Monti | 9 | 12139 |
| Matteo Renzi | 9 | 19465 |
| Matteo Salvini | 9 | 22557 |
| Maurizio Martina | 9 | 12353 |
| Mirko Tremaglia | 9 | 8600 |
| Roberto Maroni | 9 | 11438 |
| Silvio Berlusconi | 9 | 17817 |
| Anna Maria Bernini | 8 | 10345 |
| Antonio Tajani | 8 | 10158 |
| Carlo Azeglio Ciampi | 8 | 11081 |
| Giuseppe Conte | 8 | 14442 |
| Leoluca Orlando | 8 | 9383 |
| Sebastiano Musumeci | 8 | 11091 |

Table 2: Number of documents and tokens per author in the dataset.

| Political Party | Abbreviation |
|---|---|
| Lega (Nord) | LN |
| Forza Italia* | FI |
| Fratelli d'Italia | FdI |
| Movimento 5 Stelle | M5S |
| Il Popolo della Libertà | PdL |
| De Luca Sindaco d'Italia | DLSI |
| La Rete | LR |
| Lista Di Pietro - Italia dei Valori | IdV |

Table 3: Italian populist parties - * borderline case.

| Variable | Characteristics |
|---|---|
| **Family: Raw Text Properties** | |
| n_sentences | Total number of sentences |
| n_tokens | Total number of tokens |
| tokens_per_sent | Average length of sentences in a document, calculated in terms of the number of words per sentence |
| char_per_tok | Average number of characters per word (excluding punctuation) |
| **Family: Lexical Variety** | |
| ttr_lemma_chunks_100 | Type/Token Ratio (TTR) calculated with respect to the lemmata in the first 100 tokens of a document. It ranges between 1 (high lexical variety) and 0 (low lexical variety) |
| ttr_lemma_chunks_200 | Type/Token Ratio (TTR) calculated with respect to the lemmata in the first 200 tokens of a document. It ranges between 1 (high lexical variety) and 0 (low lexical variety) |
| ttr_form_chunks_100 | Type/Token Ratio (TTR) calculated with respect to the word forms in the first 100 tokens of a document. It ranges between 1 (high lexical variety) and 0 (low lexical variety) |
| ttr_form_chunks_200 | Type/Token Ratio (TTR) calculated with respect to the word forms in the first 200 tokens of a document. It ranges between 1 (high lexical variety) and 0 (low lexical variety) |
| **Family: Morphosyntactic Information** | |
| upos_dist_ADJ | Distribution of adjectives |
| upos_dist_ADP | Distribution of adpositions |
| upos_dist_ADV | Distribution of adverbs |
| upos_dist_AUX | Distribution of auxiliaries |
| upos_dist_CCONJ | Distribution of coordinating conjunctions |
| upos_dist_DET | Distribution of determiners |
| upos_dist_INTJ | Distribution of interjections |
| upos_dist_NOUN | Distribution of nouns |
| upos_dist_NUM | Distribution of numerals |
| upos_dist_PART | Distribution of particles |
| upos_dist_PRON | Distribution of pronouns |
| upos_dist_PROPN | Distribution of proper nouns |
| upos_dist_PUNCT | Distribution of punctuation |
| upos_dist_SCONJ | Distribution of subordinating conjunctions |
| upos_dist_SYM | Distribution of symbols |

*Continued on next page*

Table 4: List of features from the "UD Profiling Tool".

| Variable | Characteristics |
|---|---|
| upos_dist_VERB | Distribution of verbs |
| upos_dist_X | Distribution of other categories |
| lexical_density | Ratio of content words (nouns, proper nouns, verbs, adjectives, adverbs) over the total number of words in a document |
| **Family: Inflectional Morphology** | |
| verbs_tense_dist_Fut | Distribution of verbs in future tense |
| verbs_tense_dist_Imp | Distribution of verbs in imperfect tense |
| verbs_tense_dist_Past | Distribution of verbs in past tense |
| verbs_tense_dist_Pres | Distribution of verbs in present tense |
| verbs_mood_dist_Cnd | Distribution of verbs in conditional mood |
| verbs_mood_dist_Imp | Distribution of verbs in imperative mood |
| verbs_mood_dist_Ind | Distribution of verbs in indicative mood |
| verbs_mood_dist_Sub | Distribution of verbs in subjunctive mood |
| verbs_form_dist_Fin | Distribution of verbs in finite form |
| verbs_form_dist_Ger | Distribution of verbs in gerund form |
| verbs_form_dist_Inf | Distribution of verbs in infinitive form |
| verbs_form_dist_Part | Distribution of verbs in participle form |
| verbs_num_pers_dist_+3 | Distribution of verbs in third person |
| verbs_num_pers_dist_Plur+1 | Distribution of verbs in first person plural |
| verbs_num_pers_dist_Plur+2 | Distribution of verbs in second person plural |
| verbs_num_pers_dist_Plur+3 | Distribution of verbs in third person plural |
| verbs_num_pers_dist_Sing+1 | Distribution of verbs in first person singular |
| verbs_num_pers_dist_Sing+2 | Distribution of verbs in second person singular |
| verbs_num_pers_dist_Sing+3 | Distribution of verbs in third person singular |
| aux_tense_dist_Fut | Distribution of auxiliaries in future tense |
| aux_tense_dist_Imp | Distribution of auxiliaries in imperfect tense |
| aux_tense_dist_Past | Distribution of auxiliaries in past tense |
| aux_tense_dist_Pres | Distribution of auxiliaries in present tense |
| aux_mood_dist_Cnd | Distribution of auxiliaries in conditional mood |
| aux_mood_dist_Imp | Distribution of auxiliaries in imperative mood |
| aux_mood_dist_Ind | Distribution of auxiliaries in indicative mood |
| aux_mood_dist_Sub | Distribution of auxiliaries in subjunctive mood |
| aux_form_dist_Fin | Distribution of auxiliaries in finite form |
| aux_form_dist_Ger | Distribution of auxiliaries in gerund form |
| aux_form_dist_Inf | Distribution of auxiliaries in infinitive form |
| aux_form_dist_Part | Distribution of auxiliaries in participle form |
| aux_num_pers_dist_Plur+1 | Distribution of auxiliaries in first person plural |
| aux_num_pers_dist_Plur+2 | Distribution of auxiliaries in second person plural |
| aux_num_pers_dist_Plur+3 | Distribution of auxiliaries in third person plural |
| aux_num_pers_dist_Sing+1 | Distribution of auxiliaries in first person singular |
| aux_num_pers_dist_Sing+2 | Distribution of auxiliaries in second person singular |
| aux_num_pers_dist_Sing+3 | Distribution of auxiliaries in third person singular |
| **Family: Syntactic Features** | |
| verbal_head_per_sent | Average distribution of verbal heads in the document, out of the total of heads |
| verbal_root_perc | Average distribution of roots headed by a verb, out of the total of sentence roots |

*Continued on next page*

Table 4: List of features from the "UD Profiling Tool".

| Variable | Characteristics |
|---|---|
| avg_verb_edges | Verbal arity, calculated as the average number of instantiated dependency links (covering both arguments and modifiers) sharing the same verbal head, excluding punctuation and auxiliaries bearing the syntactic role of copula according to the UD scheme |
| verb_edges_dist_0 | Distribution of verbs with arity 0 |
| verb_edges_dist_1 | Distribution of verbs with arity 1 |
| verb_edges_dist_2 | Distribution of verbs with arity 2 |
| verb_edges_dist_3 | Distribution of verbs with arity 3 |
| verb_edges_dist_4 | Distribution of verbs with arity 4 |
| verb_edges_dist_5 | Distribution of verbs with arity 5 |
| verb_edges_dist_6 | Distribution of verbs with arity 6 |
| avg_max_depth | Mean of the maximum tree depths extracted from each sentence of a document. The maximum depth is calculated as the longest path (in terms of occurring dependency links) from the root of the dependency tree to some leaf |
| avg_token_per_clause | Average clause length, calculated in terms of the average number of tokens per clause, where a clause is defined as the ratio between the number of tokens in a sentence and the number of either verbal or copular head |
| avg_max_links_len | Mean of the longest dependency links extracted from each sentence of a document |
| avg_links_len | Average number of words occurring linearly between each syntactic head and its dependent (excluding punctuation dependencies) |
| max_links_len | The value of the longest dependency link in the document, calculated in number of tokens |
| avg_prepositional_chain_len | Average value of prepositional 'chains' extracted for all sentences of the document. A prepositional chain is calculated as the number of embedded prepositional complements dependent on a noun |
| n_prepositional_chains | Total number of prepositional 'chains' extracted for all sentences of the document |
| prep_dist_1 | Distribution of prepositional chains 1-complement long |
| prep_dist_2 | Distribution of prepositional chains 2-complements long |
| prep_dist_3 | Distribution of prepositional chains 3-complements long |
| prep_dist_4 | Distribution of prepositional chains 4-complements long |
| prep_dist_5 | Distribution of prepositional chains 5-complements long |
| **Family: Order of Elements** | |
| obj_pre | Distribution of objects preceding the verb |
| obj_post | Distribution of objects following the verb |
| subj_pre | Distribution of subjects preceding the verb |
| subj_post | Distribution of subjects following the verb |
| **Family: Syntactic Relations** | |
| dep_dist_acl | Distribution of clausal modifiers of nouns |
| dep_dist_acl:relcl | Distribution of relative clauses |
| dep_dist_advcl | Distribution of adverbial clauses |
| dep_dist_advmod | Distribution of adverbial modifiers |

*Continued on next page*

Table 4: List of features from the "UD Profiling Tool".

| Variable | Characteristics |
|---|---|
| dep_dist_amod | Distribution of adjectival modifiers |
| dep_dist_appos | Distribution of appositions |
| dep_dist_aux | Distribution of auxiliaries |
| dep_dist_aux:pass | Distribution of passive auxiliaries |
| dep_dist_case | Distribution of case markers |
| dep_dist_cc | Distribution of coordinating conjunctions |
| dep_dist_ccomp | Distribution of clausal complements |
| dep_dist_compound | Distribution of compound words |
| dep_dist_conj | Distribution of conjuncts |
| dep_dist_cop | Distribution of copulas |
| dep_dist_csubj | Distribution of clausal subjects |
| dep_dist_det | Distribution of determiners |
| dep_dist_det:poss | Distribution of possessive determiners |
| dep_dist_det:predet | Distribution of predeterminers |
| dep_dist_discourse | Distribution of discourse elements |
| dep_dist_dislocated | Distribution of dislocated elements |
| dep_dist_expl | Distribution of expletives |
| dep_dist_expl:impers | Distribution of impersonal expletives |
| dep_dist_expl:pass | Distribution of passive expletives |
| dep_dist_fixed | Distribution of fixed multiword expressions |
| dep_dist_flat | Distribution of flat multiword expressions |
| dep_dist_flat:foreign | Distribution of foreign flat multiword expressions |
| dep_dist_flat:name | Distribution of names in flat multiword expressions |
| dep_dist_iobj | Distribution of indirect objects |
| dep_dist_mark | Distribution of markers |
| dep_dist_nmod | Distribution of nominal modifiers |
| dep_dist_nsubj | Distribution of nominal subjects |
| dep_dist_nsubj:pass | Distribution of passive nominal subjects |
| dep_dist_nummod | Distribution of numeric modifiers |
| dep_dist_obj | Distribution of objects |
| dep_dist_obl | Distribution of obliques |
| dep_dist_obl:agent | Distribution of agent obliques |
| dep_dist_orphan | Distribution of orphan elements |
| dep_dist_parataxis | Distribution of parataxis |
| dep_dist_punct | Distribution of punctuation |
| dep_dist_root | Distribution of roots |
| dep_dist_vocative | Distribution of vocatives |
| dep_dist_xcomp | Distribution of open clausal complements |
| **Family: Use of Subordination** | |
| principal_proposition_dist | Distribution of principal clauses |
| subordinate_proposition_dist | Distribution of subordinate clauses |
| subordinate_post | Distribution of subordinate clauses following the main clause |
| subordinate_pre | Distribution of subordinate clauses preceding the main clause |
| avg_subordinate_chain_len | Average length of subordinate chains, where a subordinate 'chain' is calculated as the number of subordinate clauses embedded on a first subordinate clause |
| subordinate_dist_1 | Distribution of subordinate chains 1-clause long |

*Continued on next page*

Table 4: List of features from the "UD Profiling Tool".

| **Variable** | **Characteristics** |
|---|---|
| subordinate_dist_2 | Distribution of subordinate chains 2-clauses long |
| subordinate_dist_3 | Distribution of subordinate chains 3-clauses long |
| subordinate_dist_4 | Distribution of subordinate chains 4-clauses long |
| subordinate_dist_5 | Distribution of subordinate chains 5-clauses long |

Table 4: List of features from the "UD Profiling Tool".

| Anti-elitism | Translation | People-centrism | Translation |
|---|---|---|---|
| antidemocratic* | undemocratic | abitant* | citizen |
| casta | caste | cittadin* | citizen |
| consens* | consensus* | consumator* | consumer |
| corrot* | corrupt* | contribuent* | taxpayer |
| disonest* | dishonest* | elettor* | voter |
| elit* | elite* | gente | people |
| establishment | establishm* | popol* | people |
| ingann* | deceit* | | |
| mentir* | lie* | | |
| menzogn* | lie* | | |
| partitocrazia | establishm* | | |
| propagand* | propagand* | | |
| scandal* | scandal* | | |
| tradim* | betray* | | |
| tradir* | betray* | | |
| tradit* | betray* | | |
| vergogn* | shame* | | |
| verità | truth* | | |

Table 5: Seed words of the dictionary found in Decadri and Boussalis (2020) for anti-elitism and people-centrism.

| Variable | Literature Features | Selected Features |
|---|---|---|
| Intercept | –1.00±0.32** | –0.61±0.36 |
| G_index | –0.14±0.11 | - |
| char_per_tok | –0.24±0.13 | - |
| Type_token_ratio | –0.05±0.08 | - |
| word_frequency | 0.17±0.10 | - |
| avg_max_depth | –0.05±0.08 | - |
| lexical_density | 0.21±0.09* | 0.25±0.10** |
| upos_dist_PROPN | - | 0.42±0.09*** |
| Populist_words_ratio | - | 0.32±0.08*** |
| verbs_mood_dist_Cnd | - | –0.20±0.08* |
| verbs_form_dist_Fin | - | –0.43±0.09*** |
| dep_dist_det:predet | - | 0.34±0.08*** |
| verbs_num_pers_dist_Sing+2 | - | 0.24±0.08** |
| verbal_root_perc | - | –0.19±0.08* |
| upos_dist_ADJ | - | –0.47±0.10*** |
| subordinate_dist_4 | - | 0.18±0.08* |
| verb_edges_dist_1 | - | 0.19±0.08* |
| Controls | Yes | Yes |

Table 6: Comparative analysis of GLM outputs for literature and automatically selected features with estimates and standard errors. Significance codes: * $p < 0.05$, ** $p < 0.01$, *** $p < 0.001$.

| Predictor | Literature Features | Selected Features |
|---|---|---|
| Intercept | −13.90±1.92*** | −17.81±2.77*** |
| G_index | −0.40±0.31 | - |
| char_per_tok | −0.55±0.38 | - |
| Type_token_ratio | −0.03±0.27 | - |
| word_frequency | 0.33±0.27 | - |
| avg_max_depth | 0.00±0.21 | - |
| lexical_density | 0.13±0.28 | −0.37±0.35 |
| upos_dist_PROPN | - | 0.32±0.31 |
| Populist_words_ratio | - | 0.56±0.32 |
| verbs_mood_dist_Cnd | - | −0.89±0.32** |
| verbs_form_dist_Fin | - | −0.93±0.33** |
| dep_dist_det:predet | - | −0.31±0.34 |
| verbs_num_pers_dist_Sing+2 | - | 0.48±0.28 |
| verbal_root_perc | - | −0.10±0.24 |
| upos_dist_ADJ | - | 0.24±0.43 |
| subordinate_dist_4 | - | 0.76±0.31* |
| verb_edges_dist_1 | - | 0.79±0.29** |
| Controls | Yes | Yes |
| **Random Effects** | Variance ± Std.Dev. | |
| author (88) | 342.53±18.51 | 535.17±23.13 |
| transcriber (11) | 0.42±0.65 | 1.00±1.00 |

Table 7: Comparative analysis of GLMER outputs for literature and automatically selected features with estimates, standard errors, and random effects. Significance codes: * $p < 0.05$, ** $p < 0.01$, *** $p < 0.001$.

| Model | npar | AIC | BIC | logLik | Deviance | Chisq | Pr(>Chisq) |
|---|---|---|---|---|---|---|---|
| model_literature_features | 19 | 451.97 | 542.06 | -206.98 | 413.97 | | |
| model_selected_features | 24 | 416.78 | 530.58 | -184.39 | 368.78 | 45.19 | 1.33e-08 *** |

Table 8: Chi-square comparison of the mixed-effects model with predictors derived from the literature and model with the automatically selected features.

| Topic by Decade | Key Terms (Italian) | Translation |
|---|---|---|
| 1990-1999_Topic_0 | presidente, governo, paese | president, government, country |
| 1990-1999_Topic_1 | governo, paese, presidente | government, country, president |
| 1990-1999_Topic_2 | governo, paese, sinistra | government, country, left |
| 2000-2009_Topic_0 | governo, paese, presidente | government, country, president |
| 2000-2009_Topic_1 | sinistra, liberta, partito | left, freedom, party |
| 2000-2009_Topic_2 | anni, parte, governo | years, part, government |
| 2000-2009_Topic_3 | governo, partito, paese | government, party, country |
| 2000-2009_Topic_4 | legge, referendum, governo | law, referendum, government |
| 2000-2009_Topic_5 | politica, lavoro, persone | politics, work, people |
| 2000-2009_Topic_6 | sinistra, punto, potere | left, point, power |
| 2000-2009_Topic_7 | citta, parte, casa | city, part, house |
| 2010-2019_Topic_0 | paese, anni, legge | country, years, law |
| 2010-2019_Topic_1 | governo, paese, anni | government, country, years |
| 2010-2019_Topic_2 | legge, lavoro, anni | law, work, years |
| 2010-2019_Topic_3 | presidente, governo, paese | president, government, country |
| 2010-2019_Topic_4 | citta, anni, cittadini | city, years, citizens |
| 2010-2019_Topic_5 | lavoro, paese, anni | work, country, years |
| 2010-2019_Topic_6 | anni, grazie, paese | years, thanks, country |
| 2020-2023_Topic_0 | governo, presidente, ministro | government, president, minister |
| 2020-2023_Topic_1 | governo, presidente, ministro | government, president, minister |
| 2020-2023_Topic_2 | paese, anni, futuro | country, years, future |
| 2020-2023_Topic_3 | regione, persone, anni | region, people, years |
| 2020-2023_Topic_4 | ministro, giustizia, signor | minister, justice, mister |
| 2020-2023_Topic_5 | lavoro, paese, governo | work, country, government |
| 2020-2023_Topic_6 | governo, paese, presidente | government, country, president |
| 2020-2023_Topic_7 | legge, parte, anni | law, part, years |
| 2020-2023_Topic_8 | presidente, governo, anni | president, government, years |

Table 9: LDA topics by decade and key terms.

# ChatGPT as Your $n$-th Annotator: Experiments in Leveraging Large Language Models for Social Science Text Annotation in Slovak Language

**Endre Hamerlik[1,2], Marek Šuppa[1,3], Miroslav Blšták[4], Jozef Kubík[1], Martin Takáč[1], Marián Šimko[4], Andrej Findor[5],**

[1]Faculty of Mathematics Physics and Informatics, Comenius University in Bratislava, Slovakia
[2]ELKH Institute for Computer Science and Control (SZTAKI), Hungary
[3]Cisco Systems, Slovakia [4]Kempelen Institute of Intelligent Technologies, Slovakia
[5] Faculty of Social and Economic Sciences, Comenius University in Bratislava, Slovakia

## Abstract

Large Language Models (LLMs) are increasingly influential in Computational Social Science, offering new methods for processing and analyzing data, particularly in lower-resource language contexts. This study explores the use of OpenAI's GPT-3.5 Turbo and GPT-4 for automating annotations for a unique news media dataset in a lower resourced language, focusing on stance classification tasks. Our results reveal that prompting in the native language, explanation generation, and advanced prompting strategies like Retrieval Augmented Generation and Chain of Thought prompting enhance LLM performance, particularly noting GPT-4's superiority in predicting stance. Further evaluation indicates that LLMs can serve as a useful tool for social science text annotation in lower resourced languages, notably in identifying inconsistencies in annotation guidelines and annotated datasets.

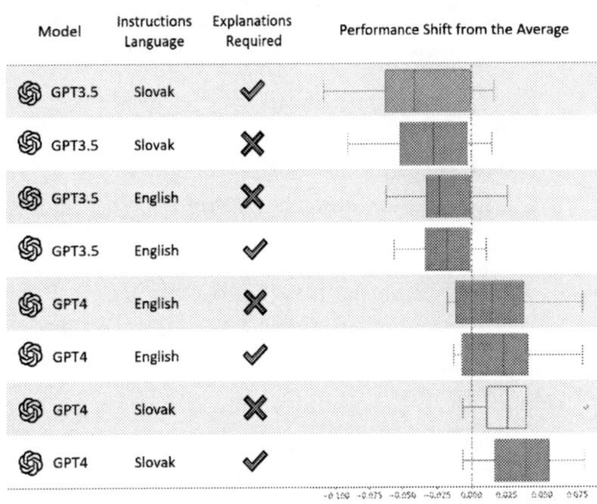


Figure 1: Prompting Strategy Grid Search: Slovak prompts exhibit the lowest effectiveness with `GPT-3.5` but secure the highest performance with `GPT-4`. Notably, incorporating explanations within prompts significantly enhances effectiveness across models. This boost is particularly pronounced for Slovak prompts used with `GPT-3.5` and English prompts with `GPT-4`. The red dashed line represents the 'zero shift' from the average performance, illustrating changes in F1 score relative to the average across all parameter combinations.

## 1 Introduction

The emergence of Large Language Models (LLMs) has not only revolutionized the field of natural language processing (NLP) (Min et al., 2023; Chang et al., 2023) but also significantly impacted social sciences (Teubner et al., 2023; Ziems et al., 2024). These models' ability to understand and generate human-like text has opened new avenues for analyzing complex social phenomena such as political discourse (Bornheim et al., 2023), public opinion (Lee et al., 2023), and media analysis (Jiang et al., 2023) with unprecedented precision.

This progress has set the stage for augmenting, or even substituting, human annotators in tasks demanding profound linguistic and semantic insights (Heseltine and Clemm von Hohenberg, 2024; Ollion et al., 2023; He et al., 2023). Our research explores the application of LLMs, coupled with sophisticated prompting strategies, to scrutinize Slovak news media content on migration, a topic with deep societal and political ramifications. The dataset, created for project MIMEDIS[1], seeks to unravel how media shapes public migration viewpoints, integrating computational and manual analysis. Our investigation pivots on employing LLMs for annotating social science materials in less commonly used languages, revealing that advanced prompting methods can position LLMs as viable alternatives or complements to traditional supervised fine-tuning. Our findings also suggest that non-English instructions could enhance LLM performance, as outlined in Figure 1. We hope that this study will help highlight the LLMs' potential as a helpful tool in annotating social science texts

[1]See https://cogsci.fmph.uniba.sk/MIMEDIS/index.html.



*Proceedings of the 58th Annual Meeting of the Association for Computational Linguistics*, pages 81–89
July 5–10, 2020. 

in lower resourced languages and instigate further development in this area.

## 2 Related Work

Large Language Models (LLMs) have garnered a significant amount of interest over the past few years, especially due to their unprecedented ability to generalize based just on zero-shot input, or from just a handful of examples, also known as few-shot learning. When combined with advanced prompting strategies such as Retrieval Augmented Generation (RAG) (Lewis et al., 2020) and Chain of Thought (CoT) prompting (Wei et al., 2022), this makes LLMs state-of-the-art methods for various NLP and text understanding tasks (Min et al., 2023).

Among other achievements, this has led to research that suggests that LLMs such as GPT-3.5-Turbo and GPT-4 can be adapted for annotation (He et al., 2023; Belal et al., 2023; Thapa et al., 2023) and in some cases even as a potential replacement for human annotation (Heseltine and Clemm von Hohenberg, 2024) as it was able to perform on-par or better than a human annotator (Gilardi et al., 2023). On the other hand, closer inspection by (Ollion et al., 2023) has found that "fewshot learners offer enticing, yet mixed results on text annotation tasks", suggesting that evidence for aforementioned claims is only partial at best.

Despite the partial evidence, LLMs still present an interesting option, particularly for languages which lack large-scale data resources and for which the cost of annotation is often significant due to the low number of native speakers and/or experts available, which is the case in our situation as well. Perhaps the most similar work to ours would be (Mets et al., 2023) in which the authors evaluate stance of sentences in Estonian news articles about immigration and compare the performance of supervised models with ChatGPT, finding that ChatGPT obtains similar performance. In contrast, in our work we explore a problem that can be viewed as multi-target and multi-class, we further consider the article-level as opposed to sentence-level stance, employ multiple LLMs (`GPT-3.5-Turbo` and `GPT-4`) and a number of advanced prompting strategies such as RAG and CoT prompting, which make our best performing LLMs capable of performing better than supervised models.

## 3 Dataset

To evaluate our models we utilize a specific Slovak dataset annotated for classification across various dimensions. The dataset aims to understand migration representation in Slovak media spanning from 2003 to 2022, targeting individual media outputs like articles and debate transcripts. We briefly outline the specific dimensions below.

**Thematic Relevance** Articles are classified based on relevance to human migration within the study period, marked as *strong*, *weak*, or *irrelevant*.

**Geographical Relevance** This categorization differentiates between articles *related to Slovakia* and those not.

**Migration Direction** It identifies if the migration is towards (*immigration*) or away from Slovakia (*emigration*).

**Stance** The media's stance toward migration is tagged as *positive*, *negative*, or *neutral* for the below listed targets: targeting migrants (*people*), facilitators of migration (*enablers*), and migration policies (*policies*). If a target is not mentioned in an article, annotators assign a label indicating the target is *not mentioned*.

As the scope of the Slovak media outputs between 2003 and 2020 is vast (we were able to obtain on the order of 800k items that contained migration-related keywords[2]), they were sampled in a stratified way on per-year basis. Each media output in the dataset was annotated by at least three different annotators via an Argilla[3] interface and only instances in which majority agreement was observed were included in the final dataset.

A visualization of the lengths of the media output contained in the respective subsets of the final dataset can be found in Figure 2.

As the majority of the media outputs in the final dataset are shorter, the truncation to 2,500 characters impacted 36%, 36% and 34% of the samples across the train, validation and test splits.

We conducted a similar analysis using the `gerulata/slovakbert` tokenizer[4] which is part of the SlovakBERT model.

The resulting distribution across the three splits can be seen in Figure 3. As the distribution in the figure suggests, the majority of media outputs

[2] See Table 2 for the list of the keywords.

[3] `https://argilla.io`

[4] `https://huggingface.co/gerulata/slovakbert`

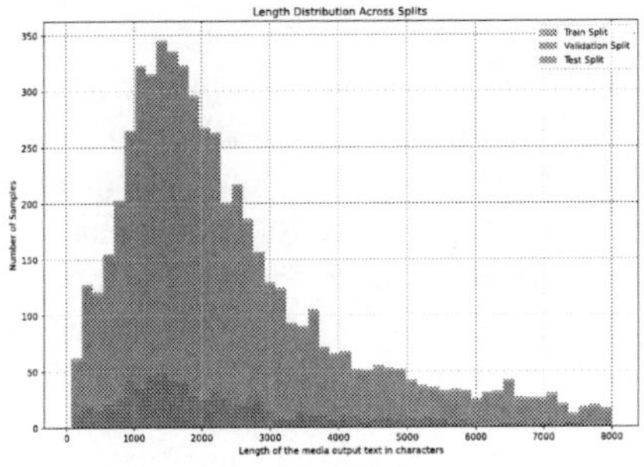


Figure 2: Character length distribution in the final dataset.

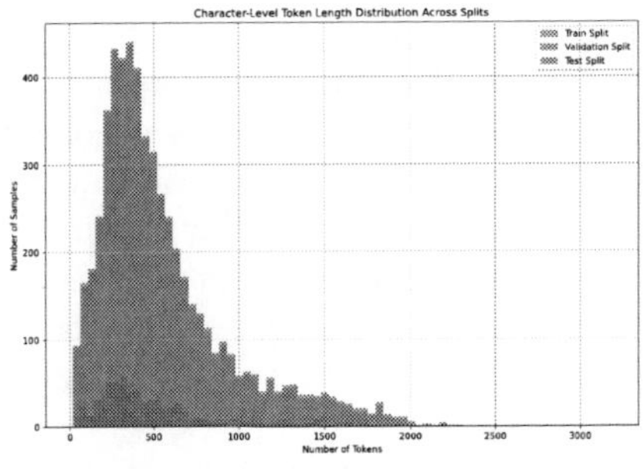


Figure 3: Token length distribution in the final dataset.

contained in the final dataset are shorter than 512 tokens. That being said, truncating the input to this token length impacted 41%, 40% and 40% of the samples in the train, validation and test set, respectively.

More information on dataset creation can be found in Section A.1.

The final dataset contains about 7.2k annotated articles, making it the largest Slovak classification dataset and the biggest in the realm of Political Social Science. More detailed statistics of the dataset can be found in Section A.2.

## 4 Methods

Our experimental methodology was informed by three key guidelines to ensure uniformity and comparability of results. To standardize input data, articles were cut to 2500 characters. This length not only aligns with the maximum input capacity of our baseline models but also helps in managing OpenAI credit usage efficiently.

The evaluation of annotations was carried out on the test split of the pre-annotated dataset. The experiments were structured with a single-task focus, i.e. there was a dedicated model for each task. Each model was tasked to predict a single label.

### 4.1 Grid search for prompting strategies

We initiated our experiments by evaluating different prompting strategies to identify critical hyperparameters, focusing on GPT-3.5 Turbo (specifically `gpt-3.5-turbo-0125`) and GPT-4 (`gpt-4-0125-preview`). Our analysis included examining the effect of prompting language on the process, particularly emphasizing that Slovak is considered troublesome in prompt engineering.[5] We compared the use of English and Slovak prompts, noting that prompts requiring detailed responses were more effective. This led to tests with and without such prompts.

### 4.2 Retrieval Augmented Generation

We incorporated Retrieval Augmented Generation (RAG) (Lewis and Oguz, 2020) into our experiments, leveraging its blend of retrieval-based and generative methods to augment prompts with relevant documents, thus improving response generation. SentenceBERT (Reimers and Gurevych, 2019) was used to embed data, aiding in the retrieval of the top-k (k=3 has been chosen based on preliminary tests and cost considerations) articles from the train set for model input. These articles, selected based on similarity in a vector database, were presented with the model prompts, details of which can be found in Appendix A.3. Our tests on `GPT-3.5` and `GPT-4` examined the effectiveness of various prompt languages and requiring explanations, in terms of the language used for prompts and the incorporation of explanation requests within the prompts.

### 4.3 Chain of Thoughts

Chain of Thought (CoT) prompting in Large Language Models (LLMs) is a strategic approach that prompts the model to reveal step-by-step reasoning before arriving at a conclusion, thereby improving the depth and logic of its outputs (Ma et al., 2023; Kojima et al., 2022). In our study, we embed CoT prompting within a dual-stage framework as discussed in Section 4.1. Initially, the prompt sets the stage with specific instructions, providing two annotated example articles and a system message highlighting the task's objective. Following this,

[5] See for instance `https://community.openai.com/t/slovak-language-not-working-well/579305`

the second stage of the prompt presents a system directive to choose an appropriate task label and includes a succinct request for the annotation of a given article. The detailed structure of this prompting strategy can be found in Appendix A.3.

### 4.4 Finetuned baselines

In order to provide a direct comparison with models within the standard supervised finetuning framework, we employ a selection of well established baselines relevant for the Slovak language: the mBERT model,[6] the multilingual version of BERT (Devlin et al., 2018), XLM-R,[7] (Conneau et al., 2019) a larger-scale pre-trained multilingual model based on the RoBERTa architecture and SlovakBERT,[8] (Pikuliak et al., 2021) a BERT-based model pretrained specifically on a large Slovak corpus and the current state-of-the-art model for many Slovak tasks. To provide uniformity across the evaluated models, we finetune all of them for five epochs using the AdamW optimizer and learning rate set at 2e-5. The models were provided the concatenation of the headline and the main text of the media output, and the inputs were further truncated at 512 tokens in order to conform to the requirements of BERT models.

## 5 Results

### 5.1 Baselines

As illustrated in Table 1, each baseline model surpassed the majority class baseline. Among them, the `slovakbert` models stood out, achieving the highest scores across most categories, with only a slight exception in `theme_relevance` where the difference was negligible and `target_people` where the difference was more pronounced.

### 5.2 Grid search for prompting strategies

The grid-search analysis showed performance differences across various setups. `GPT-3.5` performed best with English prompts, reaching a 70.22 F1 score, but slightly dropped to 69.44 when explanations were added. Conversely, `GPT-4` excelled with Slovak explanation prompts, achieving a 76.97 F1 score, a substantial rise from 75.21 with English prompts without explanations. This suggests that the explored task has a high language dependency and benefits from prompting in the language native to the input (Liu et al., 2024). Figure 1 elucidates the influence of various prompting parameters on the models' performance. Furthermore, Table 4 compiles the F1 scores for the different setups across all tasks within the dataset in a descending order, highlighting the relative advantages of specific configurations.

### 5.3 RAG and CoT experiment evaluations

The performance of `GPT-4 RAG` was notable in the collection of classification tasks, showing higher average accuracy. Its proficiency was especially prominent in geo-relevance prediction, where it outperformed other LLM experiments. Table 1 presents the top-performing configuration for each model. The success of `GPT-4 RAG` indicate the benefits of Retrieval Augmented Generation (RAG) in enhancing model capabilities, providing a significant enhancement compared to baseline models and underscoring the value of integrating external knowledge sources.

In a detailed comparison, `GPT-4 RAG` consistently surpassed `GPT-3.5 RAG`, with an impressive average F1 score difference of up to 6 F1 points. This underscores the advancements in `GPT-4`'s architecture and training compared to its predecessor. Interestingly, when employing the Chain of Thought (CoT) method, `GPT-3.5` achieved notable results in theme relevance and matched `GPT-4 RAG` in direction prediction accuracy, as indicated in the corresponding F1 scores.

However, the performance of `GPT-4 CoT` fell short of expectations, suggesting that the CoT method's performance might be task-dependent or influenced by specific model characteristics. This discrepancy invites further investigation into the CoT methodology's application in LLMs, potentially leading to innovative approaches like Retrieval Augmented Thoughts (Wang et al., 2024), which could merge the strengths of RAG and CoT for even more refined performance. This area represents a promising direction for future research, utilizing the synergy between different prompting strategies to enhance task-specific outcomes.

## 6 Discussion

The results in Table 1 show that RAG and CoT enhancements led `GPT-3.5` and `GPT-4` models to out-

[6] `bert-base-multilingual-cased`: https://huggingface.co/google-bert/bert-base-multilingual-cased

[7] `xlm-roberta-base`: https://huggingface.co/FacebookAI/xlm-roberta-base

[8] `slovakbert`: https://huggingface.co/gerulata/slovakbert

| model | theme_relevance | geo_relevance | direction | target_people | target_enablers | target_policies |
|---|---|---|---|---|---|---|
| majority class | 74.6898 | 62.3894 | 74.3386 | 36.6782 | 47.4637 | 30.6667 |
| bert-base-multilingual-cased | **79.9007** | 93.8053 | 78.8359 | 53.6332 | 47.8261 | 49.6667 |
| xlm-roberta-base | 78.1638 | **94.6903** | 80.9524 | **59.1696** | 50.0000 | 51.6667 |
| slovakbert | 79.1563 | 94.2477 | **82.8042** | 53.9792 | **52.1739** | **53.6666** |
| GPT-3.5 RAG | 85.4749 | 74.7967 | 90.9496 | 63.1090 | 47.1545 | 59.3968 |
| GPT-3.5 CoT | **85.6346** | 54.7170 | **93.1686** | 63.1090 | 45.9016 | 57.0755 |
| GPT-4 RAG | 83.5227 | **96.7598** | **93.1686** | **69.7572** | **48.3871** | **65.3333** |

Table 1: Micro F1 scores for various models and model types on the test set. As per the parameter search, GPT models were prompted in Slovak. The best performance is in bold.

perform finetuned baselines by up to 11 F1 points in most categories, except for `target_enablers`. However, some categories had low absolute F1 scores, the lowest being 48.3871. Analysis of RAG models in Figure 4 indicated a preference for "No Target" over "Positive" or "Negative" labels, suggesting these models aren't ready to replace human annotators in complex political topics like migration, yet. Although, a manual review of the models' explanations by one of the authors found them mostly logical, hinting at potential issues in the annotation guidelines or process rather than the models' capabilities. This is also reflected in the Inter-Annotator Agreement in Table 3, measured by Krippendorff's alpha (Castro, 2017), which indicated a relatively low agreement for many tasks.

In summary, while LLMs with advanced prompting have progressed, we do not yet find them to be viable replacements for human annotators in text annotation in the realm of Computational Social Science. They are, however, valuable for highlighting problems in annotation guidelines and datasets, effectively serving as an additional, or as the paper's title suggests, $n$-th, annotator. We leave further exploration of this concept as well as its potential implication to future work.

## 7 Conclusion

This study evaluates the performance of LLMs in automating stance classification tasks within a Slovak news media dataset, emphasizing the impact of advanced prompting strategies and native language instructions. The results indicate that while large language models (LLMs), particularly GPT-4, significantly outperform BERT-based baseline models, they still lack the ability to fully replace human annotators in complex tasks such as stance classification in political texts under the conditions of our experiments. However, their ability to uncover inconsistencies in annotation guidelines and datasets highlights their potential as valuable tools in social science research. The findings from this study have enabled the MIMEDIS project team to refine the annotation manual and to distinguish between inherently difficult tasks and those that are simply underdefined. Just like if chatGPT was our $n$-th expert annotator.

## Limitations

- As our analysis has been done on a dataset in Slovak language, its conclusions might not be directly applicable to other languages.
- The analysis has been done using models which are accessed via paid APIs and might hence not be widely accessible.
- While article-level annotation and single-label classification were chosen to align with the goals of our project, we acknowledge that these choices may not suit all potential tasks, such as mention detection or cases involving multiple overlapping themes. Lower-level annotations would significantly increase the complexity and duration of the annotation process, making it impractical for our purposes. Additionally, we recognize that the lower IAA agreement observed for certain tasks may partially stem from these choices.
- We recognize the potential inconsistency in our methodology, where annotators had access to the full article text, while models like the LLM and transformer encoders processed only truncated versions (up to 2,500 chars or 512 tokens, respectively). This discrepancy could contribute to differences in performance and agreement.

## Acknowledgments

We thank the 100 annotators who were instrumental in creating the dataset central to this work. This project was supported by grant APVV-21-0114.

## References


Mohammad Belal, James She, and Simon Wong. 2023. Leveraging chatgpt as text annotation tool for sentiment analysis. *arXiv preprint arXiv:2306.17177*.

Tobias Bornheim, Niklas Grieger, Patrick Gustav Blaneck, and Stephan Bialonski. 2023. Speaker attribution in german parliamentary debates with qlora-adapted large language models. *ArXiv*, abs/2309.09902.

Santiago Castro. 2017. Fast Krippendorff: Fast computation of Krippendorff's alpha agreement measure. `https://github.com/pln-fing-udelar/fast-krippendorff`.

Yupeng Chang, Xu Wang, Jindong Wang, Yuan Wu, Linyi Yang, Kaijie Zhu, Hao Chen, Xiaoyuan Yi, Cunxiang Wang, Yidong Wang, et al. 2023. A survey on evaluation of large language models. *ACM Transactions on Intelligent Systems and Technology*.

Alexis Conneau, Kartikay Khandelwal, Naman Goyal, Vishrav Chaudhary, Guillaume Wenzek, Francisco Guzmán, Edouard Grave, Myle Ott, Luke Zettlemoyer, and Veselin Stoyanov. 2019. Unsupervised cross-lingual representation learning at scale. *CoRR*, abs/1911.02116.

Jacob Devlin, Ming-Wei Chang, Kenton Lee, and Kristina Toutanova. 2018. BERT: pre-training of deep bidirectional transformers for language understanding. *CoRR*, abs/1810.04805.

Fabrizio Gilardi, Meysam Alizadeh, and Maël Kubli. 2023. Chatgpt outperforms crowd workers for text-annotation tasks. *Proceedings of the National Academy of Sciences*, 120(30):e2305016120.

Xingwei He, Zhenghao Lin, Yeyun Gong, Alex Jin, Hang Zhang, Chen Lin, Jian Jiao, Siu Ming Yiu, Nan Duan, Weizhu Chen, et al. 2023. Annollm: Making large language models to be better crowdsourced annotators. *arXiv preprint arXiv:2303.16854*.

Michael Heseltine and Bernhard Clemm von Hohenberg. 2024. Large language models as a substitute for human experts in annotating political text. *Research & Politics*, 11(1):20531680241236239.

Yan Jiang, Ruihong Qiu, Yi Zhang, and P. Zhang. 2023. Balanced and explainable social media analysis for public health with large language models. In *Australasian Database Conference*.

Daiki Kojima, Sho Oura, Yusuke Iwasawa, and Yutaka Matsuo. 2022. Large language models are zero-shot reasoners. *arXiv preprint arXiv:2205.11916*.

S. Lee, T. Q. Peng, M. H. Goldberg, S. A. Rosenthal, John E. Kotcher, Edward W Maibach, and Anthony Leiserowitz. 2023. Can large language models capture public opinion about global warming? an empirical assessment of algorithmic fidelity and bias. *ArXiv*, abs/2311.00217.

Patrick Lewis and Sergey Edunov Danqi Chen Mandar Joshi Mike Lewis Luke Zettlemoyer Veselin Stoyanov Oguz, Bhuwan Dhingra. 2020. Retrieval-augmented generation for knowledge-intensive nlp tasks. *arXiv preprint arXiv:2005.11401*.

Patrick Lewis, Ethan Perez, Aleksandara Piktus, Fabio Petroni, Vladimir Karpukhin, Naman Goyal, Heinrich Kuttler, Mike Lewis, Wen tau Yih, Tim Rocktäschel, Sebastian Riedel, and Douwe Kiela. 2020. Retrieval-augmented generation for knowledge-intensive nlp tasks. *ArXiv*, abs/2005.11401.

Chaoqun Liu, Wenxuan Zhang, Yiran Zhao, Anh Tuan Luu, and Lidong Bing. 2024. Is translation all you need? a study on solving multilingual tasks with large language models. *arXiv preprint arXiv:2403.10258*.

Xilai Ma, Jing Li, and Min Zhang. 2023. Chain of thought with explicit evidence reasoning for few-shot relation extraction. In *Findings of the Association for Computational Linguistics: EMNLP 2023*, pages 2334–2352, Singapore. Association for Computational Linguistics.

Marko Mets, Andres Karjus, Indrek Ibrus, and Maximilian Schich. 2023. Automated stance detection in complex topics and small languages: the challenging case of immigration in polarizing news media. *ArXiv*, abs/2305.13047.

Bonan Min, Hayley Ross, Elior Sulem, Amir Pouran Ben Veyseh, Thien Huu Nguyen, Oscar Sainz, Eneko Agirre, Ilana Heintz, and Dan Roth. 2023. Recent advances in natural language processing via large pre-trained language models: A survey. *ACM Computing Surveys*, 56(2):1–40.

Etienne Ollion, Rubing Shen, Ana Macanovic, and Arnault Chatelain. 2023. Chatgpt for text annotation? mind the hype! *SocArXiv. October*, 4.

Matú Pikuliak, Stefan Grivalsky, Martin Konopka, Miroslav Blták, Martin Tamajka, Viktor Bachrat'y, Marián Simko, Pavol Balázik, Michal Trnka, and Filip Uhl'arik. 2021. Slovakbert: Slovak masked language model. *ArXiv*, abs/2109.15254.

Nils Reimers and Iryna Gurevych. 2019. Sentence-bert: Sentence embeddings using siamese bert-networks. *arXiv preprint arXiv:1908.10084*.

Timm Teubner, Christoph M Flath, Christof Weinhardt, Wil van der Aalst, and Oliver Hinz. 2023. Welcome to the era of chatgpt et al. the prospects of large language models. *Business & Information Systems Engineering*, 65(2):95–101.

Surendrabikram Thapa, Usman Naseem, and Mehwish Nasim. 2023. From humans to machines: can chatgpt-like llms effectively replace human annotators in nlp tasks. In *Workshop Proceedings of the 17th International AAAI Conference on Web and Social Media*.

Zihao Wang, Anji Liu, Haowei Lin, Jiaqi Li, Xiaojian Ma, and Yitao Liang. 2024. Rat: Retrieval augmented thoughts elicit context-aware reasoning in long-horizon generation. *arXiv preprint arXiv:2403.05313*.

Jason Wei, Xuezhi Wang, Dale Schuurmans, Maarten Bosma, Ed Huai hsin Chi, F. Xia, Quoc Le, and Denny Zhou. 2022. Chain of thought prompting elicits reasoning in large language models. *ArXiv*, abs/2201.11903.

Caleb Ziems, William Held, Omar Shaikh, Jiaao Chen, Zhehao Zhang, and Diyi Yang. 2024. Can large language models transform computational social science? *Computational Linguistics*, pages 1–55.

# A Appendix

## A.1 Dataset creation

In order to arrive at a dataset representative of the migration-related discourse in Slovak media, a multi-step approach was applied.

First, an export of all Slovak media outputs that contained at least one of the migration-related keywords in one of their possible lexical forms. The full list of lemmas can be found in Table 2. This process has yielded 802,503 media outputs in total.

Second, the media outputs were filtered for length, where only those with the length of less than 8,000 characters (on the order of 1,000 words) as these were found to be long listings of for instance the TV programme for a specific day or listings of news agency output for a specific day, which would not materially contribute to the aim of our analysis. This process has filtered out 78,763 media outputs, representing 9.82% in total.

Finally, the export was sampled on per-year basis in a stratified in order for smaller batches of media output to be supplied to the annotators. This was done primarily to ensure the distribution of migration-related media outputs in the final dataset across the years is as close as possible to that of the aforementioned export, which is thought to be derived from all of the media output produced in Slovak between 2003 and 2020.

## A.2 Dataset statistics

The Table 5 describes the distribution of samples across the various configurations which are based on the categories discussed in Section 3.

| Slovak Lemma | English Translation |
|---|---|
| migrant | migrant |
| migrantka | female migrant |
| imigrant | immigrant |
| imigrantka | female immigrant |
| emigrant | emigrant |
| emigrantka | female emigrant |
| utečenec | refugee |
| utečenka | female refugee |
| utečenkyňa | female refugee (alternative form) |
| odídenec | displaced person |
| odídenka | displaced female |
| odídenkyňa | displaced female (alternative form) |
| azylant | asylum seeker |
| azylantka | female asylum seeker |
| cudzinec | foreigner |
| cudzinka | female foreigner |
| expat | expat |
| expatka | female expat |
| expatriant | expatriate |
| expatriantka | female expatriate |
| vysťahovalec | emigrant |
| vysťahovalkyňa | female emigrant |
| vyhnanec | exile |
| vyhnankyňa | female exile |
| exulant | exile |
| exulantka | female exile |
| vysťahovalectvo | emigration |
| azyl | asylum |
| migrácia | migration |
| imigrácia | immigration |
| emigrácia | emigration |
| migračný | migration-related |
| migrantský | migrant-related |
| imigrantský | immigrant-related |
| emigrantský | emigrant-related |
| utečenecký | refugee-related |
| odídenecký | displaced-related |
| cudzinecký | foreigner-related |
| vysťahovalecký | emigrant-related |
| migrantov | migrants (plural) |
| migrantkin | female migrants (plural) |
| utečencov | refugees (plural) |
| utečenkin | female refugees (plural) |
| imigrantov | immigrants (plural) |
| imigrantkin | female immigrants (plural) |
| odídencov | displaced persons (plural) |
| odídenkin | displaced females (plural) |
| emigrovať | to emigrate |
| imigrovať | to immigrate |
| migrovať | to migrate |

Table 2: The terms used to search for Slovak migration-related news outputs and their English translations

### A.3 Prompting strategy

**CoT Prompt structure**

`sys message1:`
*Try to think about why the given annotations might be correct*

`human message1:`
**Extract from the Annotation manual, including 2 annotated examples**

`response1:`
*The Annotations are correct...*

`sys message2:`
*You are an expert Slovak annotator. Your answers should ONLY contain ONE of the following labels:*
**labels**

`human message2:`
*'These are just a few examples. Please annotate the text below following the scheme of the examples provided above:*
**Article to be annotated**

`response2:`
**Annotations**

**RAG Prompt structure**

`sys message:`
*You are an expert Slovak annotator. Your answers should ONLY contain ONE of the following labels:*
**labels**

`human message:`
*First, I will give you some annotated examples:*
**##Annotated examples from the vector db of train and valid sets##**

*'These are just a few examples. Please annotate the text below following the scheme of the examples provided above:*
**Article to be annotated**

`response:`
**Annotations**

### A.4 Inter Annotator Agreement

| Task | Krippendorff's alpha |
|---|---|
| theme_relevance | 0.3258 |
| geo_relevance | 0.7375 |
| direction | 0.3627 |
| target_people | 0.1754 |
| target_enablers | 0.1167 |
| target_policies | 0.1958 |

Table 3: Inter Annotator Agreement between the human annotators represented as Krippendorff's alpha.

### A.5 Grid search results

| Parameters | | | Average F1 Score |
|---|---|---|---|
| model_name | sk_prompts | explanations | |
| GPT-4 | True | True | 76.9660 |
| GPT-4 | True | False | 76.2066 |
| GPT-4 | False | True | 75.6418 |
| GPT-4 | False | False | 75.2091 |
| GPT-3.5 | False | False | 71.4464 |
| GPT-3.5 | False | True | 71.3757 |
| GPT-3.5 | True | False | 70.2208 |
| GPT-3.5 | True | True | 69.4447 |

Table 4: Average F1 Scores for different prompting strategies (grid search results).

| Configuration | Train | Validation | Test |
|---|---|---|---|
| default | 5828 | 728 | 729 |
| theme_relevance | 3316 | 413 | 403 |
| geo_relevance | 3727 | 455 | 452 |
| direction | 3097 | 395 | 378 |
| target_people | 2394 | 296 | 289 |
| target_enablers | 2317 | 275 | 276 |
| target_policies | 2423 | 290 | 300 |

Table 5: Dataset statistics across various subsets

### A.6 Confusion Matrices

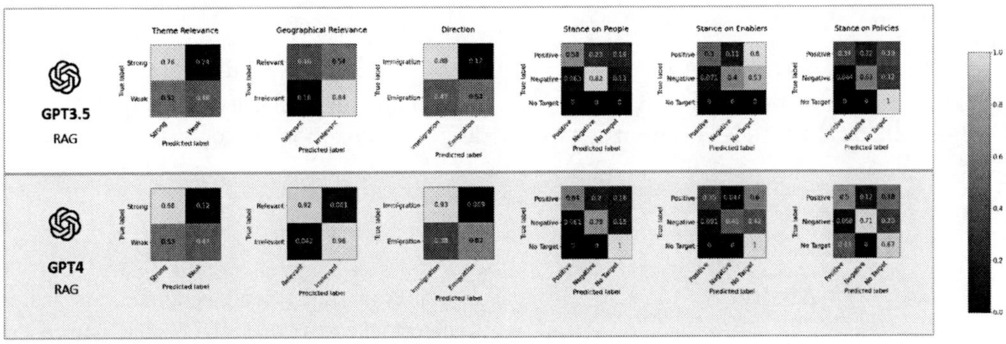

Figure 4: Confusion Matrices for `GPT-3.5 RAG` and `GPT-4 RAG`

# Detecting emotional polarity in Finnish parliamentary proceedings

**Suvi Lehtosalo***
University of Tübingen
suvi.lehtosalo@student.uni-tuebingen.de

**John Nerbonne**
Groningen, Freiburg & Tübingen
j.nerbonne@rug.nl

## Abstract

Few studies have focused on detecting emotion in parliamentary corpora, and none have done this for the Finnish parliament. In this paper, this gap is addressed by applying the polarity lexicon–based methodology of a study by Rheault et al. (2016) on speeches in the British Parliament to a Finnish corpus. The findings show an increase in positive sentiment over time. Additionally, the findings indicate that politicians' emotional states may be impacted by the state of the economy and other major events, such as the Covid-19 pandemic and the Russian invasion of Ukraine.

## 1 Introduction

### 1.1 Goal

The goal of this paper is to apply the methodology used by Rheault et al. (2016) on British parliamentary speeches to a Finnish dataset, in order to determine whether the findings – increase in emotional polarity over time and correlation with the state of the economy – can be replicated with a different corpus in another language. Additionally, comparison to other major events, namely the Covid-19 pandemic and the Russian invasion of Ukraine, is drawn in order to investigate which other topics may impact emotional polarity.

### 1.2 Background

This study is a contribution to the field of *affective computing*, that is, the detection of emotion in human language and expression. Recent studies in this field have examined various topics, such as the applications of emotion detection in medicine (Saffar et al., 2023), and using emotion analysis to detect fake news on social media (Hamed et al., 2023; Luvembe et al., 2023).

Rheault et al. (2016) performed a study detecting emotion in British parliamentary proceedings, and found an increase in polarity over time, as well as a correlation between the state of the economy and polarity. Since then, other works have addressed detecting anxiety (Rheault, 2016) and general emotionality (Gennaro and Ash, 2022) in parliamentary proceedings. A systematic analysis performed by Abercrombie and Batista-Navarro (2020) summarises efforts in the area of detecting sentiment or opinion in parliamentary debates. Detecting emotion is rarely done in isolation; most studies have focused on tasks such as detecting agreement/disagreement, vote prediction, and ideology detection. The use of a polarity lexicon is one of the common methods, the other most common method being the use of statistical machine learning.

A few studies have been performed involving automated analysis of Finnish parliamentary proceedings. These include the use of semantic tagging to detect discussions of Everyman's Rights (Kettunen and La Mela, 2022), and identifying topics in parliamentary speech using a Machine Learning approach (Ristilä and Elo, 2023). No previous studies could be found that focus on detecting emotion or use a polarity lexicon–based approach.

In addition to detecting emotion, this study aims to uncover some of the factors affecting emotionality in parliament. The impact of the economy on happiness is well-studied (Frey and Stutzer, 2000; Oswald, 1997), and a correlation between state of the economy and emotion in parliament was already found by Rheault et al. (2016). In recent years, the outbreak of war in Ukraine, as well as the Covid-19 pandemic have had a profound effect on peoples' lives, with the mental and emotional impact of the latter having been widely studied

*SL took part in a course "Digital Humanities from a Computational Linguistics perspective" taught by JN. SL presented the paper by Rheault et al. (2016) there and suggested trying a similar technique on the Finnish parliamentary protocols. SL found data for this, suitable prior work for detecting sentiment in Finnish and wrote the first version of the paper. JN supervised the work but finds that he added only a little.



*Proceedings of the 58th Annual Meeting of the Association for Computational Linguistics*, pages 90–100
July 5–10, 2020. ©2020 Association for Computational Linguistics

(Boden et al., 2021; Talevi et al., 2020; Terry et al., 2020). In this study the correlation between these major events and emotion in parliament is studied, in addition to the correlation with the economy.

## 2 Method

### 2.1 Data and preprocessing

The parliamentary proceedings were acquired from the ParliamentSampo project, which has compiled all speeches in the Parliament of Finland from 1907 onwards (Hyvönen et al., 2024). As this study focuses solely on Finnish, all Swedish-language speeches were removed; after this, the dataset consisted of 168 million tokens. The corpus was lemmatised and Part of Speech–tagged using the *libvoikko* Python library (Voikko, n.d.). All proper nouns and digits were removed. As the word *arvoisa*, meaning *honourable*, is frequently used to address the Speaker or Members in expressions such as "Honourable Speaker", it was also removed from the corpus.

The economic data was obtained from Statistics Finland (Statistics Finland, 2024a,b,c,d). As their economic measures, Rheault et al. (2016) used GDP growth, unemployment rate, the misery index and a measure of labour disputes. The same measures were used here, but as the unemployment rate and misery index data were only available from 2010 onwards, two additional economic measures were added: growth in the Cost of Living Index (CLI) and the Consumer Price Index (CPI). The economic measures used are shown in Table 3 in Appendix A.

The Covid-19 incidence data was obtained from the Finnish National Infectious Diseases Register (Finnish Institute for Health and Welfare, 2024). The dataset includes country-wide data on Covid testing and the number of cases. A measure was calculated from these data by dividing the number of cases by the number of tests done, in order to approximate the proportion of positive test results.

### 2.2 Detecting emotion

Emotion detection was performed using a polarity lexicon–based approach. As existing Finnish polarity lexicons are not specifically tailored for political data, a new lexicon was constructed based on the parliamentary corpus. This involved generating word embeddings and selecting positive and negative seed lemmas, and then using these to calculate polarity scores to create the lexicon. This lexicon could then be used to calculate polarity scores for time periods of arbitrary length.

The word embeddings were generated from the corpus using the GloVe algorithm (Pennington et al., 2014), also used by Rheault et al. (2016). GloVe embeddings were employed to maintain consistency with the original work; additionally, they appear to perform well in comparison with other context-independent word embedding methods, as shown in works such as Toshevska et al. (2020) which compared multiple word embedding methods with human similarity judgements, and Jain et al. (2021), which compared multiple word embedding methods for hate speech detection.

Words with fewer than 50 occurrences were removed to eliminate typos and rare words. A list of seed lemmas with 100 positive and 100 negative lemmas was compiled, filtering out words relating to political topics such as war and disease. Further details on embedding generation and seed lemma selection are available in Appendix A.

**Calculation of word polarities** Word polarities were calculated based on cosine similarity, as done by Rheault et al. (2016):

$$s_i = \sum_{p=1}^{P} \cos(\mathbf{v}_i, \mathbf{v}_p) - \sum_{q=1}^{Q} \cos(\mathbf{v}_i, \mathbf{v}_q) \quad (1)$$

where $s_i$ is the score for lemma $i$, positive seed lemmas are indexed by $p$ and negative seed lemmas by $q$, and $\cos(\mathbf{v}_i, \mathbf{v}_p)$ represents the cosine of the angle between vectors $\mathbf{v}_i$ and $\mathbf{v}_p$.

After calculating the scores, the 2000 lemmas with the highest scores and the 2000 lemmas with the lowest scores were added to the polarity lexicon, making the size of the lexicon 4200, including the original seed lemmas.

**Calculation of polarity in a time period** For calculating the polarity in a time period, the equation by (Rheault et al., 2016) was used:

$$y_t = \frac{\sum_{i=1}^{n_i} \mathbf{1}\{w_{it} \in L\} s_i \theta_{it}}{\sum_{i=1}^{n_i} \mathbf{1}\{w_{it} \in L\}} \quad (2)$$

Here, $\mathbf{1}\{w_{it} \in L\}$ is a filter, returning 1 when the word $w_{it}$ is included in the polarity lexicon, and 0 otherwise; $s_i$ is the word score retrieved from the polarity lexicon. $\theta_{it}$ is another filter, which is intended to eliminate negated words. This is to avoid, for example, evaluating phrases like *not happy* as positive or *not angry* as negative. The filtering is

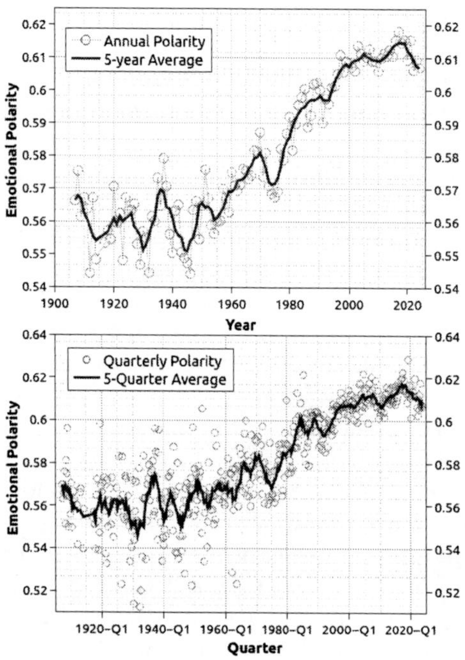


Figure 1: Emotional polarities calculated for each year and each quarter, showing both the original data points and 5-point rolling averages.

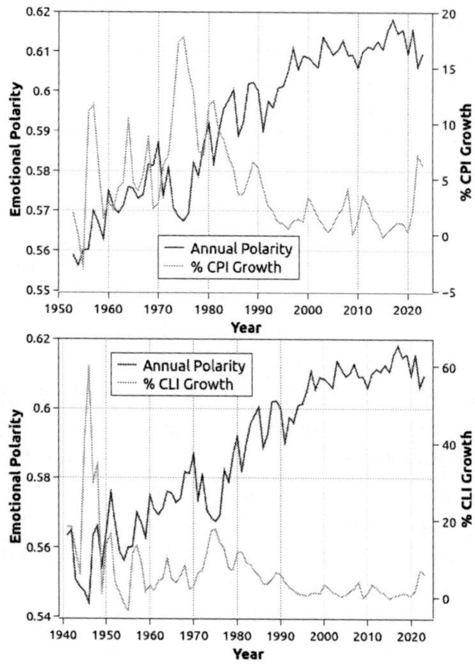


Figure 2: Change in Consumer Price Index and Cost of Living Index plotted against emotional polarity.

performed by checking whether the word $w_{it}$ is located between a negation word and a punctuation mark.

## 3 Results

### 3.1 Emotion in the Finnish parliament

The annual and quarterly emotional polarities are shown in Figure 1. The sentiments become increasingly positive over time, mirroring the similar findings by Rheault et al. (2016). This clear rise can be seen from the late 1940s to the late 2010s. More variation in the polarities can be seen before the 1960s. Overall, the polarities fall in a range [0.54,0.62], with the possible range being [-1.0,1.0]. As the focus is change in polarity over time, the specific values do not matter, but this shows that words with negative polarities were much less common in the corpus than positive words.

### 3.2 Comparison with economic data

The different economic measures were plotted against emotional polarity to examine potential correlations. Figure 2 shows the plots for CPI and CLI growth, which showed the clearest visual correlation. Both measures show a peak in the 1970s, which coincides with more negative sentiments. CLI growth also shows a similar phenomenon in the 1940s. Both graphs show a decrease in growth from the 1980s to the late 2010s, which is reflected as an increase in positive sentiments. These graphs seem to strongly suggest a relationship between emotional polarity and measures of inflation. Plotting the misery index also showed potential correlation, though not as clearly (see Figure 3).

In order to further investigate the findings from plotting the data, pairwise Granger causality tests were performed on each of the economic measures and emotional polarity. Bonferroni correction (Dunn, 1961) was applied to the *p*-values to address the multiple comparisons problem. The resulting *p*-values can be seen in Table 4 (see Appendix A). Before correction, the *p*-values for CLI growth and emotional polarity and CPI growth and emotional polarity fall below the threshold of 0.05, supporting a possible relationship; after correction, only CLI growth is below this threshold at 0.034. The *p*-value of the Misery Index–Polarity relationship is well above this threshold, indicating no relationship.

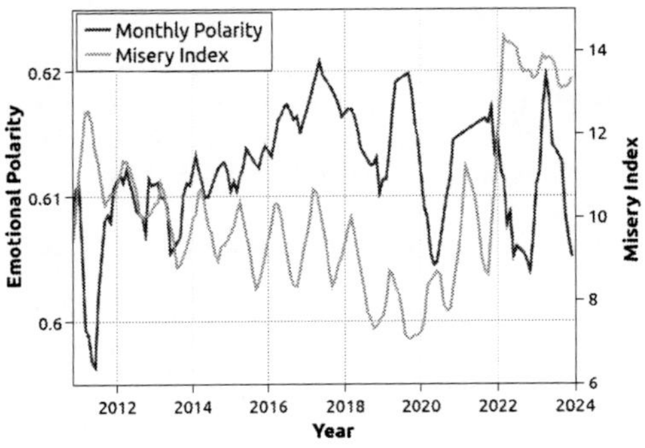


Figure 3: 4-month rolling averages of the misery index and emotional polarity.

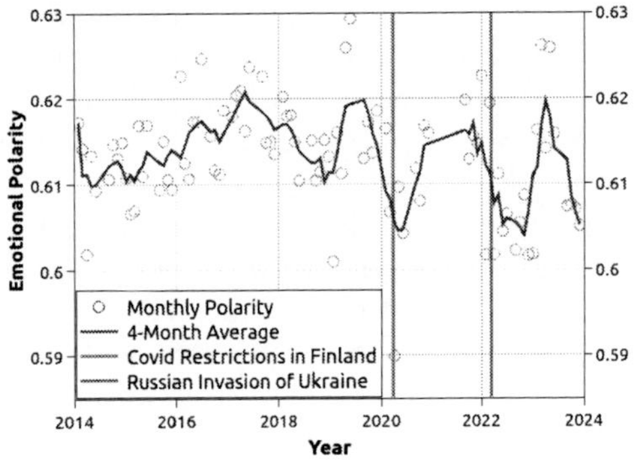


Figure 4: Emotional polarity and recent events.

### 3.3 Comparison with recent events

Another topic of investigation was the impact of recent major events on emotional polarity. The two events chosen for this were the Covid-19 pandemic and the Russian invasion of Ukraine.

Figure 4 shows monthly polarities in the last decade, as well as vertical lines indicating the significant dates. The first date is the first implementation of Covid-19 restrictions in Finland, the 17th of March 2020. This specific date was chosen (as opposed to other dates, such as the first incidence of Covid-19 in Finland), as it shows when Covid-19 was first seen as a national emergency in Finland. The second date shown is the start of the ongoing Russian invasion of Ukraine, the 24th of February 2022. Both dates coincide with periods of significant negativity in the parliament, suggesting a possible correlation.

As statistical data is easily available for Covid-19, the correlation between Covid-19 and emotional polarity was further investigated with statistical testing. Granger causality testing performed on the measure of positive test rates resulted in a Bonferroni-corrected $p$-value of 0.029 (see Table 4 in Appendix A), supporting the possibility of a correlation.

## 4 Discussion

**Interpretation of results** An overall rise in emotional polarity was seen from the mid-20th century to the 2010s. This mirrors the findings by Rheault et al. (2016), showing that this may be a universal phenomenon rather than specific to the British parliament.

A correlation was found between measures of inflation and emotional polarity. This also aligns with the findings by Rheault et al. (2016), although the specific measures used were different; a correlation could not be shown using labour disputes or the misery index as the economic measures, and after Bonferroni correction only one economic measure showed a statistically significant relationship to emotional polarity. As the findings are dependent on the specific measures used, it is difficult to assert a general relationship between economy and emotional polarity.

A possible correlation was seen between emotional polarity and the Covid-19 pandemic and the Russian invasion of Ukraine, although the latter was assessed only visually due to scarcity of statistical data. It is difficult to assess whether these correlations may simply be caused by the words associated with these events being labelled as negative. While the seed lemma selection attempted to avoid this effect by filtering out any related lemmas, it cannot be guaranteed that this was entirely effective.

**Limitations** Rheault et al. (2016) evaluated their approach using an IMDB film review dataset; as the approach here closely follows theirs, no new evaluation was performed. It is, however, possible that some minor differences in the approaches (or differences between the languages) could have caused a difference in performance, so a new evaluation could be useful. For example, the FinnSentiment social media corpus (Lindén et al., 2020) could be used for this, although the casual and contemporary nature of the language used on social media makes it less applicable to parliamentary speech. Additionally, as the evaluation performed by Rheault et al. (2016) also used a contemporary film review dataset, the approach of using a single polarity lexicon to measure emotion over many decades has not been validated. In practice, this kind of validation would be difficult to perform, due to a lack of labelled data spanning a long period of time.

A more careful approach to generating the polarity lexicon may be beneficial. While the initial list of seed lemmas was filtered to remove words related to politics or other words that could skew the results, the other 4000 lemmas in the polarity lexicon were selected solely based on the calculated similarity to the seed lemmas, with no further filtering. Searching the lexicon for words relating to topics such as disease or war and filtering these out could help avoid skew, though performing a thorough search would be quite labour-intensive.

## 5 Conclusion

The results broadly align with those shown by Rheault et al. (2016), with an increase in positive sentiment over time, and correlation between polarity and certain economic measures. However, this correlation could only be seen with certain measures, and the measures involved were slightly different between this study and Rheault et al. Links between labour disputes and polarity and the misery index and polarity could not be demonstrated. Further investigation into the topic is needed in order to conclusively determine whether economic measures impact the emotion shown in parliamentary speech. One future avenue of research that would likely prove fruitful is sentiment analysis through a Machine Learning approach, as this can achieve a higher accuracy compared to polarity lexicon–based methods, although at the expense of interpretability (Hartmann et al., 2023). Additionally, utilising contextual word embedding methods such as ELMo (Peters et al., 2018) or BERT (Devlin et al., 2019) would be worthwhile, as these may perform better compared to older word embedding methods such as GloVe (Jain et al., 2021).

Some correlation was also seen between the other studied events and emotional polarity. Further evaluation could determine whether this can be explained by words related to these events being evaluated as negative, or whether discussions unrelated to these topics also show a lowered polarity. Future study could classify speeches by topic, a task which has already been performed with Finnish parliamentary data (Ristilä and Elo, 2023), and eliminate speeches related to the events in question, in order to only focus on the unrelated speeches.

## References


Gavin Abercrombie and Riza Batista-Navarro. 2020. Sentiment and position-taking analysis of parliamentary debates: a systematic literature review. *Journal of Computational Social Science*, 3(1):245–270.

Matt Boden, Lindsey Zimmerman, Kathryn J. Azevedo, Josef I. Ruzek, Sasha Gala, Hoda S. Abdel Magid, Nichole Cohen, Robyn Walser, Naina D. Mahtani, Katherine J. Hoggatt, and Carmen P. McLean. 2021. Addressing the mental health impact of COVID-19 through population health. *Clinical Psychology Review*, 85:102006.

CSC - IT Center for Science. 2004. Frequency Lexicon of the Finnish Newspaper Language.

Jacob Devlin, Ming-Wei Chang, Kenton Lee, and Kristina Toutanova. 2019. BERT: Pre-training of Deep Bidirectional Transformers for Language Understanding. *arXiv preprint*. ArXiv:1810.04805 [cs].

Olive Jean Dunn. 1961. Multiple comparisons among means. *Journal of the American statistical association*, 56(293):52–64.

Finnish Institute for Health and Welfare. 2024. Covid-19 cases in the infectious diseases registry. https://sampo.thl.fi/pivot/prod/en/epirapo/covid19case/summary_tshcddaily.

Bruno S Frey and Alois Stutzer. 2000. Happiness, economy and institutions. *The economic journal*, 110(466):918–938.

Gloria Gennaro and Elliott Ash. 2022. Emotion and Reason in Political Language. *The Economic Journal*, 132(643):1037–1059.

Suhaib Kh Hamed, Mohd Juzaiddin Ab Aziz, and Mohd Ridzwan Yaakub. 2023. Fake news detection model on social media by leveraging sentiment analysis of news content and emotion analysis of users' comments. *Sensors*, 23(4):1748.

Jochen Hartmann, Mark Heitmann, Christian Siebert, and Christina Schamp. 2023. More than a Feeling: Accuracy and Application of Sentiment Analysis. *International Journal of Research in Marketing*, 40(1):75–87.

Eero Hyvönen, Laura Sinikallio, Petri Leskinen, Senka Drobac, Rafael Leal, Matti La Mela, Jouni Tuominen, Henna Poikkimäki, and Heikki Rantala. 2024. Publishing and Using Parliamentary Linked Data on the Semantic Web: ParliamentSampo System for Parliament of Finland. In *Semantic Web*.

Minni Jain, Puneet Goel, Puneet Singla, and Rahul Tehlan. 2021. Comparison of various word embeddings for hate-speech detection. In *Data Analytics and Management: Proceedings of ICDAM*, pages 251–265. Springer.

Kimmo Kettunen and Matti La Mela. 2022. Semantic tagging and the Nordic tradition of everyman's rights. *Digital Scholarship in the Humanities*, 37(2):483–496.

Krister Lindén, Tommi Jauhiainen, and Sam Hardwick. 2020. FinnSentiment – a Finnish Social Media Corpus for Sentiment Polarity Annotation.

Alex Munyole Luvembe, Weimin Li, Shaohua Li, Fangfang Liu, and Guiqiong Xu. 2023. Dual emotion based fake news detection: A deep attention-weight update approach. *Information Processing Management*, 60(4):103354.

Andrew J Oswald. 1997. Happiness and economic performance. *The economic journal*, 107(445):1815–1831.

Jeffrey Pennington, Richard Socher, and Christopher D. Manning. 2014. Glove: Global vectors for word representation. In *Empirical Methods in Natural Language Processing (EMNLP)*, pages 1532–1543.

Matthew E. Peters, Mark Neumann, Mohit Iyyer, Matt Gardner, Christopher Clark, Kenton Lee, and Luke Zettlemoyer. 2018. Deep contextualized word representations. *arXiv preprint*. ArXiv:1802.05365 [cs].

Ludovic Rheault. 2016. Expressions of Anxiety in Political Texts. In *Proceedings of the First Workshop on NLP and Computational Social Science*, pages 92–101, Austin, Texas. Association for Computational Linguistics.

Ludovic Rheault, Kaspar Beelen, Christopher Cochrane, and Graeme Hirst. 2016. Measuring Emotion in Parliamentary Debates with Automated Textual Analysis. *PLOS ONE*, 11(12):e0168843. Publisher: Public Library of Science.

Anna Ristilä and Kimmo Elo. 2023. Observing political and societal changes in Finnish parliamentary speech data, 1980–2010, with topic modelling. *Parliaments, Estates and Representation*, 43(2):149–176. Publisher: Routledge _eprint: https://doi.org/10.1080/02606755.2023.2213550.

Pedro L. Rodriguez and Arthur Spirling. 2022. Word Embeddings: What Works, What Doesn't, and How to Tell the Difference for Applied Research. *The Journal of Politics*, 84(1):101–115. Publisher: The University of Chicago Press.

Alieh Hajizadeh Saffar, Tiffany Katharine Mann, and Bahadorreza Ofoghi. 2023. Textual emotion detection in health: Advances and applications. *Journal of Biomedical Informatics*, 137:104258.

Statistics Finland. 2024a. Official Statistics of Finland (OSF): Annual national accounts [online publication]. https://www.stat.fi/en/statistics/vtp.

Statistics Finland. 2024b. Official Statistics of Finland (OSF): Consumer price index [online publication]. https://www.stat.fi/en/statistics/khi.

Statistics Finland. 2024c. Official Statistics of Finland (OSF): Labour force survey [online publication]. https://www.stat.fi/en/statistics/tyti.

Statistics Finland. 2024d. Official Statistics of Finland (OSF): Statistics on labour disputes [online publication]. https://www.stat.fi/en/statistics/tta.

Synonyymit.fi. n.d. Synonyymit.fi: Synonyymisanakirja netissä.

Dalila Talevi, Valentina Socci, Margherita Carai, Giulia Carnaghi, Serena Faleri, Edoardo Trebbi, Arianna di Bernardo, Francesco Capelli, and Francesca Pacitti. 2020. Mental health outcomes of the CoViD-19 pandemic. *Rivista di Psichiatria*, 55(3):137–144.

Peter C. Terry, Renée L. Parsons-Smith, and Victoria R. Terry. 2020. Mood Responses Associated With COVID-19 Restrictions. *Frontiers in Psychology*, 11. Publisher: Frontiers.

Martina Toshevska, Frosina Stojanovska, and Jovan Kalajdjieski. 2020. Comparative analysis of word embeddings for capturing word similarities. *arXiv preprint arXiv:2005.03812*.

Voikko. n.d. Voikko – Free linguistic software for Finnish. https://voikko.puimula.org/.

# A Appendix

## A.1 Word embedding parameters

The GloVe algorithm (Pennington et al., 2014) was used to generate word embeddings. Words with fewer than 50 occurrences were ignored to eliminate typos and rare words. Rheault et al. (2016) set this threshold at 200; due to the smaller size of the Finnish dataset, a lower threshold was selected here. The window size was set at 15, and the generated vectors are 300-dimensional. These parameters were chosen as they were used by Rheault et al. (2016); based on other research (Rodriguez and Spirling, 2022), the window size may be larger than necessary, but it did not pose a significant computational burden for this project.

## A.2 Seed lemma selection

The method for selecting seed lemmas followed that used by (Rheault et al., 2016).

The initial positive words *hyvä*, *rakkaus*, and *onnellinen* (*good*, *love*, and *happy*), and negative words *paha*, *viha*, and *surullinen* (*bad*, *anger*, and *sad*) were chosen. Synonyms for these words were then recursively extracted from the online synonym dictionary Synonyymit.fi (n.d.). The resulting lists were filtered, first automatically to filter out any words that could not be lemmatised using *libvoikko*, and then manually. In the manual filtering, words were removed if they were not unambiguously either negative or positive, or if they were related to topics often discussed in parliament, such as "predator" (wolves are a recurring topic in the Finnish parliament) or "illness" (this was likely more common during the Covid-19 pandemic).

After filtering, the 100 most common words in each of the two lists were retained as seed lemmas. The word frequency data for this was obtained from the Frequency Lexicon of the Finnish Newspaper Language (CSC - IT Center for Science, 2004). As no general or political frequency lexicon was found, this lexicon was considered suitable for the task.

## A.3 Seed lemmas

| Lemma | PoS | Translation |
|---|---|---|
| hyvä | adj. | good |
| tärkeä | adj. | important |
| apu | noun | aid |
| voitto | noun | win |
| mahdollinen | adj. | possible |
| vahva | adj. | strong |
| selvä | adj. | clear |
| helppo | adj. | easy |
| merkittävä | adj. | significant |
| tyytyväinen | adj. | satisfied |
| palkinto | noun | reward |
| kaunis | adj. | beautiful |
| reilu | adj. | fair |
| hieno | adj. | fine |
| taito | noun | skill |
| myönteinen | adj. | positive |
| selkeä | adj. | clear |
| kiinnostunut | adj. | interested |
| arvostaa | verb | appreciate |
| tehokas | adj. | efficient |
| mukava | adj. | nice |
| mielenkiintoinen | adj. | interesting |
| hyöty | noun | utility |
| rakkaus | noun | love |
| ilo | noun | joy |
| turvallinen | adj. | safe |
| arvokas | adj. | valuable |
| kyky | noun | ability |
| tasainen | adj. | even |
| aktiivinen | adj. | active |
| luottamus | noun | trust |
| iloinen | adj. | joyful |
| suosikki | noun | favourite |
| täydellinen | adj. | perfect |
| aito | adj. | genuine |
| erinomainen | adj. | excellent |
| positiivinen | adj. | positive |
| edullinen | adj. | affordable, beneficial |
| rauhallinen | adj. | calm |
| upea | adj. | gorgeous |
| järkevä | adj. | rational |
| sankari | noun | hero |
| mahtava | adj. | mighty |
| rakastaa | verb | love |
| lahja | noun | gift |
| onnellinen | adj. | happy |
| into | noun | enthusiasm |
| voimavara | noun | asset |
| kiva | adj. | nice |
| viisas | adj. | wise |

| Lemma | PoS | Translation |
|---|---|---|
| tyydyttää | verb | satisfy |
| lämpö | noun | warmth |
| järki | noun | sense |
| yhtenäinen | adj. | united |
| vakaa | adj. | steady |
| sopu | noun | agreement |
| kirkas | adj. | clear |
| maltillinen | adj. | moderate |
| inhimillinen | adj. | humane |
| innokas | adj. | eager |
| vankka | adj. | robust |
| ihana | adj. | lovely |
| ainutlaatuinen | adj. | unique |
| ihailla | verb | admire |
| halukas | adj. | eager |
| huima | adj. | wild |
| palkkio | noun | reward |
| huikea | adj. | breathtaking |
| ylpeä | adj. | proud |
| suosittu | adj. | popular |
| luotettava | adj. | reliable |
| yhtyä | verb | unite |
| innostunut | adj. | enthusiastic |
| kultainen | adj. | golden |
| rakas | adj. | beloved |
| tykätä | verb | like |
| oleellinen | adj. | essential |
| laadukas | adj. | high quality |
| luonteva | adj. | natural |
| yhteisymmärrys | noun | understanding |
| riemu | noun | jubilation |
| reipas | adj. | brisk, cheerful |
| armo | noun | mercy |
| ahkera | adj. | diligent |
| lahjakas | adj. | talented |
| perusteellinen | adj. | comprehensive |
| rehellinen | adj. | honest |
| kunnollinen | adj. | proper |
| asiallinen | adj. | proper |
| plussa | noun | plus |
| tyylikäs | adj. | stylish |
| uskottava | adj. | credible |
| siisti | adj. | neat |
| uskollinen | adj. | loyal |
| viisaus | noun | wisdom |
| ystävyys | noun | friendship |
| ehjä | adj. | intact |
| hyödyllinen | adj. | useful |
| intohimo | noun | passion |
| mieluisa | adj. | pleasing |

Table 1: Positive seed lemmas used.

| Lemma | PoS | Translation |
|---|---|---|
| vaikea | adj. | difficult |
| paha | adj. | bad, evil |
| huono | adj. | bad |
| kriisi | noun | crisis |
| kaivata | verb | yearn |
| vaikeus | noun | difficulty |
| virhe | noun | error |
| heikko | adj. | weak |
| vastainen | adj. | against |
| vahinko | noun | damage |
| loukkaantua | verb | be offended |
| mahdoton | adj. | impossible |
| pelko | noun | fear |
| vaarallinen | adj. | dangerous |
| hankala | adj. | difficult |
| hyökkäys | noun | attack |
| raju | adj. | fierce |
| alhainen | adj. | low |
| pettymys | noun | disappointment |
| vaativa | adj. | demanding |
| väärin | seikkasana | wrong |
| vaiva | noun | inconvenience |
| kielteinen | adj. | negative |
| ankara | adj. | strict |
| kriittinen | adj. | critical |
| rankka | adj. | tough |
| synkkä | adj. | gloomy |
| syyllinen | adj. | guilty |
| ahdas | adj. | cramped |
| suru | noun | grief |
| kohtuuton | adj. | unreasonable |
| tuska | noun | pain |
| kiusata | verb | bully |
| yksinäinen | adj. | lonely |
| väkivaltainen | adj. | violent |
| väkivaltaisuus | noun | violence |
| ongelmallinen | adj. | problematic |
| tarpeeton | adj. | superfluous |
| harmi | noun | harm |
| surkea | adj. | poor |
| kehno | adj. | bad |
| kauhu | noun | dread |
| tuhoisa | adj. | disastrous |
| heikkous | noun | weakness |
| murhe | noun | grief |
| surullinen | adj. | sad |
| viha | noun | hate |
| negatiivinen | adj. | negative |
| kiusallinen | adj. | awkward |
| virheellinen | adj. | incorrect |
| puutteellinen | adj. | inadequate |
| karu | adj. | barren |
| tylsä | adj. | boring |
| tyytymätön | adj. | unsatisfied |
| epäkohta | noun | fault |
| haukkua | verb | insult |
| haitallinen | adj. | damaging |
| katkera | adj. | bitter |
| verinen | adj. | bloody |
| likainen | adj. | dirty |
| ahdistus | noun | anxiety |
| onneton | adj. | unhappy |
| liiallinen | adj. | excessive |
| julma | adj. | barbarous |
| surra | verb | mourn |
| helvetti | noun | hell |
| tyly | adj. | rude, harsh |
| traaginen | adj. | tragic |
| tyytymättömyys | noun | dissatisfaction |
| moite | noun | reproach |
| vihainen | adj. | angry |
| huonokuntoinen | adj. | in poor condition |
| syrjäytyä | verb | become alienated |
| työläs | adj. | arduous |
| synti | noun | sin |
| karkea | adj. | rough |
| erehdys | noun | mistake |
| toivoton | adj. | hopeless |
| julmuus | noun | cruelty |
| aggressiivinen | adj. | aggressive |
| kurja | adj. | miserable |
| hävetä | verb | be ashamed |
| rasite | noun | encumbrance |
| riesa | noun | nuisance |
| ankea | adj. | bleak |
| myrkyllinen | adj. | toxic |
| levoton | adj. | restless |
| ilkivalta | noun | vandalism |
| kaipuu | noun | yearning |
| epätoivoinen | adj. | desperate |
| armoton | adj. | merciless |
| jäykkä | adj. | stiff |
| tappelu | noun | fight |
| sopimaton | adj. | improper |
| riittämätön | adj. | insufficient |
| mitätön | adj. | puny |
| kurjuus | noun | misery |
| typerä | adj. | stupid |
| vääryys | noun | injustice |
| turhautua | verb | get frustrated |

Table 2: Negative seed lemmas used.

## A.4 Additional tables and figures

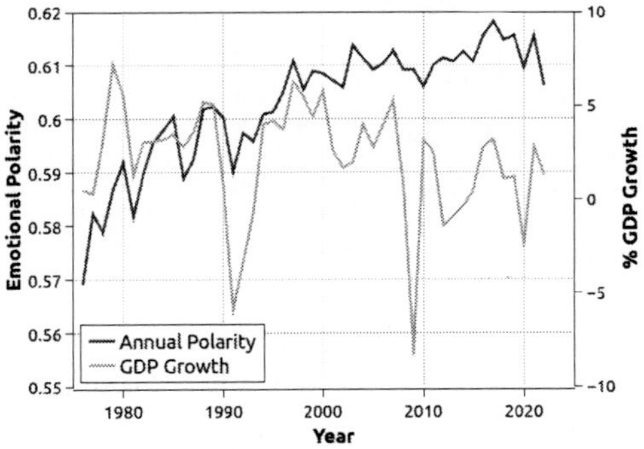


Figure 5: GDP growth and emotional polarity.

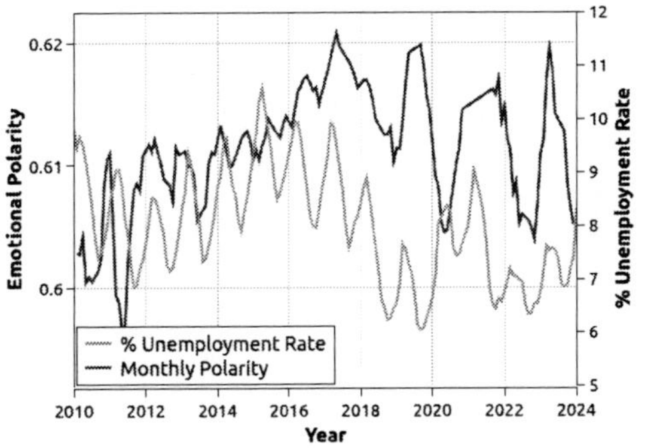


Figure 6: Unemployment rate and emotional polarity (4-month rolling average).

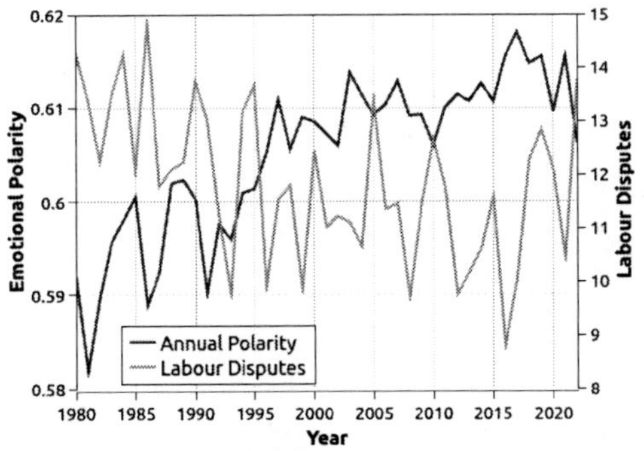


Figure 7: Labour disputes and emotional polarity.

| Name of Measure | Description | Time Period | Database |
|---|---|---|---|
| CLI Growth | % change in Cost of Living Index, annual | 1939-2023 | 2024b |
| CPI Growth | % change in Consumer Price Index, annual | 1952-2023 | 2024b |
| GDP Growth | % change in Gross Domestic Product, annual | 1976-2022 | 2024a |
| Labour Disputes | Natural logarithm of days lost to strikes, annual | 1980-2022 | 2024d |
| Misery Index | Sum of CPI growth and unemployment, monthly | 2010-2024 | 2024b; 2024c |
| Unemployment | Rate of unemployment, monthly | 2010-2024 | 2024c |

Table 3: Economic measures used.

| Cause | Effect | P | Corrected P |
|---|---|---|---|
| Polarity | CLI Growth | 0.930 | 1.000 |
| Polarity | CPI Growth | 0.537 | 1.000 |
| Polarity | GDP Growth | 0.442 | 1.000 |
| Polarity | Labour Disputes | 0.091 | 1.000 |
| Polarity | Misery Index | 0.061 | 0.732 |
| Polarity | Pos. Covid Tests | 0.350 | 1.000 |
| CLI Growth | Polarity | 0.003 | 0.034 |
| CPI Growth | Polarity | 0.040 | 0.484 |
| GDP Growth | Polarity | 0.215 | 1.000 |
| Labour Disputes | Polarity | 0.157 | 1.000 |
| Misery Index | Polarity | 0.245 | 1.000 |
| Pos. Covid Tests | Polarity | 0.002 | 0.029 |

Table 4: Results of the Granger causality tests. Rows with a corrected $p$-value below 0.05 are highlighted.

# Topic-specific social science theory in stance detection: a proposal and interdisciplinary pilot study on sustainability initiatives

**Myrthe Reuver[1], Alessandra Polimeno[3*], Antske Fokkens[1], Ana Isabel Lopes[2]**
[1] Computational Linguistics & Text Mining Lab, Vrije Universiteit Amsterdam
[2] Communication Science Department, Vrije Universiteit Amsterdam
[3] Utrecht Data School, Utrecht University
[1] firstname.lastname@vu.nl, [2] a.i.loureiro.lopes@vu.nl, [3] aapolimeno@gmail.com
[*] work completed while employed by the Vrije Universiteit Amsterdam

## Abstract

Topic-specificity is often seen as a limitation of stance detection models and datasets, especially for analyzing political and societal debates. However, stances contain topic-specific aspects that are crucial for an in-depth understanding of these debates. Our interdisciplinary approach identifies social science theories on specific debate topics as an opportunity for further defining stance detection research and analyzing online debate. This paper explores *sustainability* as debate topic, and connects stance to the sustainability-related Value-Belief-Norm (VBN) theory. VBN theory states that arguments in favor or against sustainability initiatives contain the dimensions of feeling *power* to change the issue with the initiative, and thinking whether or not the initiative tackles an urgent *threat* to the environment. In a pilot study with our *Reddit European Sustainability Initiatives corpus*, we develop an annotation procedure for these complex concepts. We then compare crowd-workers with Natural Language Processing experts' annotation proficiency. Both crowd-workers and NLP experts find the tasks difficult, but experts reach more agreement on some difficult examples. This pilot study shows that complex theories about debate topics are feasible and worthwhile as annotation tasks for stance detection.

## 1 Introduction

Online platforms see people discussing politicians (i.e., Emmanuel Macron), political issues (i.e., immigration), and cultural debates (i.e., feminist messages in the movie *Barbie*). Stance models usually classify written arguments in such debates into whether they are in favor or against the topic under discussion (Küçük and Can, 2020). The task of stance detection is often conceptualized as topic-*independent*: in datasets and papers, a stance in favour of feminism is seen as conceptually similar as one in favour of immigration.

However, it has been shown that stance models are in fact topic-*dependent*: Transformer models trained on detecting different stances in one topic do not necessarily work on unseen topics (Reuver et al., 2021b; Thorn Jakobsen et al., 2021). Recent work (Ajjour et al., 2023) attempts to tackle this limitation of topic-independent stance modelling by diversifying the number of topics in stance detection datasets, while Beck et al. (2023) update Transformer models' access to knowledge of topic context to improve cross-topic stance detection.

Instead of seeing specialization into one topic as a limitation, we argue that this topic-specificity of debates can also be an asset for stance detection research. Social science theories can play a crucial role in this challenge. Such theories can be used to develop topic-specific stance data and models, which increases the impact of stance detection on socially relevant research questions. This approach also tackles limitations of work assuming stance is topic-independent, such as models not fully capturing the underlying socio-cultural dimensions of specific topics (Reuver et al., 2021b). Social science theory can lead computational argumentation researchers to dimensions of stance that are unique for specific debate topics. These dimensions can then be annotated, and this knowledge of theories help models (and humans) navigate the unique dimensions of the debate.

We argue that defining topic-specific aspects of the debate helps analyzing, modelling, and interpreting the stances in such debates. As a case study, we apply Value-Belief-Norm (VBN) theory (Stern et al., 1999) of environmental debates to stances in environmental debates. We develop an annotation framework and test-drive this by annotating a dataset of 91 Reddit comments reacting to sustainability initiatives with stance, threat, and power. We then analyze the advantages and disadvantages of this approach for stance research on sustainability, and also on other debate topics.



*Proceedings of the 58th Annual Meeting of the Association for Computational Linguistics*, pages 101–111
July 5–10, 2020. 

This paper has the following contributions:
(1) we identify **topic-specific stance detection with social science theory** as an avenue for research in computational argumentation;
(2) we present an **annotation pipeline** for theory-driven stance detection for sustainability debates, and our findings from pilot annotations;
(3) we release **a dataset of Europe-centered debates on sustainability on Reddit**, with a small subset annotated with this annotation pipeline.

## 2 Topic-dependence and Theory in Stance

Stance detection (Küçük and Can, 2020) is a task in computational argumentation or argument mining (Lawrence and Reed, 2020) consisting of classifying arguments into pro, con, or neutral towards an idea or discussion topic. Stance detection has been used to measure support on social media for topics (Grčar et al., 2017; Scott et al., 2021). These topics are for instance vaccination, but also debate statements such as "we should abolish free speech."

Recent work has indicated that stance models are topic-*dependent* despite being designed as topic-*independent*. Reuver et al. (2021b) found that cross-topic capabilities of Transformer stance models are dependent on topical cues, and that model errors are related to a lack of understanding of socio-cultural dimensions in debates such as gun control and abortion. Thorn Jakobsen et al. (2021) found that these models learn topic-dependent signals, and use mostly topic-dependent words not related to stance as a topic-independent concept (e.g. word 'gun' rather than argumentation-related words).

Earlier work has claimed high cross-topic stance performance, but these performances have still been highly topic-dependent. Some research uses topic dependence in stance for these results, by measuring similarity between two discussion topics, and using the most related topics for cross-topic stance detection. This obtains F1 scores between .67 and .80 on stance detection in unseen topics (Xu et al., 2018; Wei and Mao, 2019; Liang et al., 2021). However, Allaway et al. (2021) do not consider topic-relatedness when modelling and obtain much more modest scores of F1 = .49 and .54 on unseen topics. A similar result can be seen in Reuver et al. (2024), where strategies for few-shot cross-topic stance detection with Transformer models lead to inconsistent performance (between F1 = .344 and F1 = .766) and are largely dependent on dataset choice rather than choices made in model design.

Approaches to improve these non-robust cross-topic capabilities of stance detection models go into two related, but distinct, directions. One is a data-centric approach that can be summarized as **improving the debate topic diversity in datasets**. Earlier work already mentioned how claims and arguments as defined in datasets are topic and context-dependent (Levy et al., 2014). Recently, Ajjour et al. (2023) have developed an ontology for defining diversity of debate topics in computational argumentation datasets.

Another direction is a more model-centric approach that can be summarized as **improving the models' use of topic knowledge**. Earlier work has also looked into improving world knowledge use in stance models (Zhang et al., 2020; Clark et al., 2021). Beck et al. (2023) recently designed a Transformer model architecture that uses real-world knowledge for classification decisions, in the form of a context encoder that "injects" domain-relevant world knowledge into stance models. See Lauscher et al. (2022) for an overview of using knowledge in computational argumentation.

While both directions have promising results, we argue there is another option for overcoming the weaknesses of topic-independent stance detection: designing datasets as well as models with relevant social science theory on the specific debates. This work argues a *debate topic* is broader than specific individual texts or statements (such as "climate change is bad"), but more narrow than what other works call *domain* (which often resorts to categories such as "legal", "social media", etc.). We define a topic as a specific area of socio-cultural discussion, with its own dimensions and aspects of debate such as "climate change", or "immigration". Our definition of *topic* most closely responds to the Level 1 and 2 topics in Ajjour et al. (2023)'s argument topic ontology. Stances in such topics have unique, topic-specific aspects, that can be captured by social science theory on the debate topic in question.

Recently, stance detection work has attempted to include dimensions of opinion beyond simply support or reject, such as argument type (Draws et al., 2022) and underlying values (Kobbe et al., 2020). These variables add underlying reasons *why* an idea is supported or rejected, often a neglected aspect of stance (Joseph et al., 2021; Scott et al., 2021). However, theories on the individual debate topics are often neglected in this exploration of aspects related to stance and arguments.

### 2.1 Social Science Theory in NLP and Stance

Previous work has outlined how a connection with social science literature and specifically theory can improve NLP tasks, analyses based on them, as well as the theory itself. Radford and Joseph (2020) describe how the traditional Machine Learning pipeline of prediction-based modelling can be enhanced by using theories that are based on the social data or social phenomenon being modelled. These theories can influence relevant sample selection, but theory can also influence the selection of research problems, design of task instructions, as well as how a successful outcome is measured. McCarthy and Dore (2023) argue that theories from the social sciences can help in connecting NLP to relevant research problems. Their work covers an extensive analysis of trends in NLP publishing, and concludes that NLP work in *ACL venues is not *grounded* in the theory about the social phenomena in text it models.

Other work has specifically connected different tasks in computational argumentation to social science theories. Lauscher et al. (2020) research theory in argument quality assessment by an extensive annotation study using theories of argument properties. Vecchi et al. (2021) find that the social science theory of deliberative quality helps solve a definition problem when trying to define and then detect argument quality. Additionally, Reuver et al. (2021a) use the theory of deliberative democracy to identify argument-related NLP tasks relevant to solving a societal problem (non-diverse news recommenders threatening democracy).

However, to our knowledge no work has yet connected social science theory on specific debate topics to the gaps in topic-independent stance detection, and the benefits of topic-dependent stance detection. We will illustrate this connection with a case study on sustainability initiatives.

## 3 Case Study: Sustainability Initiatives

A stance on sustainability initiatives can be defined as an argument in favor or against initiatives such as renewable energy in local communities (Hewitt et al., 2019) or sustainable behavior at music festivals (Bär et al., 2022). Other work within computational argumentation has looked into sustainability, for instance by annotating evidence that supports sustainability claims in scientific papers (Fergadis et al., 2021), or by detecting sustainable diet patterns in tweets (Hansen and Hershcovich, 2022).

However, the tasks and annotation variables (such as stance, claim-evidence pairs, and argument units) in these earlier papers are very similar to other computational argumentation literature. We would like the annotation procedure to be influenced directly by the sustainability literature in social science. What can a social science theory about sustainability debates tell us about stances in this debate, and how to analyze debates on sustainability?

### 3.1 Theory and Stances on Sustainability

One theory connected to sustainability and stance is the Value-Belief-Norm theory (VBN) (Stern et al., 1999) of environmentalism. We select this theory for its connection to both stance (support/rejection of initiatives) and the debate topic (sustainability).[1] This theory claims individuals who *support* a sustainability initiative have three things in common: one, they **value** the object under discussion. Two, they believe this object (in this case, the environment or society) is under **threat**. Three, they believe their actions can help restore the desired object (they feel **power to restore**). With these three conditions met, individuals will support a climate initiative. For instance, an initiative to incentivize the consumption of locally produced food might attract arguments that express a negative stance towards it. According to this theory, this negative stance does not mean that people do not support the environment (not valuing the object). A negative stance could mean consumers do not think non-local food production affects the environment (no threat to the desired object) or because they do not believe individuals changing food habits has a collective effect (no power to restore the object). This makes a stance more complex: a negative stance on a climate-related issue does not imply a negative stance on the climate or sustainability.

### 3.2 VBN aspects in Sustainability Stances

Consider some example arguments.[2] One specific initiative that is debated is *"Spanish should eat less meat to limit climate crisis, says minister"*. One commenter says: *"He's right. High levels of meat consumption and bio industry is a threat to all of humanity."*. This specific comment not only

[1] We realise this is not the only theory related to stance or sustainability: Future work could implement this approach with other theories.

[2] Examples come from our corpus on sustainability initiatives, and are also in our annotation guidelines, see below.

supports the initiative (has a positive **stance**), but also directly mentions **threat** (this issue directly threatens the environment, a valued object).

Another discussion topic has comments more clearly mentioning the **power** dimension of the stance of the commenter. On the topic *Recycling rate of plastic packaging waste*, one commenter mentions "Recycling plastic is mostly pointless. Far better to reduce the use of plastics in packaging as much as possible.", mentioning how individual action after the production process is pointless (lacks **power**). The commenter mentions a negative stance towards recycling, but clearly does support the goal of reducing plastic waste. The next section outlines our annotation pipeline and dataset for these concepts.

## 4 Data

Our dataset on European sustainability discussions, mostly in English, is obtained from the Reddit.com sub-communities (Proferes et al., 2021) called *europe*, *europeanunion*, and *europes*. We identify any sustainability discussion posted from 2017 to 2022 to contain five years of comments[3]. Our dataset consists of 2.073 discussions with 46.285 comments. Nearly half (922) of these have one or more comments. We release the entire corpus, without annotations, as the *Reddit European Sustainability Initiatives corpus*[4], for non-commercial research-use only under CC-BY-NC licence.[5].

### 4.1 Annotation

We test both crowd and expert annotation of comments on a small subset of our data, and make our annotation guidelines and task design public - see Appendix B and also our GitHub repository.[6] We also release the annotated dataset, for non-commercial research-use only under CC-BY-NC licence.[3]

**Crowd Task** A non-expert crowd of 5 annotators hired through annotation platform Prolific annotated 91 random comment-topic text pairs on whether it contained a sustainbility initiative, whether the comment expressed a stance towards it, and power/threat towards the environment. More details on task design are in Appendix B.

**Crowd characteristics** Our 5 annotators from recruitment platform Prolific were self-reported fluent speakers of English from the US, UK, Canada and Ireland. Pay was US $16 an hour, above minimum wage in highest-paying area Canada. We selected annotators with > 95% approval rating for > 100 previous tasks (Douglas et al., 2023).

**Inter-Annotator Agreement** We report moderate agreement (Landis and Koch, 1977) for annotation whether thread titles contain **sustainability initiatives** to discuss (Fleiss $\kappa$ = .47). A similar pilot annotation study on annotating debatable claim vs no claim on 100 social media comments (Bauwelinck and Lefever, 2020) reports a comparable Fleiss $\kappa$ of .45. Despite its imperfections, percentage agreement is a commonly used agreement measure for stance detection datasets (Ng and Carley, 2022). On average, 89% annotators agree per item (range: 60% to 100%) for annotating the presence of a sustainability initiative.

For **stance**, we initially see a Fleiss $\kappa$ of .31, which is considerably lower. However, one annotator shows a pattern of unreliability and consistently chooses the positive stance class in the last third of annotation decisions. Removing this annotator increases the Fleiss $\kappa$ to .39, close to moderate agreement. Stance has an average of 68% annotators agreeing per item (40% to 100%).

Agreement for **threat** is only moderate: Fleiss $\kappa$ = .33. However, there is a strong difference per item: on average, 60% of annotators agree per item for threat, but some items nearly have complete disagreement, with on 3 items even only 33% agreement. The **power** agreement is also only moderate: Fleiss $\kappa$ of .29. However, we again see a large difference per item. On average, 60% of annotators agree per item, but for 4 items the majority agrees only with 33%.

**Expert Annotation** NLP experts from the author's university attempted to improve the threat and power annotation. Four annotators annotated all 91 examples for power. This led to a Fleiss $\kappa$ of .26: very similar to the crowd annotators. On average, there was 66% agreement over items - slightly higher agreement than the crowdworkers. However, again it shows 4 items with agreement of 33%. For threat (3 annotators), this led to a Fleiss $\kappa$ of .18,

[3]We scraped with a manual keyword list expanded with pre-trained word embeddings, see Appendix A.

[4]A basic topic model analysis as well as qualitative analysis of this corpus is in Appendix C.

[5]https://huggingface.co/datasets/Myrthe/RedditEuropeanSustainabilityInitiatives

[6]https://github.com/myrthereuver/TopicSpecific_Stance_SocialScience

which is considerably lower than the crowd workers - but could be attributed to fatigue, as annotators annotated this variable after power, and the session was long. On average, there was 59% agreement over items, which is similar to the crowdworkers.

### 4.2 Per-item annotation differences

Annotating power and threat is more difficult in some comments than others. A deeper look into these comments shows why. One item that had low agreement (33%) from both experts and crowdworkers is one where on the topic *"Climate change: The rich are to blame, international study finds"*, a commenter appears to respond sarcastically: *"Incredible, truly incredible ..did they hire Sherlock for this one ?"*. This added sarcasm makes it hard to differentiate whether this commenter thinks climate change is a serious threat, for both expert and non-expert annotators. The annotation instructions do explicitly ask annotators to attempt to consider sarcasm and commenters' intent when annotating, but disagreement about intent is still possible.

A comment only crowdworkers struggled to get agreement on, is a complex comment on the initiative to use leaf plates. The commenter makes a multi-sentence argument: *'This makes no sense. A ceramic plates using hot water from a zero carbon source would last millions of cycles where as these leaf plates require some kind of glue from an outside sources. I doubt these lasted long and how do they preserve the leafs autumn when all the leafs on the trees have disintegrated away.'*. Crowd annotators struggle to obtain agreement, but experts are correctly able to parse that this does mean the commenter expresses that the environment is threatened (the need to save trees and reduce carbon).

## 5 Discussion

Our pilot study gave several insights. Firstly, we note that irony is a specific issue in argument annotation. This has been noted by earlier work integrating social science theory in computational argumentation studies, e.g. in a tutorial on the topic by Lapesa et al. (2024). Lauscher et al. (2020) also find in annotation experiments for argument quality that even experts struggle with annotating and interpreting irony in arguments when annotating with complex theories.

Secondly, using theories in natural language processing can also help connecting a theory to a phenomenon, and finding gaps between these (Radford and Joseph, 2020). Responsibility is a dimension which is not part the VBN theory or of our annotation pilot, but in annotation we found it was a clear dimension in the debate: in multiple discussions, commenters mentioned that while they supported the initiative (e.g. nudging people to produce less waste), they felt others (either the rich elite, people in China or America, or companies) were mainly responsible for climate-related problems. These comments are in line with a different, but not mutually exclusive, theory about climate debate: that of *social identity theory*, were people feel pushed to blame outside groups (Post et al., 2019). This connection may be interesting for future work on sustainability and stance.

Another question is whether the VBN theory applies to other debate topics. We note that 'power' and 'threat' may relate to stances in especially other policy-related debates. However, the two dimensions in this theory are also different, and it seems the threat dimension is more applicable to debates on debates that feel existential (e.g. *is immigration a threat?*). The power dimension (*Do we have power to restore the desired state?*), is more related to feeling whether people have influence on the outcome with their own actions, which is more applicable to debates with a central role for individual action, i.e. donating money, or voting.

Topic-specific aspects also exist beyond sustainability. Another debate topic is COVID-19 policies, popular in stance detection research (Hossain et al., 2020; Glandt et al., 2021). Topic-independent pro/con stances ignores the COVID19-specific issue of whether people disagree because the measure is too strict, or not strict enough. Without this topic-specific aspect, there are limitations to interpreting stances in this debate (Scott et al., 2021).

## 6 Conclusion

We propose to integrate topic-specific social science theories in stance detection, improving some weaknesses of topic-independent conceptualizations of stance detection. As a case study, we use Value-Belief-Norm theory (Stern et al., 1999) for stances on sustainability, and apply this theory to a pilot annotation task on 91 comments in our *Reddit European Sustainability Initiatives corpus*. The aspects are difficult to annotate, but experts annotate some difficult examples better than crowdworkers. Topic-specific theories improve stance understanding - for both models and humans.

## Limitations

We identified several limitations of our study that may lead to our results not being representative beyond this study. We invite future work to improve on these limitations.

**Small Sample** Due to time as well as funding constraints, our annotated sample is somewhat small, with 91 comments on 86 unique sustainability initiatives. Future work may address this concern by increasing the size of the data, both in size (a larger dataset) and in scope (more topics, language, and contexts, see below).

**Only One Debate Topic** This work is limited by only analyzing our proposed approach to one overarching discussion topic: that of sustainability initiatives. Our findings may not generalize well to other debate topics.

**Only One Language and Debate Context** Additionally, this topic and our dataset is limited to not only one language (English) (Bender, 2019) but also one socio-cultural context (Europe-focused online debates). This may mean our findings do not generalize well to user-generated textual debate in other contexts. Similarly, we analyze debates on Reddit.com, which is a very specific debate context: its norms, nuances, and specifics (Proferes et al., 2021) may make results on this data not applicable to other platforms.

**Online Stance not Representative of Offline Opinions** The detection of online stances is often used to predict stances of people in offline settings. However, research has shown that this has limited validity: Joseph et al. (2021) find a limited connection between people's survey responses and the same individuals' online stance-taking on social media. This may also mean that theories on offline stance-taking may not connect well to stance-taking behaviour on online platforms, as these debate contexts (online debate measurement vs offline questioning) lead to different outcomes of opinion measurement even for the same participants, which may lead to different conclusions about the debate from researchers in the social sciences than from computational researchers. We therefore also caution against any research using stance models as the sole measurement of public or individual opinion.

## Ethics Statement

The data used in this project was scraped from Reddit in December 2022 with the PushShift API, before Reddit's PushShift API restrictions from April 2023 onwards. We ensure the data is released for non-commercial use only. This is also in-line with Reddit users' concern of their data being used for training commercial LLMs or other technology.

This paper concerns debate on sensitive, political topics. We completed an ERB check from the Social Science department at the Vrije Universiteit Amsterdam, which indicated we could proceed with our scraping and analyses without harm. We encourage other authors to also seek approval and a check on ethical and legal concerns before proceeding with scraping or analyzing data. We do not process identifying information on users such as usernames or post history, and neither do we release such data.

Additionally, we employ human annotators during our study. We are aware of the power dynamics and precarity involved in annotation platform work, but found it necessary for our study. We paid our annotators a fair wage, used fair attention and test tasks, and paid all annotators completing the task.

## Acknowledgements

Alessandra Polimeno's contributions as well as crowd annotator costs were funded by a research voucher grant for the project *Reasons for online (dis)trust in sustainable initiatives* awarded to Myrthe Reuver and Ana Isabel Lopes by the Network Institute at the Vrije Universiteit Amsterdam. Myrthe Reuver and Antske Fokkens were also funded by the Netherlands Organisation for Scientific Research (NWO) through the the *Rethinking News Algorithms* project via the Open Competition Digitalization Humanities & Social Science grant (406.D1.19.073).

We thank lab members at CLTL for participating in the expert annotator sessions, and feedback sessions on earlier versions of this paper.

A preliminary version of this paper was presented at the non-archival International Communication Association (ICA) 2023 conference. We would like to thank all reviewers, whose comments improved this version and earlier versions of this paper. All remaining errors or unclarities are ours.

## References

Yamen Ajjour, Johannes Kiesel, Benno Stein, and Martin Potthast. 2023. Topic ontologies for arguments. In *Findings of the Association for Computational Linguistics: EACL 2023*, pages 1411–1427, Dubrovnik, Croatia. Association for Computational Linguistics.

Emily Allaway, Malavika Srikanth, and Kathleen Mckeown. 2021. Adversarial learning for zero-shot stance detection on social media. In *Proceedings of the 2021 Conference of the North American Chapter of the Association for Computational Linguistics: Human Language Technologies*, pages 4756–4767.

Sören Bär, Laura Korrmann, and Markus Kurscheidt. 2022. How nudging inspires sustainable behavior among event attendees: A qualitative analysis of selected music festivals. *Sustainability*, 14(10):6321.

Nina Bauwelinck and Els Lefever. 2020. Annotating topics, stance, argumentativeness and claims in dutch social media comments: a pilot study. In *Proceedings of the 7th Workshop on Argument Mining*, pages 8–18.

Tilman Beck, Andreas Waldis, and Iryna Gurevych. 2023. Robust integration of contextual information for cross-target stance detection. In *Proceedings of the 12th Joint Conference on Lexical and Computational Semantics (*SEM 2023)*, pages 494–511, Toronto, Canada. Association for Computational Linguistics.

Anya Belz, Craig Thomson, Ehud Reiter, Gavin Abercrombie, Jose M Alonso-Moral, Mohammad Arvan, Jackie Cheung, Mark Cieliebak, Elizabeth Clark, Kees van Deemter, et al. 2023. Missing information, unresponsive authors, experimental flaws: The impossibility of assessing the reproducibility of previous human evaluations in nlp. *arXiv preprint arXiv:2305.01633*.

Emily Bender. 2019. The# benderrule: On naming the languages we study and why it matters. *The Gradient*, 14.

Thomas Clark, Costanza Conforti, Fangyu Liu, Zaiqiao Meng, Ehsan Shareghi, and Nigel Collier. 2021. Integrating transformers and knowledge graphs for Twitter stance detection. In *Proceedings of the Seventh Workshop on Noisy User-generated Text (W-NUT 2021)*, pages 304–312, Online. Association for Computational Linguistics.

Johannes Daxenberger, Steffen Eger, Ivan Habernal, Christian Stab, and Iryna Gurevych. 2017. What is the essence of a claim? cross-domain claim identification. In *Proceedings of the 2017 Conference on Empirical Methods in Natural Language Processing*, pages 2055–2066, Copenhagen, Denmark. Association for Computational Linguistics.

Benjamin D Douglas, Patrick J Ewell, and Markus Brauer. 2023. Data quality in online human-subjects research: Comparisons between mturk, prolific, cloudresearch, qualtrics, and sona. *Plos one*, 18(3):e0279720.

Tim Draws, Oana Inel, Nava Tintarev, Christian Baden, and Benjamin Timmermans. 2022. Comprehensive viewpoint representations for a deeper understanding of user interactions with debated topics. In *ACM SIGIR Conference on Human Information Interaction and Retrieval*, pages 135–145.

Aris Fergadis, Dimitris Pappas, Antonia Karamolegkou, and Harris Papageorgiou. 2021. Argumentation mining in scientific literature for sustainable development. In *Proceedings of the 8th Workshop on Argument Mining*, pages 100–111.

Kyle Glandt, Sarthak Khanal, Yingjie Li, Doina Caragea, and Cornelia Caragea. 2021. Stance detection in covid-19 tweets. In *Proceedings of the 59th Annual Meeting of the Association for Computational Linguistics and the 11th International Joint Conference on Natural Language Processing (Long Papers)*, volume 1.

Miha Grčar, Darko Cherepnalkoski, Igor Mozetič, and Petra Kralj Novak. 2017. Stance and influence of twitter users regarding the brexit referendum. *Computational social networks*, 4:1–25.

Maarten Grootendorst. 2022. Bertopic: Neural topic modeling with a class-based tf-idf procedure. *arXiv preprint arXiv:2203.05794*.

Marcus Hansen and Daniel Hershcovich. 2022. A dataset of sustainable diet arguments on Twitter. In *Proceedings of the Second Workshop on NLP for Positive Impact (NLP4PI)*, pages 40–58, Abu Dhabi, United Arab Emirates (Hybrid). Association for Computational Linguistics.

Richard J Hewitt, Nicholas Bradley, Andrea Baggio Compagnucci, Carla Barlagne, Andrzej Ceglarz, Roger Cremades, Margaret McKeen, Ilona M Otto, and Bill Slee. 2019. Social innovation in community energy in europe: A review of the evidence. *Frontiers in Energy Research*, 7:31.

Tamanna Hossain, Robert L. Logan IV, Arjuna Ugarte, Yoshitomo Matsubara, Sean Young, and Sameer Singh. 2020. COVIDLies: Detecting COVID-19 misinformation on social media. In *Proceedings of the 1st Workshop on NLP for COVID-19 (Part 2) at EMNLP 2020*, Online. Association for Computational Linguistics.

Kenneth Joseph, Sarah Shugars, Ryan Gallagher, Jon Green, Alexi Quintana Mathé, Zijian An, and David Lazer. 2021. (mis)alignment between stance expressed in social media data and public opinion surveys. In *Proceedings of the 2021 Conference on Empirical Methods in Natural Language Processing*, pages 312–324, Online and Punta Cana, Dominican Republic. Association for Computational Linguistics.

Jonathan Kobbe, Ines Rehbein, Ioana Hulpuş, and Heiner Stuckenschmidt. 2020. Exploring morality in argumentation. In *Proceedings of the 7th Workshop on Argument Mining*, pages 30–40, Online. Association for Computational Linguistics.

Dilek Küçük and Fazli Can. 2020. Stance detection: A survey. *ACM Comput. Surv.*, 53(1).

J Richard Landis and Gary G Koch. 1977. The measurement of observer agreement for categorical data. *biometrics*, pages 159–174.

Gabriella Lapesa, Eva Maria Vecchi, Serena Villata, and Henning Wachsmuth. 2024. Mining, assessing, and improving arguments in NLP and the social sciences. In *Proceedings of the 2024 Joint International Conference on Computational Linguistics, Language Resources and Evaluation (LREC-COLING 2024): Tutorial Summaries*, pages 26–32, Torino, Italia. ELRA and ICCL.

Anne Lauscher, Lily Ng, Courtney Napoles, and Joel Tetreault. 2020. Rhetoric, logic, and dialectic: Advancing theory-based argument quality assessment in natural language processing. In *Proceedings of the 28th International Conference on Computational Linguistics*, pages 4563–4574.

Anne Lauscher, Henning Wachsmuth, Iryna Gurevych, and Goran Glavaš. 2022. Scientia potentia est—on the role of knowledge in computational argumentation. *Transactions of the Association for Computational Linguistics*, 10:1392–1422.

John Lawrence and Chris Reed. 2020. Argument mining: A survey. *Computational Linguistics*, 45(4):765–818.

Ran Levy, Yonatan Bilu, Daniel Hershcovich, Ehud Aharoni, and Noam Slonim. 2014. Context dependent claim detection. In *Proceedings of COLING 2014, the 25th International Conference on Computational Linguistics: Technical Papers*, pages 1489–1500, Dublin, Ireland. Dublin City University and Association for Computational Linguistics.

Bin Liang, Yonghao Fu, Lin Gui, Min Yang, Jiachen Du, Yulan He, and Ruifeng Xu. 2021. Target-adaptive graph for cross-target stance detection. In *Proceedings of the Web Conference 2021*, pages 3453–3464.

Sara Marjanovic, Karolina Stańczak, and Isabelle Augenstein. 2022. Quantifying Gender Biases Towards Politicians on Reddit. *PLoS ONE*. To appear.

Arya D McCarthy and Giovanna Maria Dora Dore. 2023. Theory-grounded computational text analysis. In *Proceedings of the 61st Annual Meeting of the Association for Computational Linguistics (Volume 2: Short Papers)*, pages 1586–1594.

Tomas Mikolov, Ilya Sutskever, Kai Chen, Greg S Corrado, and Jeff Dean. 2013. Distributed representations of words and phrases and their compositionality. *Advances in neural information processing systems*, 26.

Lynnette Hui Xian Ng and Kathleen M Carley. 2022. Is my stance the same as your stance? a cross validation study of stance detection datasets. *Information Processing & Management*, 59(6):103070.

Jeffrey Pennington, Richard Socher, and Christopher D Manning. 2014. Glove: Global vectors for word representation. In *Proceedings of the 2014 conference on empirical methods in natural language processing (EMNLP)*, pages 1532–1543, Doha, Qatar. ACL.

Senja Post, Katharina Kleinen-von Königslöw, and Mike S Schäfer. 2019. Between guilt and obligation: Debating the responsibility for climate change and climate politics in the media. *Environmental Communication*, 13(6):723–739.

Nicholas Proferes, Naiyan Jones, Sarah Gilbert, Casey Fiesler, and Michael Zimmer. 2021. Studying reddit: A systematic overview of disciplines, approaches, methods, and ethics. *Social Media+ Society*, 7(2):20563051211019004.

Jason Radford and Kenneth Joseph. 2020. Theory in, theory out: The uses of social theory in machine learning for social science. *Frontiers in Big Data*, 3.

Myrthe Reuver, Antske Fokkens, and Suzan Verberne. 2021a. No NLP task should be an island: Multi-disciplinarity for diversity in news recommender systems. In *Proceedings of the EACL Hackashop on News Media Content Analysis and Automated Report Generation*, pages 45–55, Online. Association for Computational Linguistics.

Myrthe Reuver, Suzan Verberne, and Antske Fokkens. 2024. Investigating the robustness of modelling decisions for few-shot cross-topic stance detection: A preregistered study. In *Proceedings of the 2024 Joint International Conference on Computational Linguistics, Language Resources and Evaluation (LREC-COLING 2024)*, pages 9245–9260, Torino, Italia. ELRA and ICCL.

Myrthe Reuver, Suzan Verberne, Roser Morante, and Antske Fokkens. 2021b. Is stance detection topic-independent and cross-topic generalizable?-a reproduction study. In *Proceedings of the 8th Workshop on Argument Mining*, pages 46–56.

Kristen Scott, Pieter Delobelle, and Bettina Berendt. 2021. Measuring shifts in attitudes towards covid-19 measures in belgium. *Computational Linguistics in the Netherlands Journal*, 11:161–171.

Paul C Stern, Thomas Dietz, Troy Abel, Gregory A Guagnano, and Linda Kalof. 1999. A value-belief-norm theory of support for social movements: The case of environmentalism. *Human ecology review*, pages 81–97.

Terne Sasha Thorn Jakobsen, Maria Barrett, and Anders Søgaard. 2021. Spurious correlations in cross-topic argument mining. In *Proceedings of *SEM 2021: The Tenth Joint Conference on Lexical and Computational Semantics*, pages 263–277, Online. Association for Computational Linguistics.

Eva Maria Vecchi, Neele Falk, Iman Jundi, and Gabriella Lapesa. 2021. Towards argument mining for social good: A survey. In *Proceedings of the 59th Annual Meeting of the Association for Computational Linguistics and the 11th International Joint Conference on Natural Language Processing (Volume 1: Long Papers)*, pages 1338–1352.

Penghui Wei and Wenji Mao. 2019. Modeling transferable topics for cross-target stance detection. In *Proceedings of the 42nd International ACM SIGIR Conference on Research and Development in Information Retrieval*, pages 1173–1176.

Thomas Wolf, Lysandre Debut, Victor Sanh, Julien Chaumond, Clement Delangue, Anthony Moi, Pierric Cistac, Tim Rault, Rémi Louf, Morgan Funtowicz, et al. 2020. Transformers: State-of-the-art natural language processing. In *Proceedings of the 2020 conference on empirical methods in natural language processing: system demonstrations*, pages 38–45.

Chang Xu, Cecile Paris, Surya Nepal, and Ross Sparks. 2018. Cross-target stance classification with self-attention networks. In *Proceedings of the 56th Annual Meeting of the Association for Computational Linguistics (Volume 2: Short Papers)*, pages 778–783.

Bowen Zhang, Min Yang, Xutao Li, Yunming Ye, Xiaofei Xu, and Kuai Dai. 2020. Enhancing cross-target stance detection with transferable semantic-emotion knowledge. In *Proceedings of the 58th Annual Meeting of the Association for Computational Linguistics*, pages 3188–3197, Online. Association for Computational Linguistics.

## Appendix

## A Data Scraping

We identified relevant discussions in the reddit boards (sub-communities) europe, europeanunion, and europes and define a list of 10 keywords, then extend it with with word2vec embeddings (Mikolov et al., 2013) of the Google News corpus and the Glove embeddings (Pennington et al., 2014) on the GigaWord corpus. This process led to a keyword list of 38 words: ["climate change", "climate goals "," climate activists", "climate top", "climate target", "climate crisis", "climate crises ", "climate protesters", "sustainable", "sustainability", "carbon emissions", "co2 emissions", "green energy", "green shift ", "green energy", "global warming", "global temperature", "circular economy", "recycling", "recycle", "recyclables", "recyclable", "e-waste", "waste disposal", "landfills", "landfilling", "landfill", "carbon neutrality", "carbon neutral", "biodiversity", "biodiversity conservation", "biodiversity loss", "deforestation", "desertification", "renewable energy", "ecology threats", "ecology protection", "ecology-friendly"]

We scraped discussions from 2017 to 2022 with these keywords using the Pushshift Reddit API. We filter comments of bots (common on Reddit for automatic moderation) by means of a regular expression and rule-based method (Marjanovic et al., 2022), and remove empty or deleted discussions.

## B Annotation Details

**Crowd Annotation set-up** We annotate stance of the comment towards the Reddit topic text in [comment - topic text] pairs. Stance can be *SUPPORT*, *REJECT*, or *NEUTRAL* towards the initiative in the topic text.

When the comment expresses a stance, we add two dimensions: *threat* and *power*. These aspects also have three classes: absence (no mention of this aspect in the stance), positive presence, and negative presence. Positive for threat means explicit recognition of the initiative reacting to a threat. Negative presence of threat means that the comment explicitly mentions the initiative does **not** react to a threat. Positive for power means that the comment mentions feeling power to alleviate this threat. Negative presence of power means explicitly expressing a lack of power on the issue.

We use a simple task design. First, annotators decide whether the topic text contains sustainability action, initiative or statement one can agree or disagree with.[7] Then, they annotate the stance of comments towards these initiatives. Lastly, the 68[8] comment-topic pairs determined to have a sustainability by the majority were annotated for the threat and power dimension.

The authors of this paper annotated 13 examples, with 7 used as training material for annotators and 6 used as quality check items during the task. To assure data quality, the task contained 2 attention checks per batch of around 20 items.

**Task Design and Format** Our task design used a Qualtrics survey adapted to ask the same questions over different texts with a Loop & Merge Field, in a random loop for each participant. Two attention checks early in the task removed participants not reading the task items, which removed one participant in the threat & power task.

Increasing data quality was achieved with 5 random expert-annotated items interspersed through the annotation task, with reminders of reasoning behind annotation decisions provided.

The task flow was as follows: 3 instruction slides, then 5 annotation blocks with 8 to 25 items, each followed by an attention item. The Qualtrics template is released in our GitHub repository[9], both as word file and as .qsf file ready to import into Qualtrics. We release these files inspired by research on the (non) reproducibility of human evaluation & annotation tasks noted by Belz et al. (2023).

## C Analysis of Corpus

### C.1 Methods

**SentenceBERT Clustering** Our initial exploratory analysis consisted of exploring clusters of arguments in order to identify the main topics being discussed in the Reddit Communities. We use the SentenceBERT architecture (embedding texts in a shared dimensional space) with MiniLM version 2 as pre-trained embeddings, with batch size 64.

Our initial clustering algorithm was the basic Community Detection embedded into SentenceBERT. We set this to a minimum community size

[7] A narrow definition of policy claim / debate topic such as "X should Y" (Daxenberger et al., 2017) does not capture the real-world stance-taking reactions people show online to utterances such as questions, announcements of protests, and quotes on sustainability.

[8] There were 71 items in total, but 3 items had an annotation error in the threat/power task.

[9] `https://github.com/myrthereuver/TopicSpecific_Stance_SocialScience`

of 50, and indicated that communities should have a cosine similarity threshold of at least .60. Comments not within this boundary are discarded. This divides up the large embedding space with 46.285 arguments into 25 clusters.

**BERTopic** Our second, more extensive exploratory analysis consists of BERTopic (Grootendorst, 2022), a BERT-based topic model technique based on Huggingface Transformers (Wolf et al., 2020). This out-of-the-box approach uses the SentenceBERT bi-encoding approach outlined above to embed sentences, and adds HBDSCAN as clustering algorithm and UMAP as dimensionality reduction to create and unsupervised clustering approach. The clusters receive "labels" that function as topic names with TF-IDF weighting of most prominent words per cluster. BERTopic is slightly non-deterministic due to the UMAP dimensionality reduction algorithm having a stochastic aspect: however, we found our results to be relatively stable across 3 runs due to the more deterministic results of both SentenceBERT text representation as well as HBDSCAN clustering.

### C.2 Results

**SBERT + miniLM** The input for our clustering analysis were the 46.285 comments found after our preprocessing procedure, and the goal was to find whether there were broad trends and themes in comments. Cluster size varies between 1.549 texts (Cluster 1) and 50 texts (cluster 25). Note that these are only groups that have large enough clusters to all fall within a cosine similarity boundary of .60. A manual inspection of clusters shows that many of these clusters are specific topics and argument types. The largest cluster (1.549 comments) identifies a group of similar comments on renewable energy and specifically nuclear energy as a solution. The second-largest cluster (526 elements) instead focusses on discussions and comments on China versus the west when it comes to CO2 emissions per capita. Another cluster finds all comments related to recycling and waste use, and interestingly does so from various different discussions, also discussions nuclear energy where commenters mention nuclear waste. A smaller cluster (76 texts) focusses on the difference between weather and climate. More detailed results can be found in our GitHub repository. [10]

**BERTopic** Our second preliminary analysis consisted of a BERTopic model. This model allows us to see broad trends and themes across the discussions. The input for our BERTopic model were the 2.073 individual discussions found in our preprocessing step, to see whether the discussions could be grouped into broader themes. The BERTopic model identified 19 topics. The outlier group (573 discussions) consisted mostly of general discussions on climate change and co2 emissions, and because of its lower semantic coherence should not be considered in further analysis (Grootendorst, 2022). The largest cluster (127 discussions) was one on recycling, waste, and landfills, and another large group (127 discussions) discussed student protests and activists. Most topics consisted of broader themes such as heatwaves and increased hot weather in summer (35 discussions), or a broad initiative like the circular economy (31 discussions), but smaller clusters sometimes discussed very specific incidents in the news, such as a Norwegian ban on palm oil (27 discussions) and a courtcase against Shell in the Netherlands (26 discussions). These two incidents seemed to attract attention in the discussion boards.

**Brief Qualitative Analysis** Our annotation process as well as clustering experiments found a variety of reasons why people agreed or disagreed with sustainable initiatives, indicated by the different topics brought up in the discussion. Clustering results indicate that a basic pro/con stance analysis of arguments in sustainable discussions does not do justice to the actual discussion - commenters mention many different aspects of arguments, even the same argument aspects (waste, activism) across different topics and stances in these discussions.

BERTopic models allowed us to find prominent sustainability discussions. One finding is that discussions on activism and activists as well as protests are relatively common. We also found this during our annotation process, so much so that we added "activists" as an actor of sustainability initiatives. Additionally, we found that some specific initiatives in the news (a ban on palm oil and a court case against shell) attracted more comments than others.

[10] https://github.com/myrthereuver/TopicSpecific_Stance_SocialScience

# The Echoes of the 'I': Tracing Identity with Demographically Enhanced Word Embeddings

**Ivan Smirnov**
University of Technology Sydney
ivan.smirnov@uts.edu.au

## Abstract

Identity is one of the most commonly studied constructs in social science. However, despite extensive theoretical work on identity, there remains a need for additional empirical data to validate and refine existing theories. This paper introduces a novel approach to studying identity by enhancing word embeddings with socio-demographic information. As a proof of concept, we demonstrate that our approach successfully reproduces and extends established findings regarding gendered self-views. Our methodology can be applied in a wide variety of settings, allowing researchers to tap into a vast pool of naturally occurring data, such as social media posts. Unlike similar methods already introduced in computer science, our approach allows for the study of differences between social groups. This could be particularly appealing to social scientists and may encourage the faster adoption of computational methods in the field.

## 1 Introduction

Identity is central and one of the most commonly studied constructs in the social sciences, shaping our understanding human behaviour, and society more generally (Leary and Tangney, 2003). While there is no universally accepted definition of identity, it generally refers to individual's self-perception that consists of self-ascribed personal traits, beliefs about themselves, as well as self-categorization into particular social groups and roles.

Research on identity spans disciplines from psychology to sociology, and from linguistics to political science offering rich theoretical insights into identity (Vignoles et al., 2011). However, measuring identity and related constructs remains challenging, which is why there is still a clear need for empirical studies that would allow to validate and refine existing theories (McLean and Syed, 2015). Established methods typically require the annotation of survey data by experts who have to be specially trained. Take, for instance, Loevinger theory of ego development (Loevinger, 1976) which is generally considered as one of the most empirically supported theories of personality development (Gilmore and Durkin, 2001). Traditionally, ego development is measured via the Washington University Sentence Completion Test (WUSCT) (Hy and Loevinger, 1996). That is a projective technique where participants are asked to complete sentence stems such as "What gets me in trouble..." or "A girl has a right to...". While WUSCT has been shown to be a reliable and valid method of measuring ego development (Gilmore and Durkin, 2001), its administration is resource-intensive and requires a specialized training for raters. At the same time, recent developments in computational methods suggest that social media data, at least at a macro level, can aid in assessing psychological constructs (Pellert et al., 2022). This could pave the way for alternatives to traditional survey-based assessments.

Computational approaches and natural language processing have been previously applied to study identity. In particular LIWC (Tausczik and Pennebaker, 2010) – a popular dictionary-based method – has been used to analyze responses to WUSCT (Lanning et al., 2018) or to identify salient identity in social media posts (Koschate et al., 2021). In our work, we propose using word embeddings as they allow capturing more complex semantic relationships in the text by considering the context in which words are used.

The common approach to using word embeddings in social science is to consider projections on semantic axes in word-vector space. It has been previously demonstrated that this technique could effectively recover human sentiments, judgments, and perceptions (An et al., 2018; Grand et al., 2022). This enabled computational social



*Proceedings of the 58th Annual Meeting of the Association for Computational Linguistics*, pages 112–118
July 5–10, 2020. ©2020 Association for Computational Linguistics

scientists to extract insights from large text corpora. The potential of this approach was most notably demonstrated in studies on stereotypes (Caliskan et al., 2017; Garg et al., 2018; Boutyline et al., 2023).

Typically, a word embedding model is trained on a specific corpus of interest. Then, the distance between target words and predefined reference poles, represented by opposing words or sets of words, is considered. This distance is interpreted as the semantic closeness between target words and reference poles, providing insights into underlying associations and relationships. More concretely, it has been shown that certain occupational terms, e.g. 'mechanic', are closer to words representing men ('man', 'boy', 'he', etc.), while other terms, e.g. 'nurse', are closer to words representing women ('woman', 'girl', 'she', etc.), indicating a gender bias (Garg et al., 2018). By training separate word embedding models on time-segmented historical texts, it has been further demonstrated that the changes in word distances over time reflect real-world changes in women's occupations.

Another study has found that words representing men are closer to words related to intelligence, while words representing women are closer to 'studying', reflecting a common stereotype in education: "boys are successful at school because they are smart and girls because they study a lot" (Boutyline et al., 2023). Training separate word embedding models on texts produced at different time points further showed that this stereotype emerged at specific point in time, consistent with sociological explanations of the phenomenon.

Simply computing word similarities in a given corpus is often not very informative. Therefore, researchers typically segment the corpus for comparative analysis. These segments might represent different time periods, as in the examples above, or the corpus could be split by other criteria, such as training distinct models on texts authored by Republicans versus Democrats (Rodriguez and Spirling, 2022). This approach, however, has a disadvantage as it reduces the amount of data available for training individual models, which could impair their performance. It also requires the alignment of resulting models in a common space, which could complicate the interpretation of the results (Hamilton et al., 2016).

In our work, we build upon these ideas by enhancing word embeddings with socio-demographic information and focusing on studying the self. More specifically, we replace every occurrence of the word 'I' in a large corpus of social media posts with $I_{g,a}$ tokens, where $g$ represents the gender of the post author and $a$ their age. We then train a word embedding model on the altered corpus. Projecting the resulting enhanced vectors on semantic axes allows exploring identity as expressed in social media posts. By incorporating socio-demographic information into the I-tokens, it also becomes possible to compare different social groups without splitting the original corpus.

In the remainder of this paper, we provide a more detailed description of our method. We then characterise the obtained enhanced I-tokens and verify whether they meet the criteria for face validity. To further validate our approach, we check if it can reproduce established findings on gendered self-views. Next, we investigate the robustness of the results with respect to model specifications and corpus size. Finally, we discuss how our approach can be applied in different contexts and compare it with existing methods.

## 2 Methods

### 2.1 Data & Model

To train the model, we used data on 62,707,791 posts shared over a span of 5 years by 913,230 users on VK[1]–a popular social media platform predominantly used by Russian speakers. The process of collecting the corpus and filtering out fake profiles has been previously detailed in (Smirnov, 2017) and (Sivak and Smirnov, 2019). Unlike on many other social media platforms, age and gender are mandatory fields of a user profile on VK and are publicly available via its API. This allows us to construct $I_{g,a}$ tokens for all posts in the dataset. While we use VK data for the results described in this paper, our approach could equally be applied to other data sources and to attributes beyond gender and age (see Discussion).

We normalized all adjectives and nouns in the corpus using pymorphy2, the state-of-the-art morphological analyzer and generator for Russian and Ukrainian languages (Korobov, 2015). This step is necessary because, in Russian, nouns and adjectives have distinct feminine and masculine forms. This makes words in feminine form artificially closer to $I_{woman,*}$ tokens in vector space and words in masculine form closer to $I_{man,*}$, preventing meaningful comparisons.

[1] `https://vk.com`

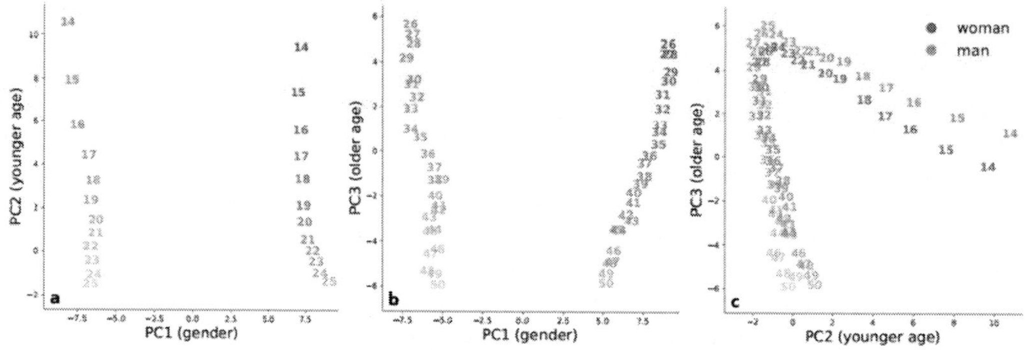

Figure 1: **The structure of enhanced I-token embeddings.** The first principal component extracted from embeddings of enhanced I-tokens corresponds to gender (a, b). Curiously, age is represented by two components: the second component corresponds to a younger age (a), while the third corresponds to an older age (b).

Next, we replaced all singular first-person pronouns used in posts with $I_{g,a}$ tokens, where $g$ and $a$ correspond to the self-reported gender of an author and their self-reported age at the time of writing, e.g. 'I_woman_42', 'I_man_19'. We then trained a continuous bag-of-words model (Mikolov et al., 2013) with 100 dimensions over 10 epochs on this modified corpus. We report the main results for this specific model configuration; however, we also examine their sensitivity to model type (CBOW vs skip-gram), number of dimensions, number of epochs, and corpus size.

We examined the geometric structure of the obtained enhanced embeddings to ensure their face validity. Specifically, we expect $I_{man,*}$ and $I_{woman,*}$ to be clearly separated in vector space. We also expect that $I_{g,a}$ tokens will be sequentially ordered by age, i.e., that $I_{g,i}$ would be between $I_{g,i-1}$ and $I_{g,i+1}$.

**Gendered self-views**

To further validate our approach, we checked if it can reproduce existing findings on sex-trait stereotypes. Sex-trait stereotypes refer to the psychological characteristics or behavioral traits believed to be more prevalent in women than in men, or vice versa (Williams and Best, 1990). A common way to assess sex-trait stereotypes is to present participants with a series of adjectives and ask them to determine whether each adjective is more commonly associated with women or men. From such studies emerged a list of adjectives that participants consistently associate more with either women or men, whether they are describing others or themselves. Examples include 'affectionate' and 'sensitive' for women, and 'courageous' and 'ambitious' for men (the full list of adjectives used in this study is available in Table 1.1 of (Williams and Best, 1990)).

We translated this list into Russian and constructed a semantic axis (*gender stereotype axis*) by subtracting the average embedding for men-associated adjectives from the average embedding for women-associated adjectives. The original list consisted of 29 adjectives for women and 32 for men. This was reduced to 27 and 28 respectively, due to some English words having identical translations in Russian. While the original list was obtained by asking Euro-American college students, recent studies demonstrate that women and men consistently rate themselves higher on corresponding traits across 62 countries (Kosakowska-Berezecka et al., 2023). Thus, if our approach is valid, we expect the projections of $I_{woman,*}$ on the *gender stereotype axis* to be positive, while projections of $I_{man,*}$ to be negative.

## 3 Results

We found that the variation between $I_{g,a}$ tokens is largely explained by gender and age variables. In particular, the first principal component extracted from these vectors corresponds to gender, clearly separating $I_{woman,*}$ from $I_{man,*}$ tokens (Figure 1a and 1b). The point-biserial correlation coefficient between gender and the first component is 0.986 ($P < 10^{-61}$).

We expected that the second principal component would correspond to age. However, the results are more nuanced: the second component corresponds to younger age (Figure 1a) with Spearman's $\rho = 0.965, P < 10^{-13}$, while the third component corresponds to older age (Figure 1b) with Spear-

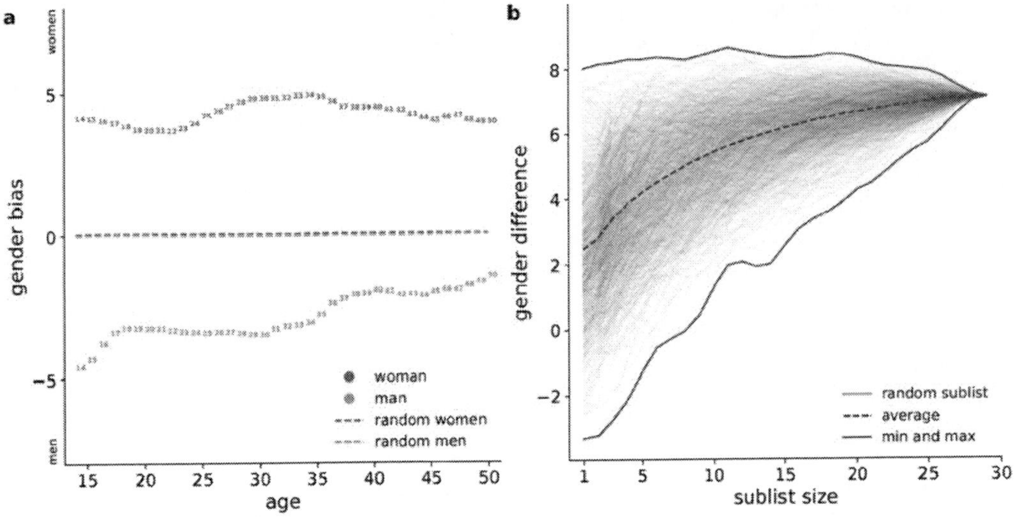


Figure 2: **Projection of enhanced I-tokens on *gender stereotype axis* reproduces established findings on gendered self-views.** $I_{woman,*}$ tokens are closer to women's pole of the axis, while $I_{man,*}$ tokens are closer to the men's pole (a). The gap between them narrows with age as $I_{man,*}$ tokens shift towards the center. The results are significant with $P < 10^{-3}$ and are robust with respect to the selection of adjectives, starting from a list size of around 10 (b). For visual clarity, a moving average with a window size of 3 is used.

man's $\rho = 0.928, P < 10^{-24}$. The interaction between these components and age is shown in Figure 1c. We hypothesise that this might be explained by graduation from university and the transition to working life, as the curve's turning point (25–26 years in Figure 1c) roughly matches the age when students typically complete their degrees in Russia.

### Gendered self-views

If our approach is valid, we expect that projections of $I_{woman,*}$ on the *gender stereotype axis* will be positive, and projections of $I_{man,*}$ will be negative. This is indeed what we observe (see Figure 2a). We tested the significance of this result by randomly shuffling adjectives used to construct the *gender stereotype axis* and projecting the enhanced I-tokens on the resulting random axes. None of the biases computed for $1,000$ random axes were as strong as the one we observed, making our results significant with $P < 10^{-3}$.

We also tested the robustness of our results with respect to dictionary size, following the method suggested in (Spliethöver and Wachsmuth, 2021). To do this, we randomly selected $k$ adjectives, with $k$ varying from 1 to 28, from both the men-associated and women-associated lists. We then used these shorter lists to construct a gender axis and compute the bias, repeating the procedure $1,000$ times. This shows that the bias is consistently detected with a list size of around 10 adjectives for each gender (Figure 2b). Note that for this analysis we did not consider age separately, but computed the differences between the projections of aggregated $I_{man}$ and $I_{woman}$ on the *gender stereotype axis*, where the aggregated vectors represent averages over all ages.

Additionally, we were able to detect changes in the strength of this relationship over the years–a result that is difficult to capture in surveys, as they are typically conducted on samples of university students (Williams and Best, 1990; Kosakowska-Berezecka et al., 2023). This demonstrates the potential of our methodology not only to reproduce established findings but also to gain new insights that might be harder to obtain via traditional methods.

### Robustness of the results

We evaluated how well the observed geometrical structure of enhanced I-tokens is preserved across different model specifications. We also checked for the robustness of the relationship between gender and gender-stereotypical adjectives. For this purpose, we computed point-biserial correlation coefficients between gender and the first principal component extracted from I-tokens, as well as between gender and the projection of I-tokens on the *gender stereotype axis* (see Figure 3).

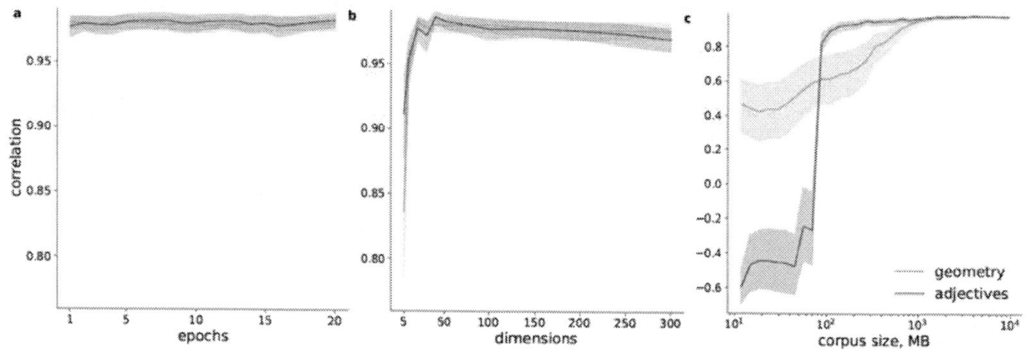


Figure 3: **Robustness of the results with respect to model specification.** We evaluated how much point-biserial correlations between gender and the first principal component extracted from enhanced I-tokens (orange), as well as between gender and the projection of I-tokens on the *gender stereotype axis* (blue), depend on model specification. We found that no further training is required beyond one epoch to reproduce the results (a). We also found that any reasonable number of dimensions can be used (b). Finally, we found that 100MB is a sufficient corpus size, but beyond that point, the performance drops for adjectives as they become too rare. The first principal component of enhanced I-tokens remains strongly associated with gender for all our experiments.

Although we trained the model for 10 epochs for the reported results, we found that further training offers little additional benefit and the main results can be reproduced after just one epoch (Figure 3a). We also found that any reasonable number of dimensions (50–300) could be used without compromising the model's performance (Figure 3b). The observed relationships are even more salient when vector sizes are between 50 and 100, which could be preferable due to the smaller model size. There was no substantial difference between the CBOW and skip-gram architectures.

We found that 100MB of data is sufficient to reproduce the results after training for one epoch (Figure 3c). For smaller datasets, performance drops for adjectives because they become too rare in the corpus. The first principal component of enhanced I-tokens is strongly correlated with gender in all our experiments. In practice, an even smaller corpus could be used. For example, the corpus of interest could be augmented by a neural one, such as a Wikipedia dump. This should result in better representations of rare words without affecting enhanced I-tokens, as they would only be present in the original corpus of interest.

## 4 Discussion

In this paper, we introduced a novel approach that leverages readily available data sources, such as social media, to study identity. Unlike traditional methods that rely on self-report surveys, our method allows for the study of identity in natural settings and on a larger scale. While we used data from VK, the same technique can be applied to other datasets as well. For example, self-reported gender and age have been extracted from posts on popular platforms such as Reddit and Twitter (Tigunova et al., 2020; Klein et al., 2022), making it possible to apply our method directly to these datasets. Attributes that can be used to construct enhanced I-tokens are not limited to gender and age. For instance, with datasets containing profession information on Reddit (Tigunova et al., 2020) or educational outcomes on VK (Smirnov, 2019), it becomes possible to study differences between various socio-economic groups. Moreover, this approach can be extended beyond social media data. Our experiments demonstrate that the corpus does not need to be exceptionally large for the method to be effective. Therefore, it could be applied to TV scripts to analyse the representation of different groups on television, building upon previous research in this area (Ramakrishna et al., 2015, 2017).

As a proof of concept, we applied our method to study gendered self-views. We found that the approach not only reproduces established results but also allows for new findings by covering a wider age range than is typically available in surveys. This method can similarly be applied to other phenomena using curated word lists. Alternatively, an open dictionary approach can be used to identify and examine words that are especially close to certain enhanced I-tokens in a corpus of interest.

The introduced method relies on natural language processing techniques that are admittedly no longer considered state-of-the-art. Since the introduction of word2vec (Mikolov et al., 2013), more advanced models have emerged, particularly fastText (Bojanowski et al., 2017), which operates at the character n-gram level and potentially offers superior embeddings for morphologically rich languages such as Russian. Later, contextual word embedding models were developed, most notably BERT (Devlin et al., 2019), which outperformed static models in a wide range of tasks. However, we believe that advances in machine learning outpace their adoption in social sciences, and there are still many opportunities for new insights to be obtained from using static continuous representations of words. While newer models have led to remarkable performance gains in machine learning applications, we believe that the higher interpretability and computational efficiency of simpler models might still make them preferable for analytical purposes and applications in social science.

The idea of using semantic projections traces its origins back to at least 2016 (Bolukbasi et al., 2016), when a gender axis was constructed to reveal biases in word embeddings. This methodology was later formally introduced in (An et al., 2018), re-introduced in (Mathew et al., 2020), and re-introduced again in (Grand et al., 2022). It was further extended to contextual word embeddings (Lucy et al., 2022; Engler et al., 2022). Despite these developments within the computer science literature, their adoption in social sciences has been relatively slow. One possible explanation is that these methods enable the identification of biases at an aggregated level of entire corpora, which, while interesting, has limited applications. In our paper, we build upon previous ideas and show how they can be extended to study differences between social groups. We believe this opens up many new possibilities that would be particularly appealing to social scientists.

## Data and Code

The data and code used to obtain the main results of this paper are available at `https://github.com/ibsmirnov/echoes-of-i`.

## References


Jisun An, Haewoon Kwak, and Yong-Yeol Ahn. 2018. SemAxis: A lightweight framework to characterize domain-specific word semantics beyond sentiment. pages 2450–2461, Melbourne, Australia.

Piotr Bojanowski, Edouard Grave, Armand Joulin, and Tomas Mikolov. 2017. Enriching word vectors with subword information. *Transactions of the Association for Computational Linguistics*, 5:135–146.

Tolga Bolukbasi, Kai-Wei Chang, James Y Zou, Venkatesh Saligrama, and Adam T Kalai. 2016. Man is to computer programmer as woman is to homemaker? debiasing word embeddings. *Advances in neural information processing systems*, 29.

Andrei Boutyline, Alina Arseniev-Koehler, and Devin J Cornell. 2023. School, studying, and smarts: Gender stereotypes and education across 80 years of american print media, 1930–2009. *Social Forces*, page soac148.

Aylin Caliskan, Joanna J Bryson, and Arvind Narayanan. 2017. Semantics derived automatically from language corpora contain human-like biases. *Science*, 356(6334):183–186.

Jacob Devlin, Ming-Wei Chang, Kenton Lee, and Kristina Toutanova. 2019. BERT: Pre-training of deep bidirectional transformers for language understanding. pages 4171–4186, Minneapolis, Minnesota.

Jan Engler, Sandipan Sikdar, Marlene Lutz, and Markus Strohmaier. 2022. SensePOLAR: Word sense aware interpretability for pre-trained contextual word embeddings. pages 4607–4619, Abu Dhabi, United Arab Emirates.

Nikhil Garg, Londa Schiebinger, Dan Jurafsky, and James Zou. 2018. Word embeddings quantify 100 years of gender and ethnic stereotypes. *Proceedings of the National Academy of Sciences*, 115(16):E3635–E3644.

John Manners Gilmore and Kevin Durkin. 2001. A critical review of the validity of ego development theory and its measurement. *Journal of personality assessment*, 77(3):541–567.

Gabriel Grand, Idan Asher Blank, Francisco Pereira, and Evelina Fedorenko. 2022. Semantic projection recovers rich human knowledge of multiple object features from word embeddings. *Nature human behaviour*, 6(7):975–987.

William L. Hamilton, Jure Leskovec, and Dan Jurafsky. 2016. Diachronic word embeddings reveal statistical laws of semantic change. pages 1489–1501, Berlin, Germany.

Le Xuan Hy and Jane Loevinger. 1996. *Measuring ego development*. Lawrence Erlbaum Associates, Inc.

Ari Z Klein, Arjun Magge, and Graciela Gonzalez-Hernandez. 2022. Reportage: Automatically extracting the exact age of twitter users based on self-reports in tweets. *PloS one*, 17(1):e0262087.

Mikhail Korobov. 2015. Morphological analyzer and generator for Russian and Ukrainian languages. In Mikhail Yu. Khachay, Natalia Konstantinova, Alexander Panchenko, Dmitry I. Ignatov, and Valeri G. Labunets, editors, *Analysis of Images, Social Networks and Texts*, volume 542 of *Communications in Computer and Information Science*, pages 320–332. Springer International Publishing.

Natasza Kosakowska-Berezecka, Jennifer K Bosson, Paweł Jurek, Tomasz Besta, Michał Olech, Joseph A Vandello, Michael Bender, Justine Dandy, Vera Hoorens, Inga Jasinskaja-Lahti, et al. 2023. Gendered self-views across 62 countries: A test of competing models. *Social Psychological and Personality Science*, 14(7):808–824.

Miriam Koschate, Elahe Naserian, Luke Dickens, Avelie Stuart, Alessandra Russo, and Mark Levine. 2021. Asia: Automated social identity assessment using linguistic style. *Behavior Research Methods*, 53:1762–1781.

Kevin Lanning, Rachel E Pauletti, Laura A King, and Dan P McAdams. 2018. Personality development through natural language. *Nature Human Behaviour*, 2(5):327–334.

Mark R Leary and June Price Tangney. 2003. The self as an organizing construct in the behavioral and social sciences. *Handbook of self and identity*, 15:3–14.

Jane Loevinger. 1976. *Ego development*. Jossey-Bass, San Francisco.

Li Lucy, Divya Tadimeti, and David Bamman. 2022. Discovering differences in the representation of people using contextualized semantic axes. pages 3477–3494, Abu Dhabi, United Arab Emirates.

Binny Mathew, Sandipan Sikdar, Florian Lemmerich, and Markus Strohmaier. 2020. The polar framework: Polar opposites enable interpretability of pre-trained word embeddings. In *Proceedings of The Web Conference 2020*, pages 1548–1558.

Kate C McLean and Moin Syed. 2015. The field of identity development needs an identity: An introduction to the oxford handbook of identity development. *The Oxford handbook of identity development*, pages 1–10.

Tomas Mikolov, Kai Chen, Greg Corrado, and Jeffrey Dean. 2013. Efficient estimation of word representations in vector space. *arXiv preprint arXiv:1301.3781*.

Max Pellert, Hannah Metzler, Michael Matzenberger, and David Garcia. 2022. Validating daily social media macroscopes of emotions. *Scientific reports*, 12(1):11236.

Anil Ramakrishna, Nikolaos Malandrakis, Elizabeth Staruk, and Shrikanth Narayanan. 2015. A quantitative analysis of gender differences in movies using psycholinguistic normatives. pages 1996–2001, Lisbon, Portugal.

Anil Ramakrishna, Victor R. Martínez, Nikolaos Malandrakis, Karan Singla, and Shrikanth Narayanan. 2017. Linguistic analysis of differences in portrayal of movie characters. pages 1669–1678, Vancouver, Canada.

Pedro L Rodriguez and Arthur Spirling. 2022. Word embeddings: What works, what doesn't, and how to tell the difference for applied research. *The Journal of Politics*, 84(1):101–115.

Elizaveta Sivak and Ivan Smirnov. 2019. Parents mention sons more often than daughters on social media. *Proceedings of the National Academy of Sciences*, 116(6):2039–2041.

Ivan Smirnov. 2017. The digital flynn effect: Complexity of posts on social media increases over time. In *Social Informatics: 9th International Conference, SocInfo 2017, Oxford, UK, September 13-15, 2017, Proceedings, Part II 9*, pages 24–30. Springer.

Ivan Smirnov. 2019. Schools are segregated by educational outcomes in the digital space. *PloS one*, 14(5):e0217142.

Maximilian Spliethöver and Henning Wachsmuth. 2021. Bias silhouette analysis: Towards assessing the quality of bias metrics for word embedding models. In *IJCAI*, pages 552–559.

Yla R Tausczik and James W Pennebaker. 2010. The psychological meaning of words: LIWC and computerized text analysis methods. *Journal of language and social psychology*, 29(1):24–54.

Anna Tigunova, Paramita Mirza, Andrew Yates, and Gerhard Weikum. 2020. RedDust: a large reusable dataset of Reddit user traits. pages 6118–6126, Marseille, France. European Language Resources Association.

Vivian L Vignoles, Seth J Schwartz, and Koen Luyckx. 2011. Introduction: Toward an integrative view of identity. In *Handbook of identity theory and research*, pages 1–27. Springer.

John E Williams and Deborah L Best. 1990. *Measuring sex stereotypes: A multination study, Rev*. Sage Publications, Inc.

# TPPMI - a Temporal Positive Pointwise Mutual Information Embedding of Words

**Paul Schmitt**
TU Wien
paulschmitt.a@icloud.com

**Zsófia Rakovics**
Eötvös Loránd University
zsofia.rakovics@tatk.elte.hu

**Márton Rakovics**
Eötvös Loránd University
marton.rakovics@tatk.elte.hu

**Gábor Recski**
TU Wien
gabor.recski@tuwien.ac.at

## Abstract

We present Temporal Positive Pointwise Mutual Information (TPPMI) embeddings as a robust and data-efficient alternative for modeling temporal semantic change. Based on the assumption that the semantics of the most frequent words in a corpus are relatively stable over time, our model represents words as vectors of their PPMI similarities with a predefined set of such context words. We evaluate our method on the temporal word analogy benchmark of Yao et al. (2018) and compare it to the TWEC model (Di Carlo et al., 2019), demonstrating the competitiveness of the approach. While the performance of TPPMI stays below that of the state-of-the-art TWEC model, it offers a higher degree of interpretability and is applicable in scenarios where only a limited amount of data is available.

## 1 Introduction

Word embedding models have become the dominant approach to modelling lexical semantics in the natural language processing (NLP) community. While contextual embeddings are now prevalent in most NLP applications, common static embedding methods such as word2vec (Mikolov et al., 2013) and GLoVe (Pennington et al., 2014) are still widely used in the computational modeling of word meaning, including the study of semantic change. Modern approaches train temporal word embeddings by learning alignments between multiple sets of word vectors (Hamilton et al., 2016; Di Carlo et al., 2019), but these approaches rely on the availability of a large amount of training data from each time period.

The efficiency and robustness of Pointwise Mutual Information (PMI) as a simple measure for word co-occurrence has been demonstrated in multiple studies (Bullinaria and Levy, 2007; Levy and Goldberg, 2014; Wendlandt et al., 2018). In this study we propose the use of Positive Pointwise Mutual Information (PPMI) to create temporal embeddings that represent the meaning of words as vectors of their PPMI with a small fixed set of context words chosen from the most frequent content words of the corpus, based on the assumption that the semantics of these words is relatively stable across time. Our experiments on the temporal word analogy task of Yao et al. (2018) demonstrate that this highly interpretable model offers a robust and competitive measure of lexical semantic change. The rest of the paper is structured as follows: Section 2 summarizes recent research on temporal word embeddings. Section 3 presents our method. Section 4 describes our experimental setup and Section 5 presents results of both quantitative and qualitative analysis. Section 6 concludes the paper. All software described here is publicly available on GitHub[1] under an MIT license.

## 2 Related Work

Word embeddings have been used extensively to study lexical semantic change. Yao et al. (2018) trains time-aware word embeddings by jointly learning multiple word embeddings and their alignment. For evaluation they train on a dataset of nearly 100,000 crawled articles from the New York Times (NYT), published between 1980 and 2016, and evaluate their method by using the resulting vector spaces to solve simple temporal reasoning tasks. One of these tasks that has since been reused for evaluating temporal embeddings, and which we also use in this paper, are *temporal analogy* questions of the form *2012:Obama = 2004:?*. In this example a temporal embedding is expected to predict *Bush* as a likely or even the most likely answer based on the assumption that the word's semantics in 2004 news texts should be (most) similar to that of *Obama* in 2012.

[1] https://github.com/FlackoJodye1/temporal-word-embeddings



*Proceedings of the 58th Annual Meeting of the Association for Computational Linguistics*, pages 119–125
July 5–10, 2020. 

Rudolph and Blei (2018) develop Dynamic Bernoulli Embeddings, a type of Exponential Family Embeddings (Rudolph et al., 2016), which capture change by modeling words as sequences of embeddings over time slices that are grounded in a space of shared context vectors. They train their models on corpora of scientific papers and U.S. Senate speeches. In addition to qualitative analysis of the resulting embeddings they also perform intrinsic evaluation that involves calculating their loss function on heldout portions for each dataset and time period. This experiment is reproduced by Di Carlo et al. (2019), who propose the TWEC method for aligning word2vec embeddings trained on data from various time periods based on a shared target vector space trained on atemporal data. They also test their method on the temporal analogy task, and it is this approach that we use for comparison when evaluating the TPPMI method.

## 3 Method

The Temporal Positive Pointwise Mutual Information (TPPMI) method models semantic change of words based on their distribution w.r.t a fixed set of the most frequent content words of the atemporal context, based on the assumption that these words exhibit relatively stable semantics. Pointwise Mutual Information (PMI) measures the co-occurrence of a word $w$ with a context word $c$ by calculating

$$\text{PMI}(w, c) = \log \frac{\hat{P}(w, c)}{\hat{P}(w)\hat{P}_\alpha(c)} - \log(k)$$

where $\hat{P}(w, c)$ is the co-occurrence probability of $w$ and $c$, $\hat{P}(w)$ is the overall probability of $w$, $\hat{P}_\alpha(c)$ is the probability of $c$ smoothed and $k$ is a shifting constant (Levy and Goldberg, 2014). In all our experiments we use $\alpha = 1$ and $k = 1$. Positive Pointwise Mutual Information (PPMI) is defined as

$$\text{PPMI}(w, c) = \max(\text{PMI}(w, c), 0)$$

TPPMI embeddings for each time period map words to vectors of PPMI values between each word and the fixed set of context words, calculated on data from the given time period. This results in word embeddings that are highly interpretable compared to standard word vectors, since dimensions directly correspond to individual context words. As a second step, the entries of the PPMI matrices are smoothed in time using a cubic spline separately for each component of the embedding vectors to stabilize the vectors in each slice.

The static set of context words is determined by removing stopwords from the atemporal corpus (the union of all time slices) and sampling from the most frequent words in the corpus. The number of words, which determines the dimensionality of the TPPMI embeddings, is a parameter of our approach. To create a set of $n$ context words we sample from the $2n$ most frequent words. Stopword removal is performed using the `nltk`[2] package. The size of the context word set greatly influences the robustness and performance of our models and should be optimized separately for each application of the TPPMI approach.

## 4 Experiment

Following the experimental setup of Di Carlo et al. (2019) we train our temporal embeddings on the NYT dataset and evaluate it on temporal word analogies (see also Section 2). We compare our model to both TWEC and to static word2vec embeddings as a trivial baseline.

### 4.1 Models

The TPPMI embeddings are trained using the process described in Section 3. The number of context words is set to 2,000. The TWEC model and the static word2vec model (SW2V) are trained usting the hyperparameters from Yao et al. (2018) and Di Carlo et al. (2019), embedding dimension is 50, the context window size is 5, and the vocabulary size is 21,000. All text is lowercased, stopwords as well as words with an overall frequency below 200 are omitted.

### 4.2 Temporal Word Analogies

We compare the TPPMI model with established methods using a modified version of the temporal analogical reasoning task introduced by Yao et al. (2018). The task of solving a temporal word analogy (TWA) can be expressed as $t1 : w1 = t2 :?$ and entails predicting the word $w2$ that at time $t2$ is semantically most semantically similar to the word $w1$ at time $t1$. In all vector space models this prediction is achieved by identifying the word whose vector in the vector space of time $t2$ is most similar to the vector of $w1$ at time $t1$.

[2] https://www.nltk.org/

The training dataset contains 99,872 crawled articles from the New York Times, all of them published between January 1990 and July 2016. The dataset was also used by Yao et al. (2018) and was provided to us by the authors. Following previous experiments we partition the articles into batches for each calendar year, resulting in a total of 27 slices. The temporal analogy queries introduced by Yao et al. (2018) are derived from publicly available records and contain the names of persons occupying various public offices in each calendar year, including U.S. President, the Chancellor of Germany, the Governor of New York, among others. In our experiments we focus only on analogies involving U.S. Presidents. The test queries contain two types of analogies:

- **Static analogies:** The target word is identical to the query word, e.g. *2003:bush* = *2004:bush*
- **Dynamic analogies:** The target word differs from the query word, e.g. *2003:bush* = *2011:obama*

Following Di Carlo et al. (2019) we evaluate our method separately on each subset. This is necessary to separate cases where the trivial strategy of the static embedding (SW2V) yields the correct answer. Evaluating on both datasets ensures that temporal embedding models strike a balance between stability and dynamism. Basic descriptive statistics about the test set are shown in Table 1.

| Analogies | Total queries | Unique queries |
|---|---|---|
| All | 8272 | 369 |
| Static | 2333 | 335 |
| Dynamic | 5938 | 369 |

Table 1: Basic statistics of the Temporal Word Analogy test set. For each unique pair of query word and year (e.g. *2012:obama*) the test set contains queries for multiple years (e.g. *1990:?*, *2000:?*, etc.), hence the total number of queries is much larger then the number of unique queries

**Named Entities** Our early experiments revealed a significant artefact of the evaluation data. Since all queries and target words are named entities, evaluation results are largely influenced by some models' tendency to predict target words that have the same part-of-speech as the query word, behavior that is characteristic of most static word embeddings. Since this behavior offers an unwanted advantage on the TWA task, we modify the experimental setup by filtering words predicted by any model to only contain named entities. This strategy increases the performance of all models, since the set of possible answers is considerably reduced, but focuses the evaluation on models' ability to predict semantic shifts. For the filtering step we use the Pantheon dataset of globally famous biographies (Yu et al., 2016), the set of possible target words is reduced to those that are listed in this dataset as person names. This strategy can trivially be extended to other entity types to allow for broader sets of TWA queries.

### 4.3 Evaluation

For each model cosine similarity is used to retrieve the vectors most similar to that of the target word, yielding a ranked list of possible answers to each query. These lists are then compared to the ground truth using two metrics, Mean Reciprocal Rank over the top 10 answers (MRR@10) and Mean Precision at various thresholds (MP@k). Both metrics are defined below.

**Mean Reciprocal Rank (MRR@10)** is the average rank that a model assigns to the correct answer. For each query $i$, $\text{rank}_i$ is the rank of the expected answer in the list of predicted answers returned by a model. The MRR of the model can then be defined as

$$\text{MRR} = \frac{1}{N}\sum_{i=1}^{N}\frac{1}{\text{rank}_i}$$

To calculate MRR@10, $\frac{1}{\text{rank}_i}$ is set to 0 if the word is not among the top 10 predicted words.

**Mean Precision (MP@k)** averages over all queries whether the expected answer is among the top $k$ predicted answers. For a query $i$ we define $P_i@k$ to be 1 if the top $k$ predicted words contain the target word and 0 otherwise. MP@k is then defined as

$$\text{MP}@k = \frac{1}{N}\sum_{i=1}^{N} P_i@k$$

MP@1 is equivalent to model accuracy, measuring the ratio of queries for which the model successfully predicted the target word as the most likely answer.

## 5 Results

### 5.1 Quantitative Analysis

Table 2 shows all scores for each of the three models. The static baseline (SW2V) that uses the same vector space for query and target words achieves 1.0 accuracy (MP@1) on the static test set and 0.0 accuracy on the dynamic test set. Its MP@3 score of 0.709 on the dynamic test set demonstrates that most target words are among those that are distributionally most similar to the query word in the atemporal space, i.e. all names of recent U.S. presidents are relatively close together in a static word embedding. This property of the corpus together with our NE filtering strategy is responsible for high MP@k scores across the board, MP@10 values show that for all models the target word is among the top 10 predicted words for 80% of static queries and between 48 and 56% of dynamic queries. The high scores achieved even by the trivial baseline SW2V on the complete dataset ("All") also illustrates the need to evaluate models separately on the dynamic subset, i.e. on those analogies where the target word is different from the query word.

Both the TWEC and TPPMI models perform robustly in static analogies, with TWEC achieving slightly higher scores. TWEC's MRR@10 is 0.668 compared to TPPMI's 0.592, and TWEC's MP@1 is 0.591 compared to TPPMI's 0.493. However, TPPMI shows strong performance with an MP@3 of 0.663 and MP@5 of 0.729, demonstrating its capability to rank relevant words highly in static contexts. This indicates that while both models effectively capture stable semantic associations, TWEC has a slight edge in precision. Nonetheless, the TPPMI model showcases its ability to produce robust temporal embeddings with a much simpler approach.

On dynamic analogies, the TWEC model significantly outperforms TPPMI, achieving an MRR@10 of 0.402 and MP@1 of 0.326 compared to TPPMI's 0.302 and 0.225, respectively. In terms of MRR the TPPMI is on par only with the static baseline, but its accuracy (MP@1) of 0.225 on the dynamic set indicates its potential for correctly predicting semantic shifts. While further research shall be necessary to improve our method, these preliminary results suggest that the TPPMI model has potential as a simple, interpretable, and computationally efficient alternative to state-of-the-art methods. The interpretability of the method is further demonstrated by the qualitative analysis in the next section.

### 5.2 Qualitative analysis

Much recent work on temporal word embeddings has performed qualitative analysis using a variety of trajectory visualizations based on 2-dimensional projections of vector spaces. In our work we focus only on relative similarity of vectors as measured by cosine similarity and conduct two simple experiments for inspecting our model's ability to capture semantic change and temporal analogies, respectively.

Figure 1 plots the cosine similarity between the word "president" and the names "obama," "biden," "clinton," and "bush" over the years 1990 to 2016. The gray dotted lines on the graph indicate the years when a new president was elected: Bill Clinton in 1992, George W. Bush in 2000, and Barack Obama in 2008. This plot is especially interesting because Bush is also the name of the U.S. President before 1992 and Clinton is also the name of the Democratic candidate in 2016, accounting for the periodicity observed in each curve.

Next we demonstrate the workings of a temporal word analogy. Given the TWA query *2004:Bush = 2012:?* the prediction of the TPPMI model will be based on the similarity of target words in 2012 to those context words that are most similar to *Bush* in 2004. Figure 2 shows the top 10 such context words and their similarities to both *Bush* in the 2004 vector space and to *Obama* in the 2015 vector space. The years 2004 and 2012 were chosen as they are the re-election years for George W. Bush and Barack Obama, respectively. We can observe that some, but not all of these context words maintain a high similarity with the name of the sitting president across time periods. While in this case the observed distinctions are trivial, e.g. that among the words most closely associated with *Bush*, *president* and *re-election* are more distinctive of his 2012 role than the word *George*, it nevertheless demonstrates the TPPMI model's ability to offer similar but less trivial insights from limited amount of temporal data.

## 6 Conclusion

We presented the Temporal Positive Pointwise Mutual Information model of lexical semantic change. TPPMI offers an interpretable and robust approach to capturing temporal semantic shifts of words, addressing the challenges of small and sparse datasets.

Table 2: Evaluation results on the Temporal Word Analogy task.

| Model | Category | MRR@10 | MP@1 | MP@3 | MP@5 | MP@10 |
|---|---|---|---|---|---|---|
| TWEC | Static | 0.668 | 0.591 | 0.723 | 0.768 | 0.818 |
| | Dynamic | **0.402** | **0.326** | **0.455** | **0.508** | **0.560** |
| | All | 0.455 | **0.383** | 0.504 | 0.551 | 0.602 |
| TPPMI | Static | 0.592 | 0.493 | 0.663 | 0.729 | 0.791 |
| | Dynamic | 0.302 | 0.225 | 0.348 | 0.409 | 0.475 |
| | All | 0.365 | 0.284 | 0.417 | 0.478 | 0.541 |
| SW2V | Static | **1.000** | **1.000** | **1.000** | **1.000** | **1.000** |
| | Dynamic | 0.322 | 0.000 | 0.709 | 0.741 | 0.813 |
| | All | **0.551** | 0.337 | **0.807** | **0.828** | **0.876** |

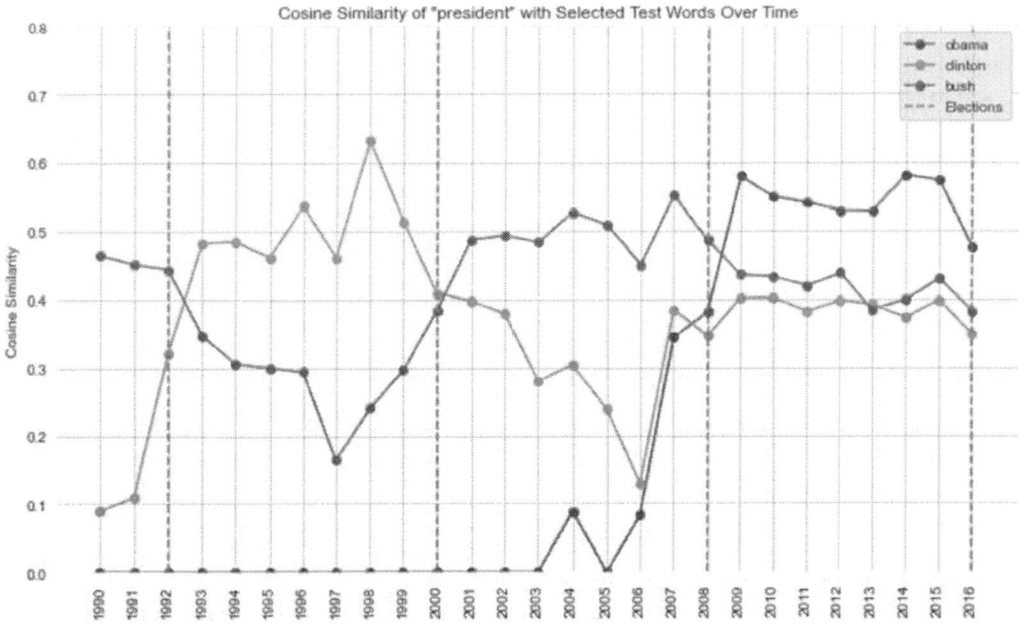


Figure 1: Yearly cosine similarities between the word 'president' and the names of U.S. Presidents between 1990 and 2016, as measured by the TPPMI model

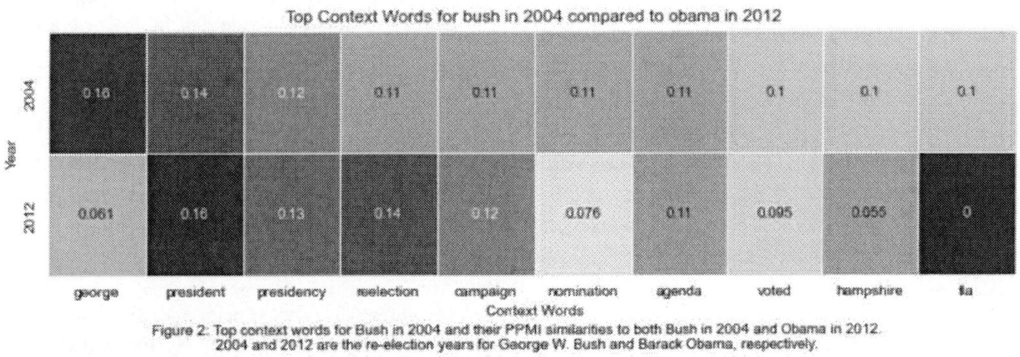


Figure 2: Top context words for *Bush* in 2004 and their PPMI similarities to both *Bush* in 2004 and *Obama* in 2012. 2004 and 2012 are the re-election years for George W. Bush and Barack Obama, respectively.

The model is evaluated on a temporal word analogy task and achieves reasonable performance on both static and dynamic analogies. Despite its inferiority to more sophisticated models like TWEC, we believe that its simplicity and computational efficiency make TPPMI a practical alternative for applications with limited data. Our qualitative analysis further demonstrates the model's ability to show semantic shifts of individual words over time and to offer explanations of such shifts based on the words corresponding to significant dimensions.

## Limitations

Despite its strengths, the TPPMI model's performance is clearly limited and appears to be inferior to state-of-the-art methods on the TWA benchmark. While the method is a practical alternative for applications with limited data and a need for explainability, it is likely not sufficiently robust for large-scale analysis of semantic change. The significance of this preliminary work is further limited by the choice of a single training dataset, a single evaluation benchmark, and a single reference system.

## Ethical considerations

As any distributional model, TPPMI embeddings may inherit and amplify harmful biases present in its training data. Mitigating this risk requires careful data selection, preprocessing, and ongoing evaluation of model bias. However, the interpretability of TPPMI embeddings offers a lowered risk of bias in temporal predictions compared to alternative methods, since the significant dimensions are directly associated with individual context words.

## Notes

The first version of the TPPMI method was presented at the conference of ELTE Angelusz Róbert College for Advanced Studies in Social Sciences and published in the associated conference proceedings (Rakovics, 2022). The improved version of the method was presented at the 8th International Conference on Computational Social Science (IC2S2) as a conference poster (Rakovics and Rakovics, 2022).

## References


John A. Bullinaria and Joseph P. Levy. 2007. Extracting semantic representations from word co-occurrence statistics: A computational study. *Behavior Research Methods*, 39(3):510–526.

Valerio Di Carlo, Federico Bianchi, and Matteo Palmonari. 2019. Training Temporal Word Embeddings with a Compass. *Proceedings of the AAAI Conference on Artificial Intelligence*, 33(01):6326–6334.

William L. Hamilton, Jure Leskovec, and Dan Jurafsky. 2016. Diachronic word embeddings reveal statistical laws of semantic change. In *Proceedings of the 54th Annual Meeting of the Association for Computational Linguistics (Volume 1: Long Papers)*, pages 1489–1501, Berlin, Germany. Association for Computational Linguistics.

Omer Levy and Yoav Goldberg. 2014. Neural word embedding as implicit matrix factorization. In *Advances in Neural Information Processing Systems*, volume 27. Curran Associates, Inc.

Tomas Mikolov, Ilya Sutskever, Kai Chen, Greg S Corrado, and Jeff Dean. 2013. Distributed representations of words and phrases and their compositionality. In *Advances in Neural Information Processing Systems 26*, pages 3111–3119. Curran Associates, Inc.

Jeffrey Pennington, Richard Socher, and Christopher Manning. 2014. GloVe: Global vectors for word representation. In *Proceedings of the 2014 Conference on Empirical Methods in Natural Language Processing (EMNLP)*, pages 1532–1543, Doha, Qatar. Association for Computational Linguistics.

Zsófia Rakovics. 2022. A Temporal Positive Pointwise Mutual Information (TPPMI) időbeli szóbeágyazási modell alkalmazásában rejlő lehetőségek demonstrálása. In *Van új a nap alatt: Az ELTE Angelusz Róbert Társadalomtudományi Szakkollégium konferenciájának tanulmánykötete*, pages 31–48. ELTE Eötvös József Kiadó; ELTE Angelusz Róbert Társadalomtudományi Szakkollégium.

Zsófia Rakovics and Márton Rakovics. 2022. Semantic evolution of words in Hungarian Prime Minister Viktor Orbán's speeches using a temporal word embedding model focusing on the issue of migration.

Maja Rudolph and David Blei. 2018. Dynamic Embeddings for Language Evolution. In *Proceedings of the 2018 World Wide Web Conference on World Wide Web - WWW '18*, pages 1003–1011, Lyon, France. ACM Press.

Maja Rudolph, Francisco Ruiz, Stephan Mandt, and David Blei. 2016. Exponential family embeddings. In *Advances in Neural Information Processing Systems*, volume 29. Curran Associates, Inc.

Laura Wendlandt, Jonathan K. Kummerfeld, and Rada Mihalcea. 2018. Factors influencing the surprising instability of word embeddings. In *Proceedings of the 2018 Conference of the North American Chapter of the Association for Computational Linguistics: Human Language Technologies, Volume 1 (Long Papers)*, pages 2092–2102, New Orleans, Louisiana. Association for Computational Linguistics.

Zijun Yao, Yifan Sun, Weicong Ding, Nikhil Rao, and Hui Xiong. 2018. Dynamic word embeddings for evolving semantic discovery. In *Proceedings of the Eleventh ACM International Conference on Web Search and Data Mining*, WSDM '18, page 673–681, New York, NY, USA. Association for Computing Machinery.

Amy Zhao Yu, Shahar Ronen, Kevin Hu, Tiffany Lu, and Cesar Hidalgo. 2016. pantheon.tsv. In *Pantheon 1.0, A Manually Verified Dataset of Globally Famous Biographies*. Harvard Dataverse.

# Augmented Political Leaning Detection: Leveraging Parliamentary Speeches for Classifying News Articles

**Charlott Jakob**
Technical University Berlin,
German Research Center for AI,
Berlin, Germany,
c.jakob@tu-berlin.de

**Pia Wenzel**
Technical University Berlin,
Berlin, Germany,
p.wenzel.2@campus.tu-berlin.de

**Salar Mohtaj**
Technical University Berlin,
German Research Center for AI,
Berlin, Germany,
salar.mohtaj@tu-berlin.de

**Vera Schmitt**
Technical University Berlin,
German Research Center for AI,
Berlin, Germany,
vera.schmitt@tu-berlin.de

## Abstract

In an era where political discourse infiltrates online platforms and news media, identifying opinion is increasingly critical, especially in news articles, where objectivity is expected. Readers frequently encounter authors' inherent political viewpoints, challenging them to discern facts from opinions. Classifying text on a spectrum from left to right is a key task for uncovering these viewpoints. Previous approaches rely on outdated datasets to classify current articles, neglecting that political opinions on certain subjects change over time. This paper explores a novel methodology for detecting political leaning in news articles by augmenting them with political speeches specific to the topic and publication time. We evaluated the impact of the augmentation using BERT and Mistral models. The results show that the BERT model's F1 score improved from a baseline of 0.82 to 0.85, while the Mistral model's F1 score increased from 0.30 to 0.31.

## 1 Introduction

In an era increasingly dominated by digital landscapes, political discussion has largely migrated online. As readers engage with posts and news articles, they encounter not only the facts but also the authors' inherent viewpoints. This phenomenon is further complicated by the prevalence of misinformation and disinformation, making it difficult for individuals to maintain objectivity and discern the embedded viewpoints.

The presence of political viewpoints in news articles poses significant challenges for the average reader, potentially leading to cognitive biases. According to a recent study by French et al. (2023), readers, among others, fall for Confirmation Bias. It reinforces pre-existing beliefs, as users tend to agree with statements that foster their own opinions. Detecting political viewpoints in textual content is thus crucial for ensuring that readers can access a comprehensive view of the information presented.

Political opinion can be categorized differently. A common way is to categorize text on a left-to-right spectrum, known amongst others as political leaning detection (Doan and Gulla, 2022).

Previous research on political leaning has predominantly focused on English-speaking contexts, yet such models are not directly transferable to the German linguistic and political landscape, where left and right viewpoints on specific topics vary significantly. For example, topics considered right-leaning in the United States, such as gun ownership rights, may not be framed similarly in Germany (Doan and Gulla, 2022).

Moreover, the dynamic nature of political landscapes means that older datasets might not accurately reflect current political climates or the evolving positions of political parties. The recent shifts in German politics with the emergence of the party Alternative für Deutschland (AfD) in the German federal parliament (Bundestag) illustrates these changes, necessitating updated and relevant datasets for analysis. Furthermore, there are differences in legislation terms as the opposition parties usually use more emotional language in their speeches when criticizing the government parties (Bissmann et al., 2016).

This paper proposes a novel system for detecting political leaning. It leverages current speeches from the Bundestag to improve the classification of Ger-



*Proceedings of the 58th Annual Meeting of the Association for Computational Linguistics*, pages 126–133
July 5–10, 2020. ©2020 Association for Computational Linguistics

man news articles by augmenting the articles with timely quotes from right-leaning and left-leaning speeches.

## 2 Related Work

A political viewpoint is defined as one of a limited number of identifiable opinions on a political subject. In the realm of automatic political viewpoint detection in English text, terms like *ideology*, *leaning*, *party*, and *political bias* are frequently used interchangeably, distinguishing classes typically along a left-to-right spectrum (Doan and Gulla, 2022). Although the specific characteristics of left and right may vary in German text, research indicates a consistent association across countries. The left is typically linked to egalitarianism, progress, social freedom, internationalism, and state intervention in the economy, while the right is associated with tradition, authority, nationalism, and market liberalization (Ferreira and Rosas, 2014; Caprara and Vecchione, 2018). For clarity, we will use the term *political leaning* to denote a viewpoint positioned on the spectrum between left and right ideologies.

Numerous studies have employed traditional machine learning models to classify political leaning (Slapin and Proksch, 2008; Barberá, 2015; Temporão et al., 2018; Goet, 2019; Rheault and Cochrane, 2020). Due to the recent advancements in Deep Learning, the utilization of Large Language Models (LLMs) is increasingly coming into focus. RoBERTa (Liu et al., 2019) in combination with a back-translation technique for augmentation proved to be effective in the CLEF *Checkthat!* shared task on political bias detection (Da San Martino et al., 2023). Maab et al. (2023) proposed another augmentation method where text samples are expanded by samples with the same target and bias.

Varies research was conducted based on the idea of comparing left and right viewpoints on the same topic to highlight differences. In 2020, Roy and Goldwasser (2020) examined the appearance of words from politically opposed news outlets regarding specific topics. Later, Liu et al. (2022) improved classification by pre-training an LLM with article pairs that presented the same story but from different ideological perspectives.

A recurring challenge in the classification of news articles is the inherent media bias. Hong et al. (2023) proposed using multi-head attention mechanisms, applying both document-level and sentence-level labels to ensure that the sentences accurately reflect the document's overall political leaning. Moreover, techniques such as Adversarial Media Adaptation and Triplet Loss Pre-training are introduced by Baly et al. (2020) to mitigate the influence of media bias on model outcomes. Chen et al. (2020) suggested modelling article-level bias by analyzing sentence-level bias along with other features like frequency, position, and sequence of biased terms.

Incorporating political speeches has shown promising results in enhancing the performance of political leaning detection models. Krestel et al. (2012) analyzed the cosine similarities between articles and speeches to classify news outlets along a political spectrum, confirming the relevance of political speeches. Bissmann et al. (2016) applied logistic regression models trained on bag-of-words vectors from German political speeches. Hajare et al. (2021) aligned social media posts with congressional speeches using TF-IDF similarity.

In this study, we augment a news article dataset with text from political speeches. Building on the ideas of Liu et al. (2022) and Bissmann et al. (2016) we leverage discussions on the same topic from different parties in the Bundestag. By using sequence pairs from the furthest left and furthest right parties in the parliament, we train the model to recognize the two most divergent political viewpoints on a given topic.

## 3 Datasets

We use two corpora, a news article dataset from Aksenov et al. (2021) and German Parliament speeches from Open Discourse (Richter et al., 2020) to evaluate our proposed approach.

### 3.1 Articles

We use the German news article dataset initially presented by Aksenov et al. (2021) as a basis. The labels were assigned based on a survey carried out by Medienkompass.org, in which subjects were asked to rate different German media outlets on a scale of left to right. Crawling the media outlets' articles resulted in a set of 47,362 articles from 34 different publishers (Aksenov et al., 2021). We rerun the open-source news crawler provided by Aksenov et al. (2021), resulting in retrieving a subset of the original dataset as some links were broken. Before cleaning, the dataset consists of

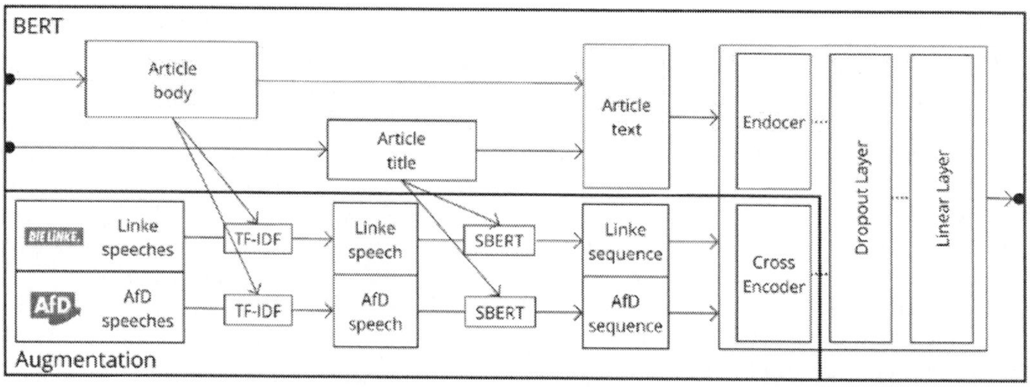


Figure 1: Augmentation pipeline and architecture of models BERT and BERT Augmented

46,191 articles from 2001 to 2021. We then filtered out articles published between March 2018 and December 2021, as AfD entered the Bundestag in October 2017 and we included speeches from six months before to six months after the article's publication date. We also removed articles with less than 100 words, which resulted in 13,831 articles in total. The length of the articles and the left- and right-side speech excerpts measured in word count are presented in Table 1

We decided to run the experiment in two scenarios that differed in the number of classes. We run the original 5 classes distribution and furthermore create new classes by splitting the news-outlet ratings from Medienkompass at quantiles 0.33 and 0.66, resulting in classes "left", "center", "right", often used in the context of political leaning detection (Doan and Gulla, 2022). The distribution of classes in both scenarios is presented in Table 2.

| Dataset | max. | avg. | std. |
|---|---|---|---|
| Articles | 16.320 | 865 | 1318 |
| AfD sequences | 185 | 45 | 20 |
| Linke sequences | 168 | 45 | 19 |

Table 1: Text length statistics within the datasets

| | Class | Total | Train | Eval. | Test |
|---|---|---|---|---|---|
| 3 Classes Absolute | left | 4.949 | 3.509 | 723 | 717 |
| | center | 5.972 | 4.136 | 921 | 915 |
| | right | 1.058 | 740 | 153 | 165 |
| 3 Classes Relative | left | 41.31 | 41.85 | 40.23 | 39.90 |
| | center | 49.85 | 49.33 | 51.25 | 50.92 |
| | right | 8.83 | 8.83 | 8.51 | 9.18 |
| 5 Classes Absolute | far-left | 210 | 148 | 31 | 31 |
| | center-left | 2.875 | 2.040 | 419 | 416 |
| | center | 2.450 | 1.726 | 373 | 351 |
| | center-right | 5.386 | 3.731 | 821 | 834 |
| | far-right | 1.058 | 740 | 153 | 165 |
| 5 Classes Relative | far-left | 1.75 | 1.77 | 1.73 | 1.73 |
| | center-left | 24.00 | 24.33 | 23.32 | 23.15 |
| | center | 20.45 | 20.58 | 20.76 | 19.53 |
| | center-right | 44.96 | 44.50 | 45.69 | 46.41 |
| | far-right | 8.83 | 8.83 | 8.51 | 9.18 |

Table 2: Label distributions across the two class scenarios

### 3.2 Speeches

The speeches are obtained from a publicly available dataset called Open Discourse (Richter et al., 2020), which is the first fully comprehensive corpus of the plenary proceedings of the Bundestag. The dataset contains speeches ranging from 9.12.1949 to 20.5.2022. We prefilter the speeches from October 2017 to July 2022 to match the article dataset. Only speeches from the factions AfD and Linke, representing the far right and far left of the German political landscape, with more than 100 words were selected. This choice aims to provide a broad range of opinions from both ends of the political spectrum for model training.

### 3.3 Augmentation

To assess political leaning in news articles, we augment the content of the articles with parliamentary speeches of two political parties. We consider the articles to be the query in an Information Retrieval sense. For both parties, we follow the following procedure. All speeches of the party are considered as documents. In the first stage, we filter the documents based on the article's publication date, selecting those that fall within a window of six months before and six months after the publication. Then, we identify the most relevant document for our article by calculating the cosine similarity between the query and the documents' TF-IDF vectors. TF-IDF is well-suited for the initial broad document search as it's able to capture the broad context of large documents. On the other side, models like SBERT are designed to embed shorter sentences and capture semantic information which is beneficial for our second stage. There, we tokenize the selected speech, removing the first and last two sentences, as they primarily include the formal opening and closing phrases that follow established protocol. Also, sentences with fewer than 10 words are excluded to remove less informative content. We then break down the speech into sentences, treating each sentence as a separate document. Each sentence is embedded as well as the article title, and we identify the most relevant sentence based on cosine similarity with the title, using SBERT embeddings (Reimers and Gurevych, 2019). The most similar sentence and its following sentence are used as the final augmentation sequence. The final augmented dataset for classification includes five columns: the article text, the 3-point scale label, the 5-point-scale label, the most similar AfD sequence, and the most similar Linke sequence. For the dataset without augmentation, the only difference is the absence of the faction sentences. A visualization of this process is provided in Figure 1. Furthermore, an example of an article with the respective augmentation sequences can be found in Figure 2.

## 4 Models

We utilize a small encoder model and a small decoder model to demonstrate the effectiveness of speech augmentation. For the encoder, we fine-tune a BERT Model (Devlin et al., 2019) pre-trained on a German corpus. To incorporate larger generative models and the concept of Retrieval Augmented Generation, we conduct inference tests with an LLM equipped with a decoder. We use Mistral-7B-Instruct (Jiang et al., 2023) as it is a small European LLM and is fine-tuned on instructions, which helps to retrieve valid JSON outputs. The prompt details for Mistral are provided in the appendix. Both models are designed as classifiers. BERT is modified by appending a dropout and a linear layer, while Mistral utilizes few-shot learning to output a JSON containing the label prediction. We then compare the baseline models of BERT and Mistral against the augmented versions.

For BERT, we enhance its capabilities by expanding it with a cross-encoder model, allowing it to incorporate the augmentation sequences. Comparing left-leaning and right-leaning sequences may help to interpret the opinions expressed in the news article. Cross-encoders are typically used for similarity calculation in retrieval processes. We exploit this feature to encode contrasting sequences. It takes two sequences as inputs, and we take its last hidden states as input for the dropout layer. The BERT model baseline and expanded BERT model are illustrated in Figure 1.

In the case of the Mistral model, the augmentation process is straightforward. Left and right-leaning sequences are included in the instructions, as detailed in the appendix 5.

## 5 Experimental Setup

We use the German BERT base model[1] and a cross-encoder for multilingual support[2]. For Mistral, we use Mistral-7B-Instruct[3]. Due to input size limitations in both models, we use a maximum token size of 512 for the articles. For evaluation, we train our BERT models with a train-eval-test split of 70%, 15% and 15%. For Mistral, we perform few-shot learning by adding a left-leaning and right-leaning news article to the prompt and running it on the test set only. For evaluation metrics, we use marco precision, recall and F1 score.

We fine-tune the BERT models using grid search and run 20 random parameter variations. We always train 4 epochs and use batch sizes [8,16,32], learning rates [1e-5, 2e-5, 3e-5, 4e-5, 5e-5], weight decays [0.01, 0.1], warm-up ratios [0.06, 0.08, 0.1] and dropout rates of [0.1, 0.2, 0.3, 0.4].

## 6 Results

The evaluation metrics for four different models over two scenarios are summarized in Table 3. For the three-class scenario, the BERT Augmented model demonstrated the highest performance with precision, recall, and F1-score all at 0.85, surpassing the standard BERT model's scores of 0.83, 0.82, and 0.82, respectively. Both versions of the Mistral

[1]https://huggingface.co/dbmdz/bert-base-german-cased

[2]https://huggingface.co/cross-encoder/msmarco-MiniLM-L6-en-de-v1

[3]https://huggingface.co/mistralai/Mistral-7B-Instruct-v0.1

Article text: „Babys an die Urne: Politiker wollen Wahlrecht ab Geburt [SEP] Babys an die Urne: Politiker wollen Wahlrecht ab Geburt Eine fraktionsübergreifende Gruppe von Bundestagsabgeordneten will das Wahlalter in Deutschland drastisch herabsetzen - auf null Jahre. Das berichtet der ""Spiegel"" in seiner neuen Ausgabe. Einen entsprechenden Antrag für ein Wahlrecht ab Geburt bereitet der FDP-Politiker und ehemalige Bundestagsvizepräsident Hermann Otto Solms vor. Die SPD-Politiker Ingrid Arndt-Brauer und Swen Schulz sowie Thomas Silberhorn von der CSU unterstützen den Vorstoß. ""Das Ziel ist mehr Generationengerechtigkeit"", sagte Solms, der bereits 2005 und 2009 versucht hat, das Wahlrecht für Kinder durchzusetzen. Der Antrag soll nach der Sommerpause ins Parlament gehen. Foto: Wähler in einem Wahllokal, über dts Nachrichtenagentur"

AfD-sequence: „Aber wir sollten dieser Ausdehnung des Wahlrechts oder, besser gesagt, der Abschaffung der Einschränkung des Wahlrechts hier nicht nur zustimmen, weil es uns Gerichte oder die UN vorgeben. Es ist eine Anerkennung der Menschenwürde, ein notwendiger Schritt des jahrzehntelangen Abschüttelns unserer alten Vorurteile gegenüber behinderten Menschen."

Linke-sequence: „Wir sollten uns zu einem Wahlrecht entschließen können – darüber sollten wir verhandeln –, das allen Parteien etwas abverlangt. Damit komme ich zu den Ideen, die aufseiten der Union vorherrschen."

Figure 2: Example article with respective augmentation sequences

model showed significantly lower metrics. The basic version results in a precision and recall of 0.32 and an F1-score of 0.30, and a small improvement was observed in the augmented version with a precision of 0.32, a recall of 0.33, and an F1-score of 0.31.

In the five-class classification, only slight improvements in precision or recall were observed. The BERT model achieved a precision of 0.67, recall of 0.69, and F1-score of 0.68, and the augmented BERT's scores of 0.67, 0.69, and 0.68. The Mistral models remained less effective, with the augmented version marginally bettering the precision and maintaining the same recall and F1-score as the non-augmented version (0.19 precision, 0.19 recall, and 0.16 F1).

| | Model | Precision | Recall | F1 |
|---|---|---|---|---|
| 3 classes | BERT | 0.83 | 0.82 | 0.82 |
| | BERT Augm. | **0.85** | **0.85** | **0.85** |
| | Mistral | 0.33 | 0.32 | 0.30 |
| | Mistral Augm. | 0.32 | 0.33 | 0.31 |
| 5 classes | BERT | **0.67** | 0.69 | **0.68** |
| | BERT Augm. | **0.67** | **0.70** | **0.68** |
| | Mistral | 0.18 | 0.19 | 0.16 |
| | Mistral Augm. | 0.19 | 0.19 | 0.16 |

Table 3: Evaluation metrics for all models

Further analysis of the class-wise performance of the BERT Augmented model for the three-class problem reveals high precision and recall across 'left' (0.84 and 0.91), 'center' (0.95 and 0.88), and 'right' categories (0.77 and 0.76), culminating in an average F1-score of 0.85 (Table 4).

| | Class | Precision | Recall | F1 | Supp. |
|---|---|---|---|---|---|
| 3 classes | left | 0.84 | 0.91 | 0.87 | 723 |
| | center | 0.95 | 0.88 | 0.92 | 921 |
| | right | 0.77 | 0.76 | 0.77 | 153 |
| | total | 0.85 | 0.85 | 0.85 | |
| 5 classes | far-left | 0.00 | 0.00 | 0.00 | 31 |
| | center-left | 1.00 | 0.97 | 0.99 | 416 |
| | center | 0.72 | 0.87 | 0.79 | 351 |
| | center-right | 0.97 | 0.91 | 0.94 | 834 |
| | far-right | 0.66 | 0.76 | 0.70 | 165 |
| | total | 0.67 | 0.70 | 0.68 | |

Table 4: Class-wise evaluation metrics for BERT Augmented

In contrast, the five-class classification shows varied performance, with the 'far-left' class failing to identify any true positives (precision and recall at 0.00), while 'center-left' and 'center-right' classes have strong performances with F1-scores of 0.99 and 0.94, respectively. The 'center' and 'far-right' classes show moderate results, contributing to an overall average F1-score of 0.68 for the model.

## 7 Discussion and Limitations

The results from Mistral appear nearly random, indicating significant room for improvement. Currently, it operates primarily through inference, which might be inadequate. Fine-tuning Mistral on a specific task using the training dataset could enhance its performance. Data augmentation didn't significantly improve Mistral's performance, potentially because Mistral was trained on bigger and more current datasets than models like BERT.

The choice of using a Cross-encoder to enhance

an encoder model warrants evaluation. Testing different configurations could reveal more effective alternatives. For instance, employing an encoder with a larger input size and directly appending speech augmentation to article tokens might optimize performance.

Our approach may reduce media bias by utilizing non-media datasets for comparison. However, the challenge of mitigating media bias persists due to our reliance on datasets labelled based on news outlets. Experimenting with a manually labelled German news dataset could provide a clearer indication of the effectiveness of our methodology.

The process of augmentation and similarity search has limitations. To improve, methods such as isolating subjective sentences could be investigated. Furthermore, considering speeches from a narrower time frame, such as within a specific two-month period, might yield more precise insights.

Our analysis currently limits itself to speeches from Linke and AfD. This restriction might oversimplify the complex political spectrum. Incorporating speeches from a broader range of political parties would add complexity and could provide a more comprehensive understanding. However, categorizing parties on a simple left-right scale is challenging as multiple dimensions influence political parties. Shared viewpoints among opposing parties might undermine the utility of the left-right scale. It raises the question of whether detecting political leaning or ideology is more suitable for analyzing the German political landscape.

## 8 Conclusion

The paper represents an initial attempt to use speeches to augment articles for the detection of political leaning. We explore this approach with two classic LLM methods: fine-tuning BERT and few-shot learning with Mistral. The study incorporated sequences from the most left-leaning and most right-leaning parties as a thematically and temporally relevant input for the articles. For both models, there were slight improvements in F1 scores, with BERT increasing from 0.82 to 0.85 and Mistral from 0.30 to 0.31. Further research is necessary to determine the effectiveness of augmentation.

## References


Dmitrii Aksenov, Peter Bourgonje, Karolina Zaczynska, Malte Ostendorff, Julian Moreno-Schneider, and Georg Rehm. 2021. Fine-grained Classification of Political Bias in German News: A Data Set and Initial Experiments. In *Proceedings of the 5th Workshop on Online Abuse and Harms (WOAH 2021)*, pages 121–131, Online. Association for Computational Linguistics.

Ramy Baly, Giovanni Da San Martino, James Glass, and Preslav Nakov. 2020. We Can Detect Your Bias: Predicting the Political Ideology of News Articles. In *Proceedings of the 2020 Conference on Empirical Methods in Natural Language Processing (EMNLP)*, pages 4982–4991, Online. Association for Computational Linguistics.

Pablo Barberá. 2015. Birds of the same feather tweet together: Bayesian ideal point estimation using twitter data. 23(1):76 – 91.

Felix Bissmann, Pola Lehmann, Daniel Kirsch, and Sebastian Schelter. 2016. Predicting political party affiliation from text. *PolText*, 14(14).

Gian Vittorio Caprara and Michele Vecchione. 2018. On the left and right ideological divide: Historical accounts and contemporary perspectives. *Political Psychology*, 39:49–83.

Wei-Fan Chen, Khalid Al-Khatib, Benno Stein, and Henning Wachsmuth. 2020. Detecting media bias in news articles using gaussian bias distributions. *arXiv preprint arXiv:2010.10649*.

Giovanni Da San Martino, Firoj Alam, Maram Hasanain, Rabindra Nath Nandi, Dilshod Azizov, and Preslav Nakov. 2023. Overview of the clef-2023 checkthat! lab task 3 on political bias of news articles and news media. *Working Notes of CLEF*.

Jacob Devlin, Ming-Wei Chang, Kenton Lee, and Kristina Toutanova. 2019. BERT: pre-training of deep bidirectional transformers for language understanding. In *Proceedings of the 2019 Conference of the North American Chapter of the Association for Computational Linguistics: Human Language Technologies, NAACL-HLT 2019, Minneapolis, MN, USA, June 2-7, 2019, Volume 1 (Long and Short Papers)*, pages 4171–4186. Association for Computational Linguistics.

Tu My Doan and Jon Atle Gulla. 2022. A Survey on Political Viewpoints Identification. *Online Social Networks and Media*, 30:100208.

Ana Rita Ferreira and João Cardoso Rosas. 2014. *Left and right: the great dichotomy revisited*. Cambridge Scholars Publishing.

Aaron M. French, Veda C. Storey, and Linda Wallace. 2023. The impact of cognitive biases on the believability of fake news. *European Journal of Information Systems*, pages 1–22.

Niels D. Goet. 2019. Measuring polarization with text analysis: Evidence from the UK house of commons, 1811–2015. 27(4):518 – 539.

Prasad Hajare, Sadia Kamal, Siddharth Krishnan, and Arunkumar Bagavathi. 2021. A Machine Learning Pipeline to Examine Political Bias with Congressional Speeches. In *2021 20th IEEE International Conference on Machine Learning and Applications (ICMLA)*, pages 239–243, Pasadena, CA, USA. IEEE.

Jiwoo Hong, Yejin Cho, Jiyoung Han, Jaemin Jung, and James Thorne. 2023. Disentangling Structure and Style: Political Bias Detection in News by Inducing Document Hierarchy. In *Findings of the Association for Computational Linguistics: EMNLP 2023*, pages 5664–5686, Singapore. Association for Computational Linguistics.

Albert Q. Jiang, Alexandre Sablayrolles, Arthur Mensch, Chris Bamford, Devendra Singh Chaplot, Diego de Las Casas, Florian Bressand, Gianna Lengyel, Guillaume Lample, Lucile Saulnier, Lélio Renard Lavaud, Marie-Anne Lachaux, Pierre Stock, Teven Le Scao, Thibaut Lavril, Thomas Wang, Timothée Lacroix, and William El Sayed. 2023. Mistral 7b. *CoRR*, abs/2310.06825.

Ralf Krestel, Alex Wall, and Wolfgang Nejdl. 2012. Treehugger or petrolhead?: identifying bias by comparing online news articles with political speeches. In *Proceedings of the 21st International Conference on World Wide Web*, pages 547–548, Lyon France. ACM.

Yinhan Liu, Myle Ott, Naman Goyal, Jingfei Du, Mandar Joshi, Danqi Chen, Omer Levy, Mike Lewis, Luke Zettlemoyer, and Veselin Stoyanov. 2019. Roberta: A robustly optimized BERT pretraining approach. *CoRR*, abs/1907.11692.

Yujian Liu, Xinliang Frederick Zhang, David Wegsman, Nick Beauchamp, and Lu Wang. 2022. POLITICS: Pretraining with Same-story Article Comparison for Ideology Prediction and Stance Detection. *arXiv preprint*. ArXiv:2205.00619 [cs].

Iffat Maab, Edison Marrese-Taylor, and Yutaka Matsuo. 2023. Target-Aware Contextual Political Bias Detection in News. In *Proceedings of the 13th International Joint Conference on Natural Language Processing and the 3rd Conference of the Asia-Pacific Chapter of the Association for Computational Linguistics (Volume 1: Long Papers)*, pages 782–792, Nusa Dua, Bali. Association for Computational Linguistics.

Nils Reimers and Iryna Gurevych. 2019. Sentence-bert: Sentence embeddings using siamese bert-networks. In *Proceedings of the 2019 Conference on Empirical Methods in Natural Language Processing and the 9th International Joint Conference on Natural Language Processing, EMNLP-IJCNLP 2019, Hong Kong, China, November 3-7, 2019*, pages 3980–3990. Association for Computational Linguistics.

Ludovic Rheault and Christopher Cochrane. 2020. Word embeddings for the analysis of ideological placement in parliamentary corpora. 28(1):112 – 133.

Florian Richter, Philipp Koch, Oliver Franke, Jakob Kraus, Fabrizio Kuruc, Anja Thiem, Judith Högerl, Stella Heine, and Konstantin Schöps. 2020. Open Discourse.

Shamik Roy and Dan Goldwasser. 2020. Weakly Supervised Learning of Nuanced Frames for Analyzing Polarization in News Media. In *Proceedings of the 2020 Conference on Empirical Methods in Natural Language Processing (EMNLP)*, pages 7698–7716, Online. Association for Computational Linguistics.

Jonathan B. Slapin and Sven-Oliver Proksch. 2008. A scaling model for estimating time-series PartyPositions from texts. 52(3):457–722.

Mickael Temporão, Corentin Vande Kerckhove, Clifton van der Linden, Yannick Dufresne, and Julien M. Hendrickx. 2018. Ideological scaling of social media users: A dynamic lexicon approach. 26(4):457 – 473.

# A Appendix

<s>[INST]
## TASK:
You are a language model tasked with analyzing the political leaning of an article. Given an article **and opinions on the topic from left and right politicians**, your goal is to:
1. Provide a brief 2-sentence elaboration on the author's perceived political viewpoint based on the article's content **and the left and right-leaning opinions**.
2. Categorize the article's political leaning as "left", "center", or "right".

## OUTPUT FORMAT:
Your response must be provided as a JSON object with the following keys and values:
```json
{{
"elaboration": "<Two sentences elaborating on the articles political leaning>",
"political leaning": "<left, center or right>"
}}
```

## EXAMPLE 1:
Article: "Die Welt bereitet sich auf einen Krieg vor [SEP] Michail Gorbatschow, hier bei seinem 85. Geburtstag im März 2016, sieht die Welt auf einen Krieg zusteuern Michail Gorbatschow ist ein Mann des Friedens. Sein Name steht für atomare Abrüstung, Perestroika und Glasnost, den Fall der Berliner Mauer und eine Annäherung der damaligen Supermächte USA und Russland. Der letzte Staatschef der Sowjetunion glaubt sein Erbe im Gefahr. „Es sieht aus, als würde die Welt sich auf einen Krieg vorbereiten", schreibt der 85-Jährige in einem Beitrag für das „Time"-Magazin. Seine Beobachtung: Es gebe ein neues Wettrüsten, das dringend gestoppt werden müsse. Doch das Gegenteil sei der Fall. Soldaten und schwere Waffen von Nato und Russland würden in Europa immer näher zusammenkommen – jeweils in Schlagdistanz. „Während Staatshaushalte darum kämpfen, die grundlegenden sozialen Bedürfnisse der Menschen zu finanzieren, wachsen die Militärausgaben." Das Geld fließe in schwere Waffen und Raketenabwehrsysteme, die die „strategische Stabilität untergraben". "
**Left leaning opinion: "Das Fazit: Der Gründungsgeist der UNO „Frieden durch Diplomatie" muss endlich wieder gestärkt werden. Die Bundesregierung hat leider mit ihrer Politik in den Vereinten Nationen mehr geostrategische NATO-Politik denn eine aktive UNO-Friedenspolitik betrieben."**
**Right leaning opinion: "Ich darf noch einmal in Erinnerung rufen: Michail Gorbatschow sprach beim Ende des Kalten Krieges vom „gemeinsamen Haus Europa". François Mitterrand sah mit dem Ende des Kalten Krieges für Europa die Möglichkeit, zu seiner eigenen Geschichte und seiner eigenen Geografie zurückzukehren, so wie man zu sich nach Hause zurückkehrt."**
Output:
```json
{{
"elaboration": "The article emphasizes the need for disarmament and criticizes the increase in military spending and aggressive political rhetoric, aligning closely with traditional left-wing values that prioritize social welfare over militarization. ",
"political leaning": "left"
}}
```

## EXAMPLE 2:
Article: "Corona: Wie gefährlich ist das Virus? Wie kann ich mich besser schützen? [SEP] Fast kein Tag vergeht mehr, wo nicht neue Verbote der Bewegungsfreiheit in Deutschland beschlossen werden. Das düstere Beispiel von Italien und Spanien vor Augen jagt eine Einschränkung die nächste. Was kommt als nächstes? Zahlen wir mit dem Kollaps unserer Wirtschaft nicht einen viel zu hohen Preis? Führt das Kontaktverbot nicht auch zu einem „Bewegungsverbot", was uns anfälliger für Corona werden lässt? Wie gefährlich ist dieser Virus, der uns allen den Atem nimmt? Wie kann ich mich vor Corona schützen? Spätestens seitdem Virologen die Macht übernommen haben, scheinen wirtschaftliche Grundregeln nicht mehr zu gelten. Wer den gigantischen Wirtschaftskreislauf runterfährt und ihn in Bereichen gar stoppt, muss triftige Gründe haben, dies zu tun. "
**Left leaning opinion: "Deshalb unterstützen wir nachdrücklich noch einmal die Forderungen des DGB und des BDI, die sagen: Auch wegen Corona müssen wir jetzt ein Zeichen setzen, dass wir aus dieser Krise herauskommen werden. – Wir fordern nochmals in den nächsten zehn Jahren zusätzliche Investitionen in Höhe von jährlich 45 Milliarden Euro."**
**Right leaning opinion: "Wir wissen jedoch schon, dass Coronaviren zu den schnell mutierenden Virusstämmen gehören. In bester sozialistischer Manier werden also Impfstoffentwickler mit Steuergeldern unterstützt, um dann Gewinne – allein die erste Impfwelle verspricht 20 Milliarden Dollar Umsatz – privat einzustreichen, und das für einen Virus, dessen Gefährlichkeit nach heutigem Wissensstand weit geringer ist, als zunächst angenommen."**
Output:
```json
{{
"elaboration": "The article conveys a right-leaning viewpoint, emphasizing skepticism towards the severity of the coronavirus and the economic repercussions of restrictive measures. It criticizes the disruption of economic norms and suggests that the virus might not justify the extensive government interventions and limitations on movement. ",
"political leaning": "right"
}}
```

## INSTRUCTIONS:
You will be provided with an article text. Your task is to analyze the content and generate a JSON object following the specified OUTPUT FORMAT. Provide your elaboration on the article's political leaning in two sentences under the "elaboration" key, and categorize it as "left", "center", or "right" under the "political leaning" key.
Strictly adhere to the JSON OUTPUT FORMAT. Do not include any other text in your response.

Article: {article}
**Left leaning opinion: {linke sequence}**
**Right leaning opinion: {afd sequence}**

[/INST]
Output: {{

Table 5: Input Sequence for Mistral and Mistral Augmented, where bold text is additionally for Mistral Augmented

# Author Index

**Association for Computational Linguistics**
209 N. Eighth Street
Stroudsburg, Pennsylvania 18360

ISBN 979-8-3313-0481-2

9 798331 304812

CURRAN ASSOCIATES INC.
proceedings.com